Interpersonal Reconciliation between Christians in a Shame-Oriented Culture

A Sri Lankan Case Study

Mano Emmanuel

© 2020 Celine Manohari Emmanuel

Published 2020 by Langham Monographs
An imprint of Langham Publishing
www.langhampublishing.org

Langham Publishing and its imprints are a ministry of Langham Partnership

Langham Partnership
PO Box 296, Carlisle, Cumbria, CA3 9WZ, UK
www.langham.org

ISBNs:
978-1-78368-809-8 Print
978-1-83973-113-36ePub
978-1-83973-114-3 Mobi
978-1-83973-115-0 PDF

Celine Manohari Emmanuel has asserted her right under the Copyright, Designs and Patents Act, 1988 to be identified as the Author of this work.

All rights reserved. No part of this publication may be reproduced, stored in a retrieval system or transmitted, in any form or by any means, electronic, mechanical, photocopying, recording or otherwise, without the prior written permission of the publisher or the Copyright Licensing Agency.

Requests to reuse content from Langham Publishing are processed through PLSclear. Please visit www.plsclear.com to complete your request.

All Scripture quotations, unless otherwise indicated, are taken from the Holy Bible, New International Version®, NIV®. Copyright ©1973, 1978, 1984, 2011 by Biblica, Inc.™ Used by permission of Zondervan.

Scripture quotations marked (NRSV) are from the New Revised Standard Version Bible, copyright © 1989 National Council of the Churches of Christ in the United States of America. Used by permission. All rights reserved.

British Library Cataloguing-in-Publication Data
A catalogue record for this book is available from the British Library.

ISBN: 978-1-78368-809-8

Cover & Book Design: projectluz.com

Langham Partnership actively supports theological dialogue and an author's right to publish but does not necessarily endorse the views and opinions set forth here or in works referenced within this publication, nor can we guarantee technical and grammatical correctness. Langham Partnership does not accept any responsibility or liability to persons or property as a consequence of the reading, use or interpretation of its published content.

There are some who supported me through their love and encouragement
and their unshakeable belief that I could accomplish this task.

Most beloved was my mother, Ranji,
who patiently waited for me to "finish writing the story" and
who entered glory two months before I completed this work.
She knew this day was coming, but may not have known how
much it meant to me to have such a devoted cheerleader.

It is with gratitude and love that I dedicate this work to her memory.

The inability to deal properly with interpersonal conflicts is causing havoc in the South Asian church today. Christians with bright prospects of usefulness in the kingdom are destroying their futures, and vibrant churches are facing God-dishonouring splits. A major reason for this poor showing in the church is an inadequate understanding of the biblical dynamics of conflict resolution and an inadequate reckoning of the cultural features that hugely influence our behaviour. This learned study discusses these issues with a deep sensitivity to both these areas. Reading and learning from this book would be a health-giving antidote to much that ails our church.

Ajith Fernando
Teaching Director, Youth for Christ, Sri Lanka
Author, *Discipling in a Multicultural World*

In this informed and engaging work, Mano Emmanuel takes us deep into important cultural issues in her context of Sri Lanka. Noting how rarely Western literature on relationships and conflict considers the challenges of those who operate with different cultural modes of shame and honor, Emmanuel provides a biblically informed, theoretically aware, and research-driven approach that tackles head-on issues of conflict with the lenses of face, honor, and shame. Based on her deep engagement with Scripture and current literature in anthropology, missiology, and face and facework theory, Emmanuel calls for the church to contextualize notions of "shameful" and "honorable." This important volume adds to the growing literature of culturally specific engagement with issues of face, honor, and shame. Scholars and practitioners alike will find in this helpful work valuable resources for navigating issues of conflict in the church.

Christopher Flanders, PhD
Associate Professor of Missions,
Abilene Christian University, Texas, USA
Assistant Editor, *Missio Dei Journal*
Member of the Executive Leadership Team, Honor-Shame Network

In this eye-opening book, Mano Emmanuel writes with the eye of an insider, an objective examination of Christian cultural thought on reconciliation in her country, and good academic research. The book can be an excellent asset for missionaries, teachers, leaders, and social workers engaged with people who view and understand their identity and their relationship with others in terms of honour and shame.

Alemayehu Mekonnen, PhD
Associate Professor of Missions,
Regent University, Virginia Beach, USA

Mano Emmanuel's Sri Lankan case study on interpersonal reconciliation between Christians uses a novel cross-cultural approach to conflict resolution. She introduces the concept of conscience orientation based on shame and guilt, its relationship to cultures, worldviews, and values, and its influence on the perception and management of conflicts. However, Mano Emmanuel not only bases her research on the social sciences but also on the Bible. This comparative approach permits the author to arrive at practical conclusions and make detailed recommendations for conflict resolution in a shame-oriented culture.

Dr. Hannes Wiher
Professor of Missiology,
Faculté Libre de Théologie Évangélique, Vaux-sur-Seine, France
Faculté Jean Calvin, Aix-en-Provence, France
Université Shalom de Bunia, Bunia, Congo, DRC

Contents

List of Figures xi

List of Tables xi

Acknowledgments xiii

Abstract xv

Chapter 1 1
   Introduction
      Overview 1
      Purpose Statement 5
      Research Question 5
      Significance of the Study 5
      Assumptions 7
      Research Methodology 7
      Definition of Terms 8
      Delimitations 9

Chapter 2 11
   Honor and Shame in Culture
      Culture, Worldviews, Shame, and Honor 11
         Defining Culture 11
         Culture and Worldview 13
         Cultural Values and Norms 16
      Understanding Guilt and Shame Cultures 23
         Defining Shame 33
         Defining Honor 40
      Characteristics of Shame-Oriented Cultures 44
         Dynamics of Shame 44
         The Dynamics of Honor 52
         Summary 59
      Dynamics of Conflict in Guilt and Shame-Oriented Cultures 60
      Conflict Resolution in Shame-Oriented Cultures 61
         Identity of Self and Group 63
         Style of Communication 70
         Conflict Resolution Style and Process 73
         Status and Power Distance 78
         Relativistic Morality 80

| Extreme Reactions to Being Shamed 89
| Summary 92
| Positive Aspects of Shame-Oriented Cultures 95
| Catalyst for Transformation 95
| Desire for Harmony 97
| Conceptual Framework 97

Chapter 3 99
Field Research Design and Implementation
    Research Design Rationale 100
    Instrument Design Rationale 102
    Ethical Considerations 104
    Data Collection Procedures 104
        Sampling Rationale 104
        Interview Protocol 105
        Case Studies 106
        Table of Characteristics 106
    Data Analysis Procedures 106

Chapter 4 109
Field Research Findings
    Cultural Characterization 109
        Sri Lanka's People, History, and Religions 109
        Basic Collectivistic Values 110
        Values Directly Related to Conflict Resolution 114
    Field Research Findings: Interviews 127
        Source Demographics 127
        Main Causes of Conflict in the Church 127
        Shame-Oriented Dynamics of Interpersonal Conflict 128
        Application of Christian Faith to Conflict 142
        The Role of the Church 143
    Field Research Findings: Case Studies 147
        Goal of Conflict Resolution 147
        Identity of Self and Group 147
        Style of Communication 148
        Conflict Resolution Style 148
        Status and Power Distance 149
        Relativistic Morality 149
        Extreme Reactions 150
    New Insights from Field Research 150
        The Fragile Nature of Identity 150

    Trust Can Be Fostered with Time and Intentionality 151
    Low Value of Relationships..152
    Differing Cultural Norms 152
    A Neglected Topic in Church 153
    Lack of Recourse to Bible or Prayer 154

Chapter 5 155
Interpersonal Conflict in the New Testament
    Honor and Shame in New Testament Culture................................156
    Direct Approach to Conflict among Church Members 158
        If Your Brother Sins (Against You) 162
        Go and Point Out Their Fault, Just between the Two of You 165
        If He Listens You Have Won Back Your Brother 169
        But If He Does Not Listen Take Witnesses 175
        If They Still Refuse to Listen, Tell It to the Church 179
        If They Refuse to Listen, Treat Them as You Would a Pagan
            or a Tax Collector 180
        Hand This Man Over to Satan (1 Cor 5:1–5, 6–13) 186
    Direct Approach to Conflict among Leaders 193
        Rebuke False and Divisive Teachers..193
        Challenge an Erring Leader 196
        Rebuke an Elder Publicly..197
    Lessons from Community Conflicts 199
        Acts 6 – Inter-ethnic Conflict 199
        Acts 15 – Doctrinal Conflict...201
    Lessons from Interpersonal Conflicts 202
        Euodia and Synteche 202
        Peter and Jesus..203
        Paul and Barnabas..205
        Philemon and Onesimus..205
        Overall Attitude Toward Those Who Need Correcting..............211
        Values and Virtues for Honor 214
        Summary...216

Chapter 6 219
Recommendations and Conclusions
    Major Discoveries Emerging from the Study...................................219
    Recommendations for the Church 220
        Goal of Conflict Resolution 221
        Identity of Self and Others..222
        Style of Communication...232

  Conflict Style 234
  Status Orientation 237
  Relativistic Morality 237
  Extreme Reactions 244
 Using Positive Aspects of Shame 245
 Theological Resources 246
  Re-envisioning the Cross 246
  Redefining "Honorable" and "Shameful" 248
 Recommendations for Further Study 249
 Conclusion 250

Appendix A 251
 Integrated Basic Values Model

Appendix B 255
 Interview Protocol

Appendix C 257
 Table of Characteristics

Appendix D 260
 Case Summaries Compared

Appendix E 265
 Case Studies
  Case Study 1: C1CODaAm 265
  Case Study 2: C2COYo 271
  Case Study 3: C3ChGiSu 275
  Case Study 4: C4ChRam 280
  Case Study 5: C5ChMaSa 283
  Case Study 6: C6ChHaJo 286

Bibliography 289

List of Figures

Figure 3.1. Data Analysis..107
Figure 4.1. The Slippery Slope..121

List of Tables

Table 2.1. Value Orientations according to Kluckhohn 18
Table 2.2. The Moral Dimensions of Parson.......................................19
Table 2.3. The Basic Values of Mayers 21
Table 2.4. Comparison of Shame and Guilt Experiences 39
Table 2.5. The Distinction between Shame and Guilt according to Flanders 39
Table 2.6. Comparative Analysis of Conflict Resolution Style and Process........93
Table 2.7. High and Low Power Distance Distinctives........................94
Table 2.8. Comparing Individualist and Collectivist Values...............95
Table 2.9. Conceptual Framework Elements and Explanation 98
Table 3.1. Summary of the Basic Values of Mayers 103
Table 3.2. The Intercultural Conflict Model of Ting-Toomey..........103
Table 4.1. Comparison of 1 Corinthians with Deuteronomy by Hays............192
Table 5.1. Conflict and Shame in the New Testament 217
Table 6.1. Conflict Management Styles in the New Testament 235
Table 6.2. Sri Lankan Conflict Resolution Recommendations 236
Table 6.3. Soteriological Model of Conscience 243

Acknowledgments

"One person cannot do a PhD" a colleague jokingly remarked to me as we discussed editing and formatting issues related to completing my thesis. He was right. Although many, many hours are spent in solitude in libraries and in front of screens, what is eventually produced contains and is enhanced by the contribution, big and small, of companions along the way. So, it is with gratitude that I acknowledge those who journeyed with me.

Thanks are due to Colombo Theological Seminary and especially to its Principal Dr. Ivor Poobalan, who encouraged me to register on the program and supported me in many ways, including allowing me sabbaticals to concentrate on research.

A special word of gratitude to Dr. Mark Young, the president of Denver Seminary, who invited me to spend a sabbatical at Denver Seminary as a visiting scholar. It was there that the thesis took shape and the major portion of it was written. I am grateful for the hospitality extended to me and the warmth of staff, faculty, and students. My thanks to Dr. Alemayehu Mekonnen, Associate Professor of Mission, who advised me and encouraged me to be confident in my findings. Professor Craig Blomberg and Dr. Heather Gingrich provided valuable advice on various aspects of my research.

Thanks also to my sister Keshy and her family, and brother Ranjan and family in whose homes in England I spent sabbaticals. I am grateful for their hospitality which provided me with a respite from other responsibilities.

I spent many hours in the library at London School of Theology. I am grateful to faculty there who have encouraged me from the time of my first undergraduate studies, especially Dr. Graham McFarlane, Mary Evans, Lish Eves, and Professor Tony Lane.

My thanks also go to those who took part in the field research surveys and interviews, and who shared case studies with me.

Thank you to those who shared their expertise with me and lent or sent me books, including their own. Among them I acknowledge Dr. Ajith Fernando, Dr. David deSilva, Dr. Hannes Wiher, and Dr. Ruth Lienhard. My thanks to Dr. Karl Dortzbach, my supervisor, who by emails, visits, skype calls, and meetings ensured that I finished well, and to Dr. Steve Hobson of the International Graduate School of Leadership, for the careful administration of my studies over these years.

Thank you also to my team of proof readers and editors including Rochelle Hakel-Ranasinghe, Denisa Poobalan, and Ranmalie Seniviratne. Special thanks to my colleague Ravin Caldera who has become the resident expert in formatting and linguistics, for his "can do" attitude and willingness to take on this task.

Many people supported me in prayer, including colleagues and students at Colombo Theological Seminary, friends from St Mary's Watford, Kollupitiya Methodist Church, and prayer supporters all over the globe. I am deeply grateful to each of you for standing in the gap for me.

Yes, no one completes a PhD on their own, neither do they complete it for themselves. My hope is that this work will benefit the church in Sri Lanka and help them build a reconciling and reconciled community that glorifies the Lord Jesus. To him be all the glory.

Abstract

This study identifies aspects of a shame-oriented culture, specifically urban Sri Lanka, that contribute to conflict and impact the effectiveness of its conflict resolution processes. This research was motivated by the phenomenon of broken relationships and unresolved conflicts between Christians in the Sri Lankan church.

The literature review surveys the fields of cultural anthropology, missiology, and communication studies. Seven elements are identified within shame-oriented cultures that relate to conflict and its resolution. These seven are (1) the goal of conflict resolution, (2) identity, (3) communication style, (4) conflict resolution style, (5) status orientation, (6) relative morality, and (7) extreme reactions.

Data collected from Christian participants were analyzed in the light of a conceptual framework comprised of the seven elements, and were examined for correspondence or divergence. The analysis of the data reveals close correspondence with the seven elements of the conceptual framework, with some additional discoveries.

Selected New Testament texts related to interpersonal conflict were exegeted and analyzed related to the shame-oriented culture of the Mediterranean to discover if they prescribe particular forms or methods of conflict resolution. The objective was to allow these texts to inform recommendations for the church in urban Sri Lanka.

The conclusion drawn from the field research findings and NT texts was that the gospel requires a transformation of worldview including the conflict script believers receive from their culture. While protecting the honor of believers, it requires a redefinition of key aspects of the culture, including one's understanding of kin group, status, conflict style, and what is to be considered honorable.

The study recommends the development of the church as a fictive kinship group: a family, where attention is given to the selection of leaders who exemplify honor as virtue and where a new conflict script is learned through re-socializing of converts.

CHAPTER 1

Introduction

This study investigates the phenomenon of interpersonal conflict in the urban church in Sri Lanka. Field research was conducted with participants drawn from the capital city, Colombo. The study seeks to identify specific characteristics within the culture which impact conflict management in Sri Lanka. Its purpose is to raise awareness in the church about the tendencies within the culture which mitigate against reconciliation, and to make recommendations for change.

Overview

Sri Lanka's tourist market is enticed by the picture of a tropical paradise island. More recently though, the island has become synonymous with conflict, death, and division. In May 2009, the civil war that had raged over almost thirty years between the north and the south came to an end. Emerging from this conflict, which engulfed a whole generation, the nation has struggled to find its way towards a united future. "Reconciliation," "unity" and "nation building" have become buzzwords. The church is and has been continuously working to bring healing, justice, and peace according to its calling. Yet within the church itself, broken relationships abound. The causes may be many but the result is often the same: unresolved conflicts, hurts, bitterness, and anger where there should be peace and unity. If we scratch the surface of the typical local church, beneath the smiles and the pleasant exterior, lie serious rifts. It has become evident that the church struggles to demonstrate in its own life the reality of the gospel of reconciliation.

What is the evidence of this? Christian counsellors testify that they are inundated with requests for help from believers struggling with broken relationships within their families and within the church.[1] Many pastors find that believers who fall out with other believers or with the pastor would sooner leave the church than seek to be reconciled. A proportion of new church plants are actually church splits. This is in spite of the fact that, in Sri Lanka, local church congregations are often more homogenous than the New Testament church which consisted of Jew and Gentile, slave and free. Local congregations tend to be made up of people of the same language group (therefore same ethnicity), same background and status.

Christian organizations find that there are hidden divisions which suddenly erupt, and conflicts and issues that are brought into the open bring division rather than healing. People leave carrying hurts and bitterness which they rarely communicate in an exit interview. People who speak out are often characterized as trouble makers so that an employee, especially a junior one, will find it preferable to leave pretending all is well, or to react in passive-aggressive ways to make their displeasure felt. One Christian leader with over thirty-years ministry experience commented that almost every significant Christian ministry in the land has faced great crisis from conflict within.

Since conflict resolution is fraught with pitfalls and failure, many leaders and pastors prefer not to get involved. The result is that there is often no clear process for church discipline and restoration. For example, a pastor who has been found guilty of a sexual assault against a member of the congregation may simply be transferred to another church. This causes great confusion and anger within the congregation as the offender continues in ministry. Yet in another case, a person who has offended in some other way, perhaps been verbally abusive in a meeting, may be severely penalized or be ostracized without any clear reason for the decision.

Certain offences, such as child abuse or spousal abuse, which would be seen as sinful and criminal in a guilt-oriented culture, are often covered up in the church because the shame of the incident being made known is considered greater than the offence. A child or wife may be told to say nothing because public knowledge of the deed would bring shame on the family. The

---

1. Since there is no official organization of Christian counsellors, this date has been gathered from conversations with Christian counsellors known to the researcher.

child's future would be ruined because she (it is more often a girl) will not be marriageable if the abuse is common knowledge.

Sri Lankan society is deeply fractured. For almost thirty years ethnic conflict divided Sinhalese and Tamils. Before and during that time, various minorities, such as the Muslims and Burghers, faced discrimination and even violence.[2] The years after the official end of the war in 2009 have been filled with the rhetoric of reconciliation but the nation remains largely divided in its vision for the future. In such a society, the witness of the church as a reconciled and reconciling community is primary to its calling. However, its witness has been faltering and inconsistent partly due to the lack of reconciliation and skills for peace-making within the church.

While Christians in all cultures will struggle to live out the ideals taught in Scripture, there is a growing feeling within the church that both conflict and the process of reconciliation are affected by Sri Lankan culture, in which honor and shame are preeminent features. This has largely been ignored in the way the gospel has been presented and in the way people have been counselled and discipled. The gospel that has been introduced to the church is predominantly aimed at addressing guilt. Furthermore, it is packaged in individualistic features that characterize the countries in the West from which it has come. Bruce Nicholls reflects that Western missionaries have rarely expounded the gospel in terms of honor and shame although many of the cultures of the Majority World are more shame-oriented than guilt-oriented.[3] The result is a church that is a collection of people whose cultures claim to value community but that, with the coming of the gospel, becomes more and more individualistic.

Increasingly, missiologists and cultural anthropologists are seeking to address the distinctiveness of shame-oriented cultures and the implications for life and ministry in those cultures. At the same time, New Testament scholars are producing literature opening up the vistas of Mediterranean culture exposing the worldview and values of the New Testament community. They declare that the pursuit of honor and avoidance of shame was a key value in the New Testament world. Thus, there is a significant multi-disciplinary

---

2. See Gehan, *Confronting the Complexities*, for a description of the various rifts and conflicts in the twentieth century.

3. Nicholls, "Role of Shame and Guilt," 231–233.

stream of literature which informs the research into conflict resolution in a shame-oriented culture.

The literature review highlights the work of scholars who have been writing on the implications of shame-oriented cultures in Asia and the Middle East. They find such cultures in world of the Japanese, Chinese,[4] Malaysians, Filipinos,[5] Koreans, and in cultures of the Middle East.[6]

The research of communication specialists Stella Ting-Toomey and John G. Oetzel was especially helpful in identifying specific conflict resolution styles, methods of communicating and attitudes to conflict most commonly associated with shame-oriented cultures. Their work is found in Ting-Toomey's *Communicating across Cultures*,[7] and Ting-Toomey and Oetzel's *Managing Intercultural Conflict Effectively*.[8]

Missiologist Marvin K. Mayers produced a table of characteristics published in his *Christianity Confronts Culture*,[9] which was subsequently tested in the Polynesian islands by Sherwood Lingenfelter (primarily among the Yapese people). The modified "model of basic values" was published in *Ministering Cross-Culturally*.[10] This model is also used by missiologist Hannes Wiher in his *Shame and Guilt: A Key to Cross-Cultural Ministry*.[11] This model was key to the researcher's conceptual framework.

Recent social-scientific interpretations of the Bible have emphasized the significance of the honor-shame culture of the Mediterranean region. In the late 1980's a group of international scholars formed the Context Group, committed to the use of the social sciences in biblical interpretation. Scholars like Bruce Malina, David deSilva, Jerome Neyrey, Halvor Moxnes and Philip Esler, drawing on the influential work of anthropologists such as J. G. Peristiany

---

4. Wu, *Saving God's Face*.

5. Santos, *Turning Our Shame into Hope*.

6. Japanese: Benedict, *Chrysanthemum and the Sword*; Lebra, "Social Mechanism of Guilt"; Chinese: Wu, *Saving God's Face*; Malaysians: Yang, *Discipline or Shame?*; Filipinos: Santos, *Turning Our Shame into Hope*; Koreans: You, "Shame and Guilt Mechanisms"; Middle East: Muller, *Honor and Shame*. Thomas Schirrmacher, in his booklet written for the World Evangelical Alliance, *Culture of Shame, Culture of Guilt*, provides a useful and concise history of the development of the categories of shame and guilt cultures (19–33).

7. Ting-Toomey, *Communicating across Cultures*.

8. Ting-Toomey and Oetzel, *Managing Intercultural Conflict*.

9. Mayers, *Christianity Confronts Culture*.

10. Lingenfelter and Mayers, *Ministering Cross-Culturally*.

11. Wiher, *Shame and Guilt*.

and Julian Pitt-Rivers called people's attention to the importance of honor in the cultures of the Mediterranean. Their work on the New Testament provided the researcher with information about shame-oriented cultures. It also aided the biblical interpretation required for chapter 6, which examines New Testament teaching on conflict and reconciliation.

These strands within cultural anthropology, missiology, and New Testament studies with the added contribution from cross-cultural counsellors like David Augsburger form the tapestry of the literature review from which the conceptual framework emerged.

Purpose Statement

This study focuses on identifying factors that impact the management of conflict between believers in the shame-oriented culture of Sri Lanka. The specific context chosen is that of the capital, Colombo.

Research Question

The subject matter of this study gave rise to several data related questions that guided the study.

1. What are the distinctive characteristics of the shame-oriented culture of urban Sri Lanka?
2. In what ways do the characteristics of the shame-oriented culture of urban Sri Lanka affect the conflict behavior of Christians there?
3. In what ways do Christians in urban Sri Lanka deal with conflict in a shame-oriented culture, compared to ways prescribed by the New Testament?
4. How has the church helped urban Sri Lankan Christians be better equipped for reconciliation?

Significance of the Study

Sri Lanka is attempting to rebuild a reconciled society after almost thirty years of civil war. The church has played a role in national reconciliation, albeit in a fragmented and inconsistent way. Can the church be the reconciling force it should be without getting its own house in order?[12] The researcher's own conviction that the church has a significant role in reconciliation, together with the experience of viewing numerous broken relationships among believers, has driven this quest for a better way of understanding reconciliation in the Sri Lankan context.

As someone involved in the training of church leaders, the researcher has an interest in understanding the dynamics of interpersonal conflict in the church. The findings of this study will be used to train church leaders through the use of formal seminary curricula. It will also be of use in mentoring programs for students, staff and faculty and church members and to counsel those involved in conflict within their own churches and organizations.

Although the Western market is flooded with books on relationships, they have rarely taken into account the significance of living in a shame-oriented culture.[13] Many books are written on styles of conflict management.[14] Few provide a multi-disciplinary approach to the problem of reconciliation in the local church. Within Sri Lanka, though there are secular writings on the ethnic conflict, no one has yet carried out significant research or writing on the specific difficulties of reconciliation in a shame-oriented culture. In conversation with people from a wide array of backgrounds, including sociologists, seminary professors, lawyers and pastors, it emerged that there is a growing recognition that Sri Lankan culture is dominated by honor-shame characteristics. However, the researcher was unable to find any published research on the implications of the honor-shame culture specifically on the process of conflict and reconciliation. In such a context, this study provides a springboard for further discussion and study.

---

12. On a national level, the great conflicts that divide communities and ethnic groups are for the most part unaddressed within the church. Tamil and Sinhala congregations often worship separately. Even in churches that have joint worship services, it is rare that one community truly understands the hope, fears, and aspirations of the other. This paper will not deal with these macro issues, although it is assumed that the principles we discover will be applicable in some measure to this problem.

13. This is beginning to change with a surge of interest in shame, for example in the popular teaching by Brene Brown in the US.

14. For example, the popular identification of conflict management styles, many based on the Thomas–Kilmann Conflict Mode Instrument (TKI). Conflict management styles are listed as competing, collaborating, compromising, accommodating, and avoiding. The researcher would list them in a different order according to the logical of the shame-guilt model: avoiding, accommodating, competing, compromising, and collaborating.

Assumptions

Primary data sources consist of seven leaders currently ministering in the capital region of the country. Due to several similarities among them, it may be asked if their perspectives are biased. All have had experience of Western education and most them have lived in a Western culture for a minimum of two years. They are fluent in English and as such make use of Western resources, such as conferences, books, and seminars. Does this help or hinder them from being careful observers of Sri Lankan culture? These leaders have been chosen because of their reputation for being theologically astute, and for their years of ministry with various groups in different parts of the country.

All of the interviewees interact with Sri Lankan believers from a wide variety of backgrounds in their churches, seminaries, and counselling ministries. In the interviews, they describe their experiences and offer cultural reflection. However, in the presentation of their cases, they were simply describing an experience of interaction between Sri Lankans without offering interpretation or conclusions. Thus, this study assumes the case stories shared will be relatively bias free.

Each of the cases presented by interviewees is assumed to be truthful and accurate. No independent verification of the case nor added input from the conflicting parties was obtained. In three of the six cases analyzed, participants were personally involved in the conflict they presented as case studies.[15] Each of the interviewees was of good repute within the church. It is thus assumed that they each had nothing to gain from embellishing or falsifying their stories.

Research Methodology

The literature review disclosed several recurring themes within shame-oriented cultures that are related to conflict. From the work of anthropologists, missiologists, and communication theorists, a conceptual framework was constructed which guided the field research data collection and analysis. Seven characteristics of shame-oriented cultures were identified as key to conflict resolution. These formed the grid through which the field data were analyzed.

---

15. Seven interviews were carried out for the purpose of the study. One interviewee did not describe a case adequately for analysis so only six cases were used.

The primary field research design was case study. Qualitative data collection was conducted through interviews. Data sources were selected Christian leaders in the city of Colombo. All of them were chosen for their ministry experience which necessitated their knowledge of the inner workings of churches and organizations, and their known involvement in conflict resolution. All those chosen currently live and work in the capital city, Colombo. However, their ministry involves working with people from many parts of the country.

The interviews were based on a semi-structured format. A set of questions was prepared (appendix B) to guide the conversation. During these interviews, each interviewee was also asked to describe a case that illustrates their own experience in interpersonal conflict. Each interviewee was also asked to complete a culture rating grid (appendix C) that ranks certain characteristics of shame-oriented cultures as they perceived them in their interactions with Christians in their churches and ministries. The data collected were then analyzed using the categories constructed from the literature review.

This study includes a chapter on New Testament analysis which informs the final recommendations. This chapter is an important inclusion providing a biblical and theological basis for the final recommendations, taking into account the shame-oriented culture of the New Testament. It adds to the multi-disciplinary approach to the study.

Definition of Terms

The literature review revealed a wide variety of terms for so-called "shame" cultures. Terms such as "honor-shame" culture and "honor" culture,[16] "shame-oriented" and "relational,"[17] could all be used interchangeably. Kaufman's suggestion that the use of "shame" culture terminology had evaluative connotations, ranking it lower than "guilt" cultures, initially made the researcher inclined to use the term "honor culture."[18] However, since this research deals primarily with the effects of feeling shame and the way such feelings evoke

---

16. Malina, *New Testament World*.

17. Wiher, *Shame and Guilt*. Presented in his class "Honor and Shame Cultures" at Colombo Theological Seminary, 2014.

18. Kaufman, *Shame*.

a response in conflict resolution that also seemed inadequate. The following points were taken into consideration.

Scholars warn that writers on this topic tend to over-generalize and ignore variations and striations in culture.[19] Culture is, as Hiebert says, not best described in black and white categories but shades of grey along a continuum.[20] So also, "shame" and "guilt" characteristics are found in all cultures.[21] Therefore, the researcher has chosen the term "shame-oriented" to describe Sri Lankan culture. Where different terminology is employed by a particular author, the researcher has retained the use of their terminology to explain their position.

Delimitations

This research was delimited to a certain demographic. This study does not take into account gender-specific issues. The role of women in conflict resolution in shame-oriented cultures and how women may perceive issues of shame and honor have not been specifically dealt with because of the additional depth of research and inquiry that would need to be taken to do the topic justice. It may well be that the role of women in peace-building is something that has been neglected in Sri Lanka and can form the basis of further research and application.

There are several other sub-groups or subcultures whose response might vary significantly from the findings here. One of those groups is urban youth who have been affected by globalization through media and the internet. Another group is the Tamil population in the North who have lived with thirty years of war. The culture of violence prevalent in the north would significantly affect the responses of this people. However, for practical reasons, since this study is laying the foundation for further studies, the researcher believes a broad-based look at the most prominent characteristics of the culture of Sri Lanka will be the most beneficial, and most practical study to carry out at this stage.

---

19. Herzfeld, "Honour and Shame."
20. Hiebert, *Transforming Worldviews*, 22.
21. Augsburger, *Pastoral Counselling*, 113.

CHAPTER 2

Honor and Shame in Culture

The motif of honor-shame brings together a variety of disciplines; the most important for our purposes being cultural anthropology, missiology, biblical studies (social/culturally informed interpretations), and psychology. This chapter reviews the literature, setting out the characteristics of shame-oriented cultures, especially as they affect interpersonal conflict. While focusing on the cultural – and therefore social – aspect of honor-shame, the research will, where possible, attempt to integrate insights from the different disciplines.[1] The first two sections of the chapter explore the justification for defining a culture in terms of shame and honor. The third section highlights specific characteristics of shame-oriented cultures. The fourth examines how these characteristics impact conflict resolution. The fifth section proposes a conceptual framework for use in guiding the field study.

Culture, Worldviews, Shame, and Honor

To begin with, we shall locate the concepts of honor and shame within culture. The interplay between culture, worldview, and values provides the context for this discussion.

Defining Culture

In 1871, pioneer anthropologist E. B. Tyler coined the use of the term "culture," the anglicized version of the German word *kultur*, to describe "the total

---

1. Chapter 6 will continue into an in-depth review of New Testament texts related to inter-personal conflict.

nonbiologically transmitted heritage of man."[2] By the mid-1950s there were more than three hundred definitions of the term.[3] Culture is the whole gamut of abilities and habits including knowledge, beliefs, art, morals, customs, and law, says Luzbetak, "a design for living"[4] which, more elaborately explained, is "a *plan*, consisting of a set of *norms*, *standards*, and associated *notions and beliefs* for *coping* with the various demands of life, shared by a *social group*, *learned* by the individual from society and organized into a *dynamic system* of control."[5] It is "everything with which an individual is concerned and involved in a society."[6] It is "a complex frame of reference that consists of patterns of traditions, beliefs, values, norms, symbols, and meanings that are shared in varying degrees by interacting members of a community"[7] or society's complex integrated coping mechanism, consisting of learned, patterned concepts and behavior, plus their underlying perspectives (worldview), and resulting artefacts (material culture).[8] Cultures have a cognitive, affective, and evaluative dimension.[9]

Culture operates on every member of a society. Mayers goes so far as to say that "every thought a person thinks, every hope he has, every step he takes, every hope he holds, and every interaction he undertakes is controlled by his culture."[10] A child is "socialized"[11] or "enculturated" into their culture. Luzbetak lists three main ways in which culture is learned: through deliberate observation and imitation, through education, and most often, through unconscious imitation, which he calls "a kind of absorption."[12] Conflict style is also learned as part of the enculturation process. People tend to demonstrate a consistent conflict style within a particular culture.[13]

If we summarize the core elements of culture from these definitions, we see that culture is shared with a group, is learned and transmitted, is integrated

---

2. Kraft, *Christianity in Culture*, 45.
3. See Luzbetak, *Church and Cultures*, 134, for examples.
4. Luzbetak, 134, 139.
5. Luzbetak, 156.
6. Mayers, *Christianity Confronts Culture*, rev ed., 97.
7. Ting-Toomey, *Communicating across Cultures*, 10.
8. Kraft, *Anthropology for Christian Witness*, 38.
9. Hiebert, *Anthropological Insights*, 31.
10. Mayers, *Christianity Confronts Culture*, 98.
11. Mayers, 98.
12. Luzbetak, *Church and Cultures*, 188–189.
13. Ting-Toomey and Oetzel, *Managing Intercultural Conflict*, 46.

in all of life, includes an observable dimension, and is undergirded by an invisible set of assumptions.

Culture operates within a society. However, within any society there will be smaller groups or societies with their own subcultures, each comprising a unique blend of ingredients from the main culture. Families, villages, religious societies, clubs, and clans each may form a distinct social group. Within a society there will be systems of control to regulate the present, learn from the past, and maintain itself into the future.[14] Social structures that incorporate these controls are primarily marriage and kinship, economic, political, and religious systems.

Culture and Worldview

Culture has been likened to an iceberg.[15] We see some of the uppermost levels but many layers lie hidden beneath the surface. To understand any culture, we need to discern and understand its underlying values and beliefs. Anthropologists have discovered that there was something deep within a culture that gave rise to the externally observable phenomena. Beneath even the beliefs and values of a people were deep assumptions, a conceptual world that was rarely questioned.[16] Some scholars divide culture into two levels, the inner and outer, identifying the inner level as these silent assumptions, and the outer level as its observable features.[17] Others distinguish these assumptions from "culture" by identifying them as the "worldview" of a people. The worldview is the submerged portion of the iceberg.

The concept of worldview has emerged as a significant one in philosophy, anthropology, and Christian scholarship and practice within the last three decades.[18] Worldview can be defined as "the foundational cognitive, affective, and evaluative assumptions and frameworks a group of people makes about the nature of reality which they use to order their lives."[19] It lies at the heart of culture, informing all aspects of it. It is the "central systematization

---

14. Mayers, *Christianity Confronts Culture*, 100.
15. Ting-Toomey, *Communicating across Cultures*, 10.
16. Hiebert, *Transforming Worldviews*, 14–15.
17. Kraft, *Anthropology for Christian Witness*, 11.
18. See Hiebert (*Transforming Worldviews*, 13–71) for a discussion of the origins and development of the term.
19. Hiebert, *Transforming Worldviews*, 25–26.

of conceptions of reality," a reality that is accepted without question and largely unconsciously.[20]

A worldview is sometimes presented as static, unchanging, and completely integrated. Opler offered a more realistic and dynamic concept of worldview. He argued that in any worldview, rather than one harmonious, integrated whole, there are conflicting themes and counter-themes that function to keep cultures from going to extremes.[21] Hiebert, who supports this view, takes the example of individualism. Individualism is a major theme in some cultures, but when taken to extremes it leads to loneliness and narcissism. Therefore, a counter-theme emerges that leads people to form families, join associations and clubs, and subscribe to common laws in order to counteract individualism.[22] Cultures are thus in constant flux, adapting and changing due to the interplay between these counter-themes, sometimes also reflecting the shift of the balance of power between different groups (for example, rich and poor) as they rise to dominance. They also adapt to a changing world. Conflict as well as change is inevitable within a culture.[23] Cultures are therefore not best described in black and white categories but shades of grey along a continuum.[24] Worldviews also are not completely integrated but contain some elements that are always in tension.

Hiebert considers it a strength of Opler's model that he offers an insight into the way a worldview may be manipulated by those in power. "Worldviews are often ideologies that those in power use to keep others in subjection. Worldviews both enable us to see reality and blind us from seeing it fully."[25]

Worldviews are informed by the myths of a people, where "myth" means the metanarrative which a people relate to comprehend the cosmos. Myths are "transcendent stories believed to be true that bring cosmic order, coherence, and sense to the seemingly senseless experiences, emotions, and ideas in the everyday world by telling people what is real, eternal, and enduring."[26] Myths contain eternal truths, fostered by imagination as well as the shared memories passed down from generation to generation. In it "people see not

---

20. Kraft, *Christianity in Culture*, 53; *Anthropology for Christian Witness*, 55.
21. Opler, "Themes as Dynamic Forces."
22. Hiebert, *Transforming Worldviews*, 21–22.
23. Hiebert, 22.
24. Hiebert, 22.
25. Hiebert, 23.
26. Hiebert, 27.

truth but reality, because truth is always about something but reality is what truth is about."[27]

Common themes within worldviews are a peoples' relationship to time and space and the concept of the self. Evaluative themes within a worldview are what give rise to the social and moral order within a culture. Worldviews provide criteria which in turn inform people about the virtues to embrace, manners to exhibit in their social interactions, and standards to which they should ascribe. These standards will guide people to be able to identify who the heroes and villains are, what qualities are to be found in the ideal man and ideal woman, and how one is to relate to others, both within their group and with strangers. Worldview will undergird people's ultimate allegiances.[28] At conversion, it is a person's worldview that must change for true transformation of character.

The worldview of a people performs many vital functions.[29] To summarize, a worldview:

1. Provides answers to the ultimate questions of life, such as who am I? Why am I here? How do humans relate to the non-human world? What lies beyond death? They explain why things are the way they are and why they should remain that way or change.
2. Provides emotional security.
3. Provides the principles of right and wrong, guiding choice of behavior. Worldviews are evaluative, justifying the culture's values, goals, and institutions.
4. Provides a more or less coherent view of reality. It integrates, systemizes, and orders society's view of reality.
5. Serves as a filter through which people receive or reject new assumptions that come across their radar.
6. Provides psychological security. In times of crisis or confusion, members of the group turn to their worldview to encourage and guide them to their next course of action. Often, this reinforcement occurs through rituals and ceremonies.

---

27. Hiebert, 28.
28. Hiebert, 60–63.
29. Hiebert, 28–30; Kraft, *Christianity in Culture*, 54–57; Luzbetak, *Church and Cultures*, 252.

7. Is adaptational. Worldviews manage to be resilient in the face of changes in perceptions of reality usually transmitted through influential persons in the group.

As we have seen, worldviews are largely unexamined and implicit.[30] The way to understand a peoples' worldview is not necessarily through direct questioning, but through observation of behavior, rituals, and choices. Although we have explained that worldviews are sometimes referred to as "core culture" and are said to be the invisible source of a culture, this can be misleading. Changes can occur in the external, visible cultural forms; for example, changes in technology can in turn change a peoples' worldview.[31]

Cultural Values and Norms

The values of a culture arise from a peoples' worldview. Values are "orientations toward what is considered desirable or preferable" within a culture.[32] They have been variously described as "unconscious canons of choice,"[33] cultural themes,[34] the unconscious system of meaning[35] and worldview.[36] They are "whatever a group or an individual within a group considers of importance."[37] Cultural values are the set of priorities that give rise to an evaluation of what is "good" or "bad," "desirable," or "undesirable." They provide the motivation for a particular course of action (harmony, competitiveness), as well as being the goal.[38] "Values underlie all that a society is and does."[39] Values are not the same as moral principles. They are more fundamental than moral principles. They are accepted from an early age, their validity and desirability are not questioned or rationalized though they may be justified by moral principles.[40] "In other words, usually either we feel our values are simply logical, rational

---

30. Hiebert, *Transforming Worldviews*, 46.
31. Hiebert, 32.
32. Zavalloni, "Values," 74.
33. Benedict, *Patterns of Culture*, 48.
34. Opler, "Themes as Dynamic Forces."
35. Sapir, *Selected Writings*.
36. Redfield cited in Zavalloni, "Values," 78. Zavalloni describes how the search for a comprehensive study of values branched off into four avenues: the culture and personality school, sociology, interdisciplinary, and intercultural comparison (79).
37. Mayers, *Christianity Confronts Culture*, rev ed., 154.
38. Ting-Toomey, *Communicating across Cultures*, 11.
39. Mayers, *Christianity Confronts Culture*, rev ed., 76.
40. Adeney, *Strange Virtues*, 109.

and obvious from experience or we attribute them to God or some other authority."[41]

Within the culture, cultural values give rise to cultural norms. Cultural norms are the foundation for society's collective expectation of what is the proper thing to do.[42] They provide the "script" that governs behavior, and so can be recognized by observing behavior, though we may not discern the values, beliefs, and traditions that lie beneath them through observation of behavior alone.[43] Norms develop the values of a society. The individual internalizes the "sum of the norms" of all the groups and subcultures in which they participate.[44] The internalization of these norms makes life within a culture relatively tension free since most actions will be an "automatic" response that is in line with the norms of the culture. However, when one has to stop and think, it is a sign that one is approaching the boundaries of cultural norms.[45] In order to maintain an authentic identity, a person will live within the range of acceptable choices within the norm. When they violats the norm ("excess of norm"), there will be a reaction of shame or guilt. However, if the person then decides that their behavior is acceptable to them and represents a better lifestyle, then that guilt or shame will disappear and the new behavior is incorporated into the norm.[46] Feelings of guilt or shame might recur occasionally and the person might decide to revert to their original norm.[47]

This explanation of values, norms, and worldviews does not mean that it is easy to ascertain why people act in the way they do. There are certain common motivations based on universal human desires for betterment of quality of life, relationships, and respect, says Heine. However, since humans are also enculturated, their responses to the environment and even universal needs will be "grounded in cultural meaning systems."[48] For a culture to be either shame or guilt oriented, there must be supportive elements within

---

41. Adeney, 109.
42. Mayers, *Christianity Confronts Culture*, rev ed., 78.
43. Ting-Toomey, *Communicating across Cultures*, 11; Mayers, *Christianity Confronts Culture*, rev ed., 78.
44. Mayers, *Christianity Confronts Culture*, rev ed., 78.
45. Mayers, 79.
46. Mayers, 82.
47. Mayers, 154.
48. Heine "Culture and Motivation," 714–734. His review of current research posits a survey of motivations including religious beliefs, desire for consistency, self-esteem and self-enhancement, face, and self-improvement. The research showed differences especially between

its worldview. Also, for an individual within that culture, socialization will tend to inculcate the values towards which that culture tends. For example, in a Japanese culture where humans are considered to be morally neutral, humans do not need to be restrained from doing evil so much as molded into those who do what is considered good.[49] Creighton suggests that morals may be internalized as either "God" or "group," giving rise to cultures with a tendency to individualism (God) or collectivism (group). Practices arise within a culture to preserve and pass on their values. Even if the value is the same in different cultures, the practices that demonstrate those values will be different. "Moral principles become practical and visible when enfleshed in specific practices."[50]

Scholars have made successive attempts to posit a set of universal moral values. Closer reflection shows, however, that if such a list exists, it can only be of the vaguest generalities. Adeney reasons that even if a concept such as justice were to emerge on such a list, there would not be universal agreement on what justice was in a given situation.[51] Others have tried to provide a set of variables that they believe can map the values of any given culture.

For example, Kluckhohn developed a classification of value orientations by studying five different communities within the USA. He suggested five variables:

Table 2.1. Value Orientations according to Kluckohn

Orientation	Values
Orientation of man to nature:	Subjugation/harmony/mastery
Time orientation:	Past/present/future
Activity:	Being/being-in becoming/doing
Relational orientation:	Lineal/collateral/individualistic
Nature of man:	Good/bad/neutral

American (individualistic) and East Asian (collectivistic) subjects proving Heine's theory that choices are influenced by context.

49. Creighton, "Revisiting Shame," 297.

50. Adeney, *Strange Virtues*, 112.

51 See Adeney (*Strange Virtues*, 107–109) for a discussion on attempts to propose moral universals.

Hiebert cites Talcott Parsons' seven moral dimensions that Parsons believes exist in all societies.[52]

Table 2.2. The Moral Dimensions of Parson[53]

Emotional expression: publicly expressed, permissive	Emotional control: disciplined, private
Group centered: collective interests, corporate decision-making and responsibility	Individual centered: personal fulfillment, individual decisions
Other-world oriented: gains evaluated from other-worldly viewpoint	This world oriented: gains evaluated from this worldly viewpoint
Emphasizes ascription: relationships and personal worth based on birth	Emphasizes achievement: relationships and personal value comes from achievements
Focus on whole picture: takes a broad holistic view of an incident, person	Specific: focuses on details of specifics
Universalist: treats everyone alike, absolute ethics, stress on universal laws, truths	Particularist: people treated differently according to status and position, every situation is unique, adapts ethics to situation, values diversity and uniqueness
Hierarchy approved of: sees people as intrinsically unequal with privileges for some, accepts patron-client relationships	Values equality: sees people as inherently equal, everybody to be treated equally and held accountable, relationships are contractual

Several observations are in order. First, the sheer variety of categorizations shows there is a lack of consensus about what is universal and what categories can be used to distinguish cultures from one another. Adeney, in his research into ethics in a multicultural world, points out that some scholars have listed as many as seventy-five categories while others have as few as three.[54] The

---

52. Hiebert, *Transforming Worldviews*, 64.
53. Hiebert, 6.
54. Adeney, *Strange Virtues*, 115.

same goes for attempts to list universal moral values. Second, such lists tend to stereotype cultures. Third, they tend to evaluate certain cultures negatively in comparison with one specified culture, usually Western. While they may describe observations about a culture, they tend not to be able to explain the motivation behind different cultural choices and, in the end, run the risk of being too simplistic.[55]

From the study of the various categorizations, it can be noted that the distinction between individualistic and collectivistic cultures recurs frequently. As we shall see, this is one of the categories that distinguish shame-oriented cultures from guilt-oriented cultures. Additionally, within the models recommended, a model of values proposed by missiologist Mayers highlights values that have a significant impact on conflict resolution styles, and other issues of social interaction pertaining to conflict. Writing from within the Christian perspective, Mayers proposed a "basic values model" that presents six opposing pairs of values, which he suggested were present in and basic to all cultures.[56]

Mayers suggests that rather than attempt to identify a person or culture by placing them within one of the two opposing categories, and so polarizing them, they should be placed on a continuum.[57] Mayers's categorization of cultures was tested by Lingenfelter in the islands of Micronesia.[58] Missiologist Hannes Wiher also makes use of the data in his research.[59] For the purpose of this research, Mayers's categorizations, together with the insights of Lingenfelter and Wiher, prove extremely helpful and highlight certain traits which impact interpersonal conflict, as we shall explore more fully below.

As this overview shows, not every person in a culture may think and act exactly as another person in the same culture. "Culture varies from town to town, family to family and sometimes even from individual to individual."[60] Every person has to negotiate their way through life interacting with their beliefs, their environment (biological antecedents, physical, social, and

---

55. See Adeney for a review of maps or models of cultural value orientations.
56. Mayers, *Christianity Confronts Culture*, rev ed., 159–160.
57. Mayers, 165.
58. Lingenfelter and Mayers, *Ministering Cross-Culturally*.
59. Wiher, *Shame and Guilt*.
60. Muller, *Honor and Shame*, 22.

Table 2.3. The Basic Values of Mayers

Dichotomistic: organizes people into categories; life is polarized in black and white categories, right and wrong, where people belong, etc.	Holistic: must see big picture and be allowed to integrate all of life.
Crisis/declarative: will seek a readily available expert, like a written authority, to advise them in a crisis situation; will look for similar situations in history to learn from them.	Non-crisis/interrogative: needs several alternatives from which to choose; may choose a different solution each time they are faced with the same situation.
Time oriented: punctuality, planning.	Event oriented: interested in the events, bringing people together; concerned that the task is accomplished however long it takes.
Goal conscious: achieving goal is primary; friendships will be formed with those who have similar goals, or else will go it alone.	Interaction: relationships with people are more important than achieving a goal; rules, deadlines even goals will be sacrificed for the sake of relationships.
Prestige achieved: person will tend to ignore formal credentials and consider personal relationship; will focus on achieving prestige in his or her own eyes rather than in the eyes of society.	Prestige ascribed: will accept the place in society ascribed to them and expect others to accord him or her the respect due to that position; will tend to associate with people of similar rank.
Vulnerability as strength: not concerned about admitting they were wrong; will reveal own experiences of weakness and be open about his or her life; ready to try new things.	Vulnerability as weakness: tries not to show weakness and keeps a close check on self to prevent errors; will resist admitting to a mistake and will argue to prove he or she was right, or cover up mistakes; will be vague about personal life and not tell stories that reveal own weaknesses; unlikely to want to be involved in something new.

Source: Mayers, *Christianity Confronts Culture*, 159–160.

cultural), reflecting on the past and preparing for the future.[61] Every person is in some ways like all others, in their essential humanity and in certain basic human needs such as the need for security, safety, inclusion, dignity, respect, control, connection, meaning, creativity, and a sense of well-being.[62] These are universals, but how people go about obtaining them will differ from culture to culture.[63] People are also more like certain others, especially those who share their culture, whom they understand and with whom they feel most comfortable. Within a culture there are "cultural universals" which are adhered to by almost everyone; for example, wearing clothes as opposed to nudity. There are also "cultural alternatives" where a person has a choice between accepted norms, like marriage or singleness. Also, there are certain cultural traits that belong to certain individuals or segments of society (e.g. the king, athletes, teenagers).[64] Finally, in some ways, people are completely unique. No one is exactly like another in the package that is made up of life experience, giftedness, personality, and human nurture. As Augsburger puts it, there is in everyone an essential humanity, cultural embeddedness, and also individual uniqueness.[65] There is greatest similarity at the biological level (food, physical development, shelter), there is more variation with regard to the psychological and spiritual aspect of a person (belonging, esteem, love, ethics) and even more variety is seen in interpersonal and social areas of life (family life, language), with the greatest variation found in the institutional (social organization, state) and "broader worldview levels," like life purpose, and loyalty.[66]

Even though every individual is unique, within a given culture, there is sufficient commonality to make people look alike to outsiders.[67] Culture is sometimes personified as if it had the power to govern a people's behavior but "the apparent power of a culture to govern a person's behavior lies in the

---

61. Hiebert, *Cultural Anthropology*, table 22.1.

62. Ting-Toomey, *Communicating across Cultures*, 10.

63. Augsburger, *Pastoral Counselling*, 51. Augsburger provides a table of eighty-one human universals, formulated by Yale University's Human Relations Area File. They include bodily adornment, cooking, courtship, inheritance rules, ethics, religious rituals, and status differentiation.

64. Hiebert, *Cultural Anthropology*, 28.

65. Augsburger, *Pastoral Counselling*, 49.

66. Augsburger, 52–53.

67. Lingenfelter and Mayers, *Ministering Cross-Culturally*, 20.

human propensity to live by habit. Culture has no power in and of itself."[68] In fact, there may be times when individuals or even a large proportion of the population might not be observing the rules of the game that is culture. People are not slaves to their culture. Because they have a free will, and because of the various pressures they face, their own preferences, biases, personalities, sins, goals and anxieties, and crises, they may at times abandon the rules of culture, or abandon them in private. Adeney calls this the difference between "the desirable" and "the desired." A peoples' stated values are not necessarily observed in their praxis.[69] Occasionally, "the theoretically ideal may in fact sometimes constitute the exception rather than the rule."[70]

Understanding Guilt and Shame Cultures

Work on identifying the characteristics of honor-shame cultures began with anthropologist Ruth Benedict whose *Patterns of Culture*, though dismissed by anthropologists as an overgeneralization, provided sufficient credibility for her to be requested to analyze the Japanese culture during World War II. In her book *The Chrysanthemum and the Sword* Benedict characterized the culture of Japan as a "shame'" culture as opposed to America's "guilt" culture. In a "shame" culture people feel shame at the disapproval of their community.[71] Shame cultures rely on external sanctions rather than on conscience to maintain good behavior.[72] Benedict claimed that in Japan, the emphasis fell on shame rather than guilt. "A society that inculcates absolute standards of morality and relies on men's developing a conscience is a guilt culture by definition, but a man in such a society may, as in the United States, suffer in addition from shame when he accuses himself of gaucheries which are in no way sins."[73] According to Benedict, in a shame culture, people feel shame over acts "which we expect people to feel guilty about."[74] In shame cultures, people do not find relief in confession. In fact, Benedict goes on to say that as

---

68. Kraft, *Anthropology for Christian Witness*, 31.
69. Adeney, *Strange Virtues*, 48.
70. Luzbetak, *Church and Cultures*, 168.
71. Benedict, *Chrysanthemum and the Sword*, 222.
72. Benedict, 223.
73. Benedict, 222.
74. Benedict, 222.

long as a person's behavior is unknown by others, "he need not be troubled and confession appears to him merely a way of courting trouble."[75] Benedict, although forced to analyze the Japanese culture from a distance, managed to make this inscrutable culture more comprehensible to a Western audience.[76] We will see below that her research and her conclusions have been both challenged and defended.

In 1954, missiologist Eugene Nida raised the question of shame-oriented cultures in his classic *Customs, Cultures and Christianity*. Questioning if "primitive people" felt a sense of guilt, he recognized three types of reactions to "transgressions of religiously sanctioned codes," that is fear, shame, and guilt. He argued that guilt was a relatively rare reaction because of humanity's egocentric way of living whereas fear and shame were more common.[77]

Early anthropologists like Benedict claimed that the primary distinction between guilt and shame cultures was the way control sanctions operated. In a guilt culture people were controlled by internal sanctions created by a conscience usually informed by religious convictions (at the time of their writing, this tended to be Christianized, Western cultures). In a shame culture, by contrast, people acted in accordance with external sanctions created by their group or society.[78]

Unfortunately, there arose with these definitions, alongside certain models of anthropology, the view that shame cultures were a more primitive or less evolved culture. Even today, there exists a tendency to view shame negatively, or as a primitive form of response which ought to be transformed into a guilt reaction. Early approaches to cultural anthropology assumed an evolutionary progression in cultures, from simple to complex.[79] Shame was seen as

---

75. Benedict, 223.

76. Reference is made to this distinction in Jacob Loewen (*Culture and Human Values*, 314) citing Mead's work.

77. Nida, *Customs, Cultures and Christianity*, 150.

78. Based on the work of Margaret Mead, *Cooperation and Competition*. Benedict, *Chrysanthemum and the Sword*, 222; Piers and Singer, *Shame and Guilt*, 63.

79. Creighton, "Revisiting Shame," 283; Flanders, "Shame," 814; Piers and Singer, *Shame and Guilt*, 59. For example, see the work of ninteenth-century social theorists Edward B. Tylor (*Primitive Culture*, 2006), who proposed that every society was capable of progress and did so independently, and Lewis Morgan (*Ancient Society*, 1877), who agreed with Tylor's basic categorization of societies as passing through savagery and barbarism to civilization. See Luzbetak (*Church and Cultures*, 139–156) for a survey of anthropological models of culture, including "neo-evolutionism" which replaced cultural evolutionism.

an external sanction indicative of a culture that had not yet advanced to the stage where inner moral sanctions would be effective.[80] Tracing the historical development of anthropology, Piers and Singer state that in the early days, guilt cultures were thought to be progressive, possessed of "absolute moral standards" enforced by the individual religious conscience, for the good of the individual, while shame cultures were "static," "industrially backward," "without absolute moral standards," and dominated by "crowd psychology."[81] Norman Kraus also picks up on the fact that not only within anthropology, but also within psychology and theology, "shame" has been depicted as being morally inferior to guilt.[82] In psychology shame was seen as a morally inferior reaction to guilt in the face of wrongdoing, an early stage in development prior to full maturity.[83] Theologically, shame was seen as part of the primitive groups' ethical tradition. Its motivation was seen as self-serving (to save face) and thus far less worthy than conscience. Shame-oriented honor cultures have been characterized as archaic, and/or primitive and violent.[84] Kaufmann argues that Benedict's theories were based on false assumptions about the Japanese people and therefore contrasted the "inferior" motivation of the shame culture of the Japanese people with the "virtuous" conscience-driven guilt culture of the Americans. This bias can be seen in the fact that the Japanese culture is labelled a "shame" culture rather than an "honor" culture.[85]

In fact, all of these conceptions about shame cultures have been challenged, including the defining characteristics themselves. Benedict's early analysis of Japan as a shame culture has been resisted by the Japanese themselves, partly because of the wide spread perception that she had also ranked a shame culture lower in moral development than a guilt culture. However, Creighton in her article analyzing Benedict's work, defends Benedict's analysis of the

---

80. Yang, *Discipline or Shame?*, 208; Piers and Singer, *Shame and Guilt*, 59.
81. Piers and Singer, *Shame and Guilt*, 59–60. These assumptions have been challenged by the progress of the so-called shame culture countries, the warmongering of the so-called guilt cultures, and Islamic cultures where religious norms are the guiding values, etc. (61–62).
82. Kraus, *Jesus Our Lord*, 208.
83. Yang, *Discipline or Shame?*, 55; Kraus, *Jesus Our Lord*, 208.
84. Kaufman, "Understanding Honor," 557. Kaufmann refutes Benedict's claims which he says were based on her misunderstanding the culture.
85. Kaufman, 562.

Japanese culture against those who have "denounced, denied, refuted and reclassified" her conclusions, arguing that Benedict has been misunderstood.[86]

First, let us consider the prevailing understanding that the major difference between a guilt culture and a shame culture is the internal-external sanctions dichotomy. This differentiation is by no means as clear and distinct as some would presume. Piers and Singer note that even Margaret Mead, on whose work Benedict built, in her categorization of guilt and shame cultures implied that shame could become an internal sanction if strongly developed.[87] There was the possibility that the audience need not be present but be imagined, meaning there was a degree of internalization.[88] Piers and Singer cite Mead's illustration that an Indian alone on a lake could feel such shame at his paddle breaking that he would kill himself.[89] Creighton argues that if, as Benedict states, the external audience can be real or imagined, it implies that the fear of shame has been internalized. In fact, Creighton says, if a person's motivation is to please God that too is a shame response since God is the external audience. Not just shame but guilt too will arouse emotions in the presence of others, or if it becomes apparent that one's actions are about to become known. The difference is that in a guilt-oriented culture, the fear will be of punishment by the group. In a shame-oriented culture it will be fear of being seen as inferior within the group.[90] Creighton cites Japanese scholars who reverse Benedict's analysis by saying that guilt is externally oriented since it is caused by the fear of external punishment while shame is internally motivated and cultivated.[91] The conclusion to which Piers and Singer arrive is that since some forms of shame are paralleled in some forms of guilt, the better mode of distinction is to say that there is a difference in the source of unconscious anxiety that arises when a person within the two different cultures has acted outside of cultural norms. In a shame culture "unconscious shame" is anxiety of abandonment due to the failure to live up to the internalized parental ideals, and in a guilt

---

86. Creighton, "Revisiting Shame," 279–307.
87. Piers and Singer, *Shame and Guilt*, 62–66.
88. Benedict, *Chrysanthemum and the Sword*, 223.
89. Piers and Singer, *Shame and Guilt*, 66.
90. Creighton, "Revisiting Shame," 286.
91. Creighton, 286.

culture "unconscious guilt" arises due to the transgression of internalized parental prohibitions accompanying fear of punishment.[92]

Kaufman wants to repudiate the widely held belief that honor is essentially an "external moral ideal" (what he calls the "honor as external thesis"), crafted by the consensus of the influential majority, and purely motivated by a desire to avoid being shamed before one's peers.[93] He suggests that, in fact, the truly honorable person chooses to live in accordance with principles they consider honorable, regardless of consequences to their safety, financial or physical well-being, and regardless of what others around them might think of them.[94] This means that, contrary to this common understanding, honor is a manifestation of an individual's moral autonomy. Honor has both an internal and external motivation. It is both one's own estimation of one's self as well as the public acknowledgment of that worth. There is an internal as well as external standard that gauges the right to honor, which many scholars play down. Kaufman argues that the internal control is "prior and more fundamental" than the outward recognition.[95] Creighton similarly states that both shame and guilt need to be internalized to be truly experienced. If not, it is just the consequences of the act that are feared rather than a real inward recognition that the consequences are earned.[96] Lynd writes of the "involvement of the whole self" in shame and even suggests that a person may feel ashamed at conforming to the values of society because of a consciousness of deeper "transcultural" values that they desire to live by, thus implying that the shame culture person may be driven by an internal motivation.[97]

> It is not that the goal of honorable behavior is simply to achieve public esteem (and the attending rewards). Rather the idea is that the honorable person demonstrates his worth by acting without thought of any reward *apart* from that esteem, that is

---

92. Piers and Singer, *Shame and Guilt*, 97.
93. Kaufman, "Understanding Honor," 557.
94. Kaufman, 559.
95. Kaufman, 559.
96. Creighton, "Revisiting Shame," 287.
97. Lynd, *On Shame*, 35–37.

in contrast to the base or mercenary material motivations of most people.⁹⁸

The person in search of honor is not a superficial person whose behavior is controlled by public opinion. Rather, they are an individual who rises above the ordinary person to shun material gain in favor of being true to their ideals, and so achieves society's ideals and their acclaim. Kaufman lists and evaluates four common ways shame cultures are contrasted with guilt cultures.⁹⁹

First, they are seen as conformist as opposed to liberated. Kaufmann refutes this, declaring that from Greek heroes to Japanese Samurai to dueling Europeans, history shows that honorable people from "shame-based" cultures were in fact non-conformist. They refused to adhere to pedestrian norms of safety, but stood up for their principles despite what it cost them. Being true to themselves, they earned the honor of their peers. Kaufmann also points out that guilt cultures can be just as conformist as the caricature of shame cultures (e.g. the Puritans).

Second, they are viewed as motivated purely by a desire for external recognition. Kaufman points out that classical Greek culture, for instance, shows that heroes like Achilles were unmoved by external rewards. In fact, the hero is acting in accordance with principles that he desires his society to value. In so doing, he contributes toward influencing his society's perception of what should be honored.

Third, they are seen as superficial in that people operating in this culture are more concerned with being seen to be a certain way than actually being that way. For example, some are more concerned with being called a liar than with lying. Kaufman contends that this blanket description of honor cultures is without foundation and that it ill-behooves a culture obsessed with fashion, Hollywood, and the celebrity culture to call another culture superficial. More likely, he says, there are superficial elements to both cultures.

Fourth, he looks at the accusation that honor cultures are hypocritical. People work hard at appearing "moral on the surface but only to conceal their corrupt machinations from others."¹⁰⁰ Kaufman cites Mead who states that in the shame society the individual "is safe as long as no one knows of

---

98. Kaufman, "Understanding Honor," 560.
99. Kaufman, 565.
100. Kaufman, 569.

his misdeed; he can dismiss his misbehavior from his mind"[101] and Benedict, who agrees that "so long as his bad behavior does not 'get out into the world,'" a man "need not be troubled"[102] whereas in a guilt culture, a man "may suffer from guilt though no man knows of his misdeed."[103] This view of honor cultures paints a portrait of a society whose people merely pretend that values like courage or integrity are precious to them, but underneath this veneer, they are found to be motivated solely by self-interest and pragmatism. In such a context, it is not the action but getting caught that is the sin. This view of honor "turns honor on its head" says Kaufman, and can only be a projection onto honor cultures of all that the Western culture rejects.[104] Noble says that in ancient Greek culture honor was seen as more positive than morality because "honor stresses obligation while morality emphasizes prohibitions."[105] Notions of honor motivate people to take action to change situations.

Kaufman points out that societies cannot function as societies unless people internalize the values of that society. A society in which the members did not internalize its values would arguably not even count as a society at all.[106] If people did not internalize values, society would have to be controlled by the use of external force – a totalitarian state. The culture would then be a fear-based rather than a shame-based culture. If we accept that a shame-oriented culture depends both on internal and external sanctions, then just because a person expects some recognition of what they have done, that does not mean that that recognition was their sole motivation. The fact that people seek external approval is perfectly consistent with their also behaving according to internalized standards.[107] Recent anthropological and psychological research concludes that both guilt and shame operate using an internalized norm, the conscience.[108] Wiher considers the phenomenon of shame and guilt from a variety of perspectives, psychological, missiological, theological,

---

101. Mead cited in Kaufman, *Honor and Revenge*, 164.
102. Benedict, *Chrysanthemum and the Sword*, 223.
103. Mead cited in Kaufman, "Understanding Honor," 569.
104. Kaufman, 569.
105. Noble, *Naked and Not Ashamed*, 8.
106. Kaufman, "Understanding Honor," 567.
107. Kaufmann (567) cites the example of professional athletes who might demand high remuneration for their performance but who cannot then be characterized as performing purely out of mercenary motives.
108. Flanders, "Shame," 814.

biblical, and anthropological. He uses the concept of the conscience as his tool, which he sees as oriented towards either guilt or shame. The conscience is the center of personality; it is "activated" by the fall, for it is through the fall that mankind realizes that it is separated from God. This separation is marked by both shame and guilt.[109]

> The conscience gives man contact with God and orientation in society. It enables him to internalize norms, values and goals of society, and religion and avoid their violation. It is given to every man as an innate disposition in form of potential elements and is developed and formed by the social context. Formed and adapted through culture, it directs decisions and behavior. The process of modulation is a lifelong process, which in Christian life is directed by the Holy Spirit. The conscience relates to largely unconscious, cognitive, emotional, volitional and spiritual processes, which induce an internalized moral control of behavior.[110]

Kaufman goes on to show that guilt cultures, no less than honor cultures, have both an internal and external element of motivation. Guilt can refer to one's internal awareness of a breach of one's own conscience but it can also mean a public verdict, as in a court. If so, then guilt also operates as a form of external sanction – both through punishment and the stigma of public disapproval – as well as an internal one (indeed, the two are tightly connected). Guilt, no less than shame, can be a physical manifestation visible on a person's face, a blush for shame, and a look of "the cat that swallowed the canary" for guilt.[111] Similarly, shame is not merely exposure to the censure of others but also exposure to oneself. Shame can be experienced in relation to a failure to meet one's own standards as well as those of another.[112] A sense of shame may accompany a sense of guilt. A person feels guilt for a wrongdoing and then a sense of shame at what people might say or how they appear in their own eyes. Or a person may feel shamed and then angry and then guilty.[113] Piers

---

109. Wiher, *Shame and Guilt*, 161.
110. Wiher, 165.
111. Kaufman, "Understanding Honor," 567.
112. Kraus, *Jesus Our Lord*, 209.
113. Pattison, *Shame*, 44.

and Singer show how "guilt-shame cycles" can occur within one individual. They give the example of behavior arising from experiencing hostility. The experience first gives rise to aggression. A feeling of guilt arises which leads to inhibition and passivity. The passivity gives rise to an interaction in which the passive participant now feels shame. To compensate, the participant becomes aggressive, giving rise to guilt once again.[114] They conclude that guilt and shame, though distinct, can lead from one to another or conceal one another.[115]

Another important characterization of shame cultures, arising from the discussion above, is that people are "dyadic" or collectivistic. Newbold uses the terms "amoebic" and "encapsulated." Personality types may be either "encapsulated" or "amoebic." An encapsulated personality is one that exists as a clearly demarcated compartment, influencing rather than being influenced by its environment. This is the guilt personality type. An amoebic personality type is the opposite; it is more easily influenced and less well demarcated, more fluid, revolving around the shame axis.[116] According to Newbold, it is hard to disentangle the characteristics of the two types because they "alternate with, reinforce and conceal one another."[117]

As we can see, there seems to be consensus that guilt and shame are both internalized. Both effects may arise within an individual even within a single interaction with another. Both guilt and shame occur in cultures, whether they are labelled guilt cultures or shame cultures.

Augsburger, arguing for a new organization of theory and therapy that neither ignores nor advocates the eradication of shame and guilt, sets out the following theses.

1. Anxiety, shame, and guilt are the natural, normal, and universal sequence of controls in human personality in every culture. All three are normal reactions that occur in the first three years of a child's life in that order. Different cultures will tend towards one or the other of these as a means of social control and children will be socialized according to the dominant mode.[118]

---

114. Piers and Singer, *Shame and Guilt*, 32.
115. Piers and Singer, 44.
116. Newbold, "Personality Structure and Response," 199.
117. Newbold, 200.
118. Augsburger, *Conflict Mediation*, 82.

2. Cultures are not uniformly shame cultures or guilt cultures and cannot be labelled thus. However, one culture may stress one of the three control patterns more than the others. Augsburger explains how Japanese culture, usually the stereotypical shame culture, has a strong element of guilt, which goes unnoticed. However, unlike in individualistic cultures, that guilt does not arise from comparisons with an abstract or supernatural universal standard, but arises from the system of in-group loyalties of traditional society.[119] Augsburger calls shame the "overt social control process" and guilt the "covert," in Japan, while it is the other way around in Western culture.[120]
3. All three processes occur in every person, group, and culture but with different intensities and patterns.
4. Although in human development, shame does occur prior to guilt, this does not mean one is superior.
5. The evaluation of shame cultures as "incompletely socialized" or of guilt cultures as "superior in moral conscience formation" is faulty and is not supported by actual cases or observations.
6. The negative valuation of shame by therapists, theologians, and theorists betrays their own prejudice which blinds them to the wisdom to be gained from these cultures.
7. Full acceptance, integration, and reconciliation of all three can release their healing potential and release blocks to recovery and growth.
8. All find resolution in authentic forgiveness and grace.[121]

Creighton offers a helpful analogy from left-hand right-hand dominance. It is preferable to have two hands over one hand or none. Having some measure of dexterity in both is optimal. Those who are truly ambidextrous are few and the majority of people are either right-handed or left-handed. Finally, neither left-handedness nor right-handedness can be said to be superior to the other.[122]

---

119. Augsburger, *Pastoral Counselling*, 125.
120. Augsburger, 126.
121. Points 3–8 above are from Augsburger, *Pastoral Counselling*, 113.
122. Creighton, "Revisiting Shame," 293.

What seems to be apparent is that no individual or culture operates totally in either the guilt or shame arena.[123] The internal versus external sanctions dichotomy is also more nuanced than first thought. While it is still common to categorize cultures in this way, what must be kept in mind is that "such strong dichotomies are naïve and simplistic."[124] What Benedict and Creighton claim is supported by Japanese scholars; that is, "shame sanctions play a greater role in regulating behavior in Japan than guilt sanctions."[125] Guilt and shame reactions are both internalized at some point in development.[126] Piers and Singer say there is no evidence to justify calling certain cultures backward. "What evidence there is tends to support the conclusion that the sense of guilt and the sense of shame are found in most cultures, and that the quantitative distribution of these sanctions has little to do with the 'progressive' or 'backward' character of a culture."[127]

Defining Shame

In shame-oriented cultures, shame is the loss of honor.[128] Shame is a complex phenomenon that can be described and analyzed from several perspectives including psychoanalytical, sociological, ethical and cultural points of view.[129] One of the difficulties in describing the phenomenon of shame is that there is only one English term, "shame," which covers a range of meanings.[130] "Shame is as central to the human existence as anxiety or suffering, yet is far more elusive in nature."[131] Like an onion, shame is made up of enfolded and overlapping but also discrete meanings and understandings; "there is no 'essential onion' or 'essential shame' at the center of meaning or experience."[132] The

---

123. Augsburger, *Pastoral Counselling*, 113; Tennent, *Theology in the Context*, 79.
124. Flanders, "Shame," 814.
125. Benedict, *Chrysanthemum and the Sword*; Creighton, "Revisiting Shame," 282.
126. Creighton, 282.
127. Piers and Singer, *Shame and Guilt*, 99.
128. Noble, *Naked and Not Ashamed*, 2.
129. See Pattison (*Shame*), Albers (*Shame*), and Heller ("Five Approaches") for different approaches to understanding shame.
130. Augsburger, *Pastoral Counselling*, 115. Augsburger points out that many languages have at least two or more words to describe shame. He critiques the fact that we can easily see the positive and negative sides of anxiety and guilt but not of shame.
131. Kaufman, "Understanding Honor," 7.
132. Pattison, *Shame*, 39.

word "shame" derives from notions of covering and concealing. From the Germanic root *skam/skem* it is traced back to the Indo-European *kam/kem* meaning "to cover, to veil, to hide."[133] The notion of hiding is intrinsic to and inseparable from the concept of shame. However, this aspect of concealment more accurately describes the reaction to shame rather than shame itself. This urgent desire to hide, cover, or disappear derives from a feeling of exposure (e.g. Adam and Eve and the fig leaves).[134] Pattison suggests that shame be approached on the basis of "family resemblance" which denies that every use of a concept should contain the same content and meaning. Rather, a concept might be used in different ways and contexts with only some commonalities with usages in other contexts. Instead of a set of defining characteristics, there is a network of similarities overlapping and crisscrossing like the resemblances and differences in the features of children from one family.[135]

In psychoanalytical terms, shame originates in unconscious events and processes, and has been categorized as the failure of the ego to conform to the expectations of the ego ideal.[136] However, even this definition has been challenged. For instance, Augsburger claims that in collectivistic cultures the disparity is less between the ego and the ego ideal and more between the ego and the social ideal as represented by the ideals of the group or family.[137]

While shame occurs when a goal is not reached, and is thus a "shortcoming" or failure, guilt arises when a boundary set by the super-ego is transgressed.[138] In essence, "guilt tells us we have *gone beyond what was allowed*, while shame points to the fact that we have *fallen short of what was expected*."[139] Behind the feeling of shame is the fear of being abandoned or treated with contempt.[140]

---

133. Pattison, 40.
134. Pattison, 40.
135. Hick cited in Pattison, *Shame*, 62.
136. Pattison, *Shame*, 45–47; Piers and Singer, *Shame and Guilt*, 16–17. Guilt is the response to the failure of the ego in response to the superego, the internalization of the parent figure, real or imagined.
137. Augsburger, *Conflict Mediation*, 83.
138. Piers and Singer, *Shame and Guilt*, 24–25.
139. Binau, "Shame and the Human Predicament," 129.
140. Piers and Singer, *Shame and Guilt*, 29. See Smedes (*Shame and Grace*, 9–15) for clarification on what shame is not. Shame is distinguished from embarrassment, discouragement, depression, and frustration.

Smedes suggests that certain personalities are more prone to shame. Those who allow guilt to spread from one act to an overwhelming shame, those who have an overdeveloped sense of responsibility, those who are constantly comparing themselves to others, obsessive moralizers for whom everything is right or wrong, those who crave the approval of others, those who feel undeserving, and those who have some deep shame in their past that haunts them, are prime candidates for taking on themselves shame that is undeserved.[141] Shame also plays a part in shaping the personality. In a sociological sense, shame is

> a wound to one's self esteem. A painful feeling or sense of degradation excited by the consciousness of having done something unworthy of one's previous idea of one's own excellence. It is also a particularly painful feeling of being in a situation that incurs the scorn or contempt of others.[142]

Shame is less attached to a specific act that can be rectified and more to a sense of inadequacy, or inferiority. "It is associated with a way of being that leads to an embarrassed sense of loss and emptiness, a failing of the ideal."[143] In a cultural sense, shame is experienced as a sense of failure that arises when a person feels they have let down their community, their ancestors, or their gods. In this aspect of shame, there is little sense of transgressing a universal moral law. What has been transgressed is what is normative in society, that is, "group norms."[144] "Shame is a dynamic that pressures people to conform to their group and so maintain harmony and peace."[145]

Anthropologically, shame is a synonym of dishonor. "Honor and shame are two sides of a coin."[146] The function of shame is to prevent dishonorable behavior and guide a person towards doing what is considered honorable. "Anticipated shame serves as a powerful force for social control."[147] Auli says of the Chagga culture, "shame is interpreted as an emotional response to

---

141. Smedes, *Shame and Grace*, 16–27.
142. Pattison, *Shame*, 53; see also Lynd, *On Shame*, 23–24.
143. Augsburger, *Conflict Mediation*, 83.
144. Hiebert, *Gospel in Human Contexts*, 111.
145. Hiebert, 111.
146. Noble, *Naked and Not Ashamed*, 7.
147. Noble, 7.

falling short of the social norm. In other words, shame is the feeling that one does not correspond to the culturally defined behavior that is attached to a particular social role."[148] Shame can be broadly divided into two categories. Negatively, to behave in a way that is contrary to the values and ideals of the group brings shame and disgrace. It is "losing face" or losing the esteem of the group. On the positive side, shame is also sensitivity to the opinions of the group. When one refuses to behave in a certain way because it would bring disgrace, then one is demonstrating a positive character trait.[149] To be without a sense of shame is to be shameless. Riezler points out that there is something deep within the "soul" of the person which resonates with the external demand for a particular type of behavior. If a person is completely shameless, the only external sanction can be fear, not shame. Externally also, what others think is important because we are social beings. A person is both who they are and who they are to others. We are part what we think of ourselves and part what others think of us. Additionally, if we fail at our self-image, we try to compensate with what others think of us.[150]

This type of shame has an ethical element to it. It has the function of maintaining boundaries, allowing privacy, and maintaining modesty for ourselves and others.[151] If all self-respect is lost, the person feels no shame but only self-contempt. Shame reveals that the person cares deeply about themselves in relation to society. In shame one is judged by one's inner idea. This means there is still an ideal. Another way of defining these two types of shame is as "disgrace" shame and "discretionary" shame.[152] Riezler's description of the pain of shame is widely cited: "your image of yourself is broken. . . . You despise yourself. You will hate the one who puts you to shame. This hate is the most bitter of all, the most difficult to heal. It has the longest memory. Shame burns . . ."[153]

In the face of others, shame may project outwardly as rage. Pure shame is experienced before the self. "Shame is self-estrangement, self-rejection,

---

148. Auli, "Shame, Guilt and Church," 64.
149. Yang, *Discipline or Shame?*, 61; Noble, *Naked and Not Ashamed*, 2.
150. Riezler, "Comment on the Social Psychology," 458.
151. Albers, *Shame*.
152. Albers.
153. Cited in Augsburger, *Pastoral Counselling*, 107; Yang, *Discipline or Shame?*, 53.

even revulsion."[154] Shame provokes anger towards oneself at being less than the ideal, and towards others for humiliating us.[155] Shame causes isolation because it is extremely difficult to talk about. To talk about it is to compound the shame. It makes the shame more widely known and so makes one more shameful. Whereas sharing one's guilt may be therapeutic, sharing one's shame exacerbates it. Shame experiences are also difficult to recount because to recount is to experience afresh. "Shame experiences are incommunicable. The listener too is rendered impotent. What can they say to lessen the shame?"[156] Binau suggests that shame tends to arise within relationships in a way that guilt does not, possibly because shame occurs earlier in the developmental stage when we are first discovering our identity within relationships in the family.[157]

> Shame always stands between people and pushes them apart. It never draws people together. It makes for concealment not disclosure of self. It leads to lies, anger and avoidance . . . never leads to confession and reconciliation. It leads to concealment and avoidance . . . it makes for distrust not trust, self-defence not affirmation of the other.[158]

Shame alienates from another but still longs to be connected. This shows a continuing desire for relationship. While guilt asks, "What will happen to me?" shame focuses on the relationship asking, "What will happen to this relationship?"[159] Thus shame contains reason for hope. Whereas with disgust the other is rejected, with shame there is a yearning, a longing for reconnection.[160] Bonhoeffer, one of the earliest theologians to write on the pain of shame, described it as one of the ways humans perceive their alienation from God and from others; when they are laid bare and devoid of the covering they would have from God and others.[161] Bonhoeffer describes shame

---

154. Donald Capp cited in Yang, *Discipline or Shame?*, 53.
155. Yang, *Discipline or Shame?*, 54.
156. Yang, 54.
157. Binau, "Shame and the Human Predicament," 132.
158. MacLeod quoted in Augsburger, *Pastoral Counselling*, 114–115. Yang, *Discipline or Shame?*, 55.
159. Binau, "Shame and the Human Predicament," 133–134.
160. Augsburger, *Pastoral Counselling*, 118.
161. Bonhoeffer, *Ethics*, 20.

as "man's ineffaceable recollection of his estrangement from the origin; it is grief for this estrangement and the powerless longing to return to unity with the origin." Shame arises from this loss of something "essential to his original character, to his wholeness."[162] Shame exists in every sphere because we are estranged from God and from ourselves. "Shame is overcome only in the shaming through the forgiveness of sin, that is to say, through the restoration of fellowship with God and men. This is accomplished in confession before God and men."[163] Binau stresses the relational aspect of shame. Shame arises when we realize our relationships are askew. The theological concept of covenant deals with this aspect of shame, placing us in a relationship we can trust, where we belong.[164]

Guilt feelings are easier to deal with. There are formal remedies like confession and atonement. Shame has no such remedies. "Shame is an acute, painful, inarticulable experience. It leaves those who experience it feeling exposed, passive and impotent."[165] The contrast between guilt and shame can be set out as in table 2.4.

Many scholars argue that shame is not the reaction to falling short of group ideals. On a deeper level, shame is being exposed to oneself, being made aware that we are not who we want to be. In that aspect of shame lies the possibility of great transformation. For shame to be extinguished, a person's first level of defense is usually to move away and hide or even commit suicide. In many cases, this is where the experience of shame leaves people, but if we push past that temptation to the inner level of shame, we learn to face the truth about ourselves, and seeing it, we seek help to be transformed.[166] Flanders's comparison of guilt and shame is summarized in table 2.5.

---

162. Bonhoeffer, 20.
163. Bonhoeffer, 23.
164. Binau, "Shame and the Human Predicament," 138–139.
165. Pattison, *Shame*, 44.
166. Lynd, *On Shame*; Noble, *Naked and Not Ashamed*, 12.

Table 2.4. Comparison of Shame and Guilt Experiences

Guilt axis	Shame axis
Transgression of a boundary set by super-ego, that is, a contradiction between who we are (ego) and what we should do (super-ego)	Failure to meet expectations of ego ideal, that is, a contradiction between who we are (ego) and what we want to be (ego ideal)
Concerned with an individual act	Concerns the whole person
Transgression of a known code Involves competition, choosing acts prescribed as desirable	Falling short of an ideal Involves acting in accordance with demands of oneself, more rigorous than external codes; "each act partakes of the quality of the whole"
Involves an "additive" process of deleting wrongs and replacing them with right	Involves total insight, more than can be achieved by addition
Exposure of acts to self	Exposure of self to others and to oneself
Guilt is removed through penalty paid	Shame is overcome by acceptance, covenant relationship
Removal of guilt is innocence/righteousness	Transcending shame may lead to freedom, sense of identity
Needs assurance of forgiveness	Needs word of acceptance
Fear of punishment	Fear of abandonment

Source: Noble, *Naked and Not Ashamed*, 23; Lynd, *On Shame*, 208–209; Piers and Singer, *Shame and Guilt*, 23; Binau, "Shame and the Human Predicament," 129, 141.

Table 2.5. The Distinction between Shame and Guilt according to Flanders [167]

Guilt	Shame
Experienced as regret, remorse, self-condemnation	Experienced in feelings of inadequacy, powerlessness, unworthiness
Desire to confess, repair	Desire to hide, escape, retaliate

---

167. Flanders, *About Face*, 61.

Defining Honor

Despite the fact that, as we have seen, scholars disagree about the actual distinction between shame and guilt, several cultures have been identified as shame-oriented cultures. They tend to lie primarily between what is referred to in missiology as the 10/40 window. Some cultures which had had influential writing on the subjects are the Islamic cultures of the Middle East, Japan, China, the Philippines, Korea, and Malaysia.[168]

In shame-oriented cultures honor is a value and shame is to be avoided. Honor has been defined by British anthropologist Julian Pitt-Rivers in his seminal article as "the value of a person in his own eyes, but also in the eyes of his society. It is his estimation of his own worth, his *claim* to pride, but it is also the acknowledgment of that claim, his excellence, recognized by society, his *right* to pride."[169] Honor is a sense of freedom and self-respect based on one's identification with one's selected values, free from arrogance towards others.[170] Bruce Malina, in his highly influential work, *The New Testament World*, on which many others draw, sets honor and shame within the framework of values. Honor and shame, he states, are "pivotal" cultural values.[171] Honor is a "dynamic and relational concept," a combination of self-respect and the respect of others.[172] Honor is a "social construct, an idea that different societies fill with meaning in different ways."[173] It is a "register of social rating" or "creditworthiness" in society.[174] Gilmore calls it a "master symbol."[175] Honor may be ascribed or acquired, as will be explained below, but in either case, it must be acknowledged by some body or tribunal such as public opinion, the monarch, the law, or the deity. One may consider oneself honorable if one embodies the virtues of one's community or group. However, this self-evaluation is not sufficient. The group (which scholars label "the public court

---

168. Middle East (Roland Muller, *Honor and Shame*), Japan (Ruth Benedict, *Chrysanthemum and the Sword*; Lebra, "Social Mechanism of Guilt"), China (Wu, *Saving God's Face*), the Philippines (Santos, *Turning Our Shame into Hope*), Korea (You, "Shame and Guilt Mechanisms") and Malaysia (Yang, *Discipline or Shame?*).

169. Pitt-Rivers, "Honor and Social Status," 22.

170. Lynd, *On Shame*, 252.

171. Malina, "Understanding New Testament Persons," 51, 58.

172. deSilva, *Honor, Patronage, Kinship*, 25.

173. Neyrey, *Honour and Shame*, 15.

174. Malina and Neyrey, "First Century Personality," 26.

175. Gilmore, *Honor and Shame*, 17.

of reputation") must recognize this value. To make a claim to honor and have that claim rebuffed would lead to humiliation and ridicule. Neyrey calls honor a process, the culmination of which is the award of reputation, worth, and honor.[176] When honor is recognized, it confers a particular social identity which in turn produces status.[177]

There are two sources of honor. Ascribed honor is honor that is received through birth and lineage. It is received simply through virtue of belonging to a family that has a certain standing in the community. Not only aristocracy but even the smallest community will recognize certain families as having a superior reputation or standing, sometimes based on wealth.[178] Within a family, certain members may have greater honor than others depending on their position. For example, the eldest son has greater honor than the youngest, and a male greater honor than a female. In Arab countries marriage brings honor.[179] Ascribed honor can also be gained from political institutions, for example through appointments by the emperor, king, or deity. Ideally, a person who has honor through birth would display the character of an honorable person. "The well born are assumed to possess by inheritance the appropriate character and sentiments which will be seen in their conduct…"[180] However, this is not always the case in reality. However, since such people have status and power, no one dares challenge or question them and they would be accorded the honor they claim. Honor may be ascribed to a person whose power is such that no one dares dissent, question, or dispute the title. "The reputation of a dangerous man is liable to assure him precedence over a virtuous man … in the field of honor might is right."[181] In the case of such people, their honor is not based on virtue but on status. They possess what Pitt-Rivers dubs "honor = precedence" (status) rather than "honor = virtue."[182]

---

176. Neyrey, *Honour and Shame*, 15.

177. Pitt-Rivers, "Honor and Social Status," 21.

178. Neyrey, *Honour and Shame*, 16; Malina, *New Testament World*, 32; Muller, *Honor and Shame*, 90.

179. Muller, *Honor and Shame*, 91.

180. Pitt-Rivers, "Honor and Social Status," 23.

181. Pitt-Rivers," 25.

182. Pitt-Rivers, 23. See however, Gosnell, "Honor and Shame," 110, who distinguishes between honor and status. He points out that Pitt-Rivers does not say that "honor" is ascribed by birth but that "status" is. What is ascribed is not honor but the boundaries (status) within which one must function.

Achieved honor is earned by the individual. The traditional avenues for achieving honor in the Mediterranean world of the New Testament were the military, civic benefaction, athletic games and competitions in drama and poetry.[183] Honorable pursuits would normally differ between the sexes. A man's role might be to protect and provide while a woman would be considered honorable for displaying the virtues the culture recognizes. Often this would include modesty and chastity. In Arab countries, honor comes from education and wealth, qualities such as wisdom and charisma and physical strength. Someone with strong alliances has honor. Qualities such as bravery and loyalty are considered honorable along with the willingness to engage in violence to protect one's honor.[184]

An honorable person embodies the ideals of the community and is thus recognized as such. There is a particular status that is given to the honorable person. It is vital that the person receives the acknowledgment of their reputation as an honorable person. The question is, from whom? In an ideal society, where there is consensus, the leaders or political authority would uphold the values of the society and bestow honors on those who exemplified their society's values. However, in most societies, there are areas where there is a lack of consensus. In addition, there may be times where the power is held by those who do not uphold what others, perhaps even the majority in that community, hold as honorable. Since honor can be bestowed on a person by certain individuals in society, like the monarch, an undeserving person may receive honor through dishonorable means. "Honors have often been for sale by a sovereign with empty coffers."[185] In that case, honors may be bestowed on those whom some people would consider dishonorable.[186] Similarly, Gosnell points to the story of Odysseus, a Greek hero who is famous for his cunning. For Odysseus to lie to his enemy Cyclops is considered honorable, both because of his own reputation, and because Cyclops is "shame-able" as a result of his own lesser status. "Heroes always remain heroes, regardless of what they do."[187]

---

183. Neyrey, *Honour and Shame*, 16.
184. Muller, *Honor and Shame*, 90–97.
185. Pitt-Rivers, "Honor and Social Status," 24.
186. Pitt-Rivers, 22–23.
187. Gosnell, "Honor and Shame Rhetoric," 109.

There is another complication. In a society of equals, perhaps the highest honor to be obtained would be to be recognized by one's peers. However, if there are honors to be bestowed by those of a higher status, there is an element of competition. There will be a hierarchy of honor.[188] In such circumstances, the reputation of the victor is enhanced by the humiliation of his vanquished competitor.[189]

What is honorable is decided by each society or group (subcultures, sects, etc.) within society. As such, it will vary over time and be different in every culture, even if honor as a value remains constant.[190] Generally speaking the virtues and values that ensured the stability and survival and growth of the group were honored. For example, bravery, since the city depended on men brave enough to fight to protect the city, and generosity because the community depended on the wealthy donating to civic improvements. Those whose behavior threatened the group by adultery, cowardice, ingratitude, etc. were considered shameful.[191] Pitt-Rivers warns that a system of values is never obeyed by all in a given culture.[192] Neither can values be easily found out by a process of questioning people in the culture, but rather emerges with observation. Values form an inter-related cluster of concepts which each subculture applies as appropriate to its own setting.[193] J. C. Baroja shows how continual power struggles bring with them new definitions of honor and shame. Different groups and classes have different definitions. He shows how, in Spain, from the fifteenth to the seventeenth century, the values associated with honor gradually changed. At first, honor was based on virtue, according to Christian and classical sources, but then, the nobility constructed a different concept of honor in which they gave honor to conquest, revenge, and competition. With the rise of the merchant class, values like efficiency, utility, and the common good were associated with honor while competition and revenge now lived on as values in the lower, criminal classes.

---

188. Pitt-Rivers, "Honor and Social Status," 23.
189. Pitt-Rivers, 24.
190. Malina and Neyrey, "First Century Personality," 27
191. deSilva, *Honor, Patronage, Kinship*, 35–36; *Hope of Glory*, 2–3.
192. As we will see, this warning is not well heeded by many scholars who are being critiqued for making over-generalizations about honor-shame cultures. See Lawrence, *Ethnography of the Gospel*, for a critical assessment of the honor-shame motif in NT studies.
193. Pitt-Rivers, "Honor and Social Status," 39.

In her writing on "facework," Stella Ting-Toomey reiterates that all people want to be respected and to present and protect their self-image. While the social self-concept of face originated in Eastern cultures, people of all cultures share certain aspects of face. The concept of face that Ting-Toomey explores is one in which a person both claims a certain self-worth as well as recognizing the worth of the other. Face is thus "a cluster of identity and relational based issues" associated with respect, honor, status, credibility, competence, relationships, and obligations.[194] As we will see, this characterization of cultures has an important impact on conflict styles, processes and goals.

Honor and shame are not polar opposites. One feels shame but one does not feel honor. The opposite of shame, which is affective, is pride. Lynd says shame and guilt are distinguishable but not opposites.[195] Flanders warns against two errors made by missiologists and others. One is to equate honor and face, and the other is to assume that the concept of honor is the same in all so-called honor cultures.[196]

Characteristics of Shame-Oriented Cultures

The wide-ranging discussions comparing and contrasting guilt and shame cultures help give insight into the social forces operating in shame and honor cultures. This section of the chapter examines the social dynamics of shame and honor.

Dynamics of Shame

Shame has been described and its characteristics mapped in several cultures. The factors contributing to the motivations and energy of shame will now be explored.

Collectivistic identity

Hiebert states that shame, rather than guilt, is prominent in group-oriented communities.[197] Individualism is the "broad value tendencies of people in a

---

194. Ting-Toomey and Oetzel, *Managing Intercultural Conflict*, 36–37.
195. Lynd, *On Shame*, 207.
196. Flanders, *About Face*, 56–57.
197. Hiebert, *Transforming Worldviews*, 111.

culture to emphasize individual identity over group identity and individual rights over group obligations" while collectivism is "the broad value tendencies of people in a culture to emphasize the group identity over the individual identity and group-oriented concerns over individual wants and desires."[198] Ting-Toomey and Oetzel, citing research by Hofstede and Triandis, identify individualism as "a cultural pattern in most northern and western regions of Europe and North America," and collectivism prevalent in "Asia, Africa, the Middle East, Central and South America, and the Pacific Islands."[199] This means two thirds of the world's population have "high group-oriented value tendencies."[200] Collectivism does not mean that the individual does not matter. Rather, it assumes that it is in the best interests of the individual to maintain the well-being of the group.[201] Group values and shame are linked by several scholars. Creighton proposes that "the Japanese worldview and low cultural value given to individualism is related to the effectiveness and predominance of shame as a behavioral sanction."[202] Shame is prominent in group-oriented communities, says Hiebert.[203] Hofstede links collectivism in China and "other Asiatic countries" with the concept of "face."[204]

Missiologist Hannes Wiher cites H. Wheeler Robinson, an Old Testament scholar whose work, *The Christian Doctrine of Man*, produced in 1911 used the term "corporate personality" and talked of a "psychical unity" between members of the same social group.[205] African theologian John Mbiti writes that in traditional African society, the community must make or create the individual. "I am because we are. Since we are, therefore I am."[206] Rituals and rites of passage play an important part in this identity formation.[207] In short, this collectivistic view of personality is part of the consciousness of major

---

198. Ting-Toomey and Oetzel, *Managing Intercultural Conflict*, 30.
199. Ting-Toomey and Oetzel, 30.
200. Ting-Toomey and Oetzel, 30–31.
201. Hofstede, *Culture's Consequences*, 151.
202. Creighton, "Revisiting Shame," 280.
203. Hiebert, *Transforming Worldviews*, 111.
204. Hofstede, *Culture's Consequences*, 151.
205. Wiher, *Shame and Guilt*, 300.
206. Wiher, 300. This is what Archbishop Desmond Tutu popularized as *Ubuntu* theology.
207. Wiher, 300.

portions of the world's population. Clifford Geertz's oft-quoted insight on collectivism is that

> The Western conception of the person as a bounded, unique, more or less integrated motivational and cognitive universe, a dynamic center of awareness, emotion, judgment, and action organized into a distinctive whole and set contrastively both against other such wholes and against its social and natural background, is, however incorrigible it may seem to us, a rather peculiar idea within the context of the world's cultures.[208]

In guilt-oriented cultures, the self is autonomous and independent. Individual identity is valued over group identity. The uniqueness of the person is valued and their autonomy is respected.[209] Self-expression, individual rights, and justice are important with a lesser importance attached to responsibility to the group. A person is expected to have their personal opinion and not be afraid to express it. Openness and honesty are valued. There is a strong emphasis on personal accountability for one's own actions and opinions. There is nothing wrong with expressing personal emotions.[210] Identity is an "I" identity, whereas in a collectivistic society it is a "we" identity.[211] Augsburger illustrates the differences communicated to a child who is not behaving. In an individualistic culture, the parent threatens to make the child stay in as a discipline, whereas in the collectivistic culture, the parent threatens to make the child stay outside the home.[212] In collectivistic cultures, the goal of maturity is interdependence, not independence.[213]

In a shame-oriented culture, group expectations take precedence over individual goals. The Japanese proverb "the nail that sticks up will get pounded down" and the Ecuadorian proverb "the longest blade of grass is the first to be cut down" reflect a collectivistic community's value for conformity.[214]

---

208. Geertz, "From the Native's Point," 59.
209. Ting-Toomey, *Communicating across Cultures*, 65.
210. Ting-Toomey, 202.
211. Ting-Toomey, 67.
212. Augsburger, *Pastoral Counselling*, 89.
213. Augsburger, 90.
214. Elmer, *Cross-Cultural Connections*, 136.

The community is generally hierarchical. Hierarchy is more than accepted; it is seen as necessary and good. An example would be the caste system in India.[215] Parents are to be respected as are all those in authority. Status comes with seniority.[216] Security comes from belonging and knowing one's role, responsibilities and obligations, and where one belongs within the hierarchy. Members of the family are closely involved in each other's lives. "They feel comfortable with controlling and being controlled, with regulating and being regulated."[217] Hsu[218] describes the collectivistic Chinese as follows: the world of the Chinese is characterized by ties that bind close relatives in family and clan.[219] While to a person in a guilt-oriented culture the other is external, to the person in a shame-oriented culture, the others, or at least some of them, "are parts of himself as he is part of them."[220] People see themselves through the eyes of at least one other person from their group. Such persons would always recognize their particular position, both in relation to others of a similar status (horizontal relationship) and in relation to those above them (vertical relationship). They understand themselves in terms of how others view them and internalize that sense of identity.

Prestige is ascribed, through birth and based on formal credentials like age, birth, rank, and title. Achieved honor is also part of a person's identity but to a lesser level than in individualistic cultures where one's personal achievements are the greater source of honor. Along with an individual honor, a person shares a collective honor with those held superior or "vertically sacred" (e.g. parents, God, king) as well as "horizontally" sacred (e.g. family, tribe, ethnic group). So, an affront can be offered by insulting someone associated with you.[221] Similarly a person may take up a challenge levelled at someone associated with him, because their honor is also entwined. Loyalty to the group tends to overshadow other considerations. Behavior towards those outside

---

215. Hiebert, *Transforming Worldviews*, 240.
216. Augsburger, *Pastoral Counselling*, 90.
217. Augsburger, 90.
218. Hsu, in *Clan, Caste and Club*, identified three "worlds" or "ways of life": the American individual centred, the Chinese situation centred, and the Indian "supernatural centred."
219. Hsu, *Clan, Caste and Club*, 2.
220. Lynd, *On Shame*, 236.
221. Malina, *New Testament World*, 42.

the group can be governed by a different set of ethics than behavior towards the "in-group."²²²

Ting-Toomey and Oetzel distinguish between "low power-distance" cultures, which tend to be Western countries, and "high power-distance" cultures, which tend to be East Asian and Arab countries. Low power-distance cultures tend to emphasize individual expertise, democratic decision-making, equal relationships and equal rights, equitable punishments, and rewards based on performance, while high power-distance cultures emphasize status-based expertise and credibility, asymmetrical role-based relations, benevolent autocratic decision-making processes, and rewards and punishment based on status, age, rank, and seniority.²²³

Since what people think is so important, a leader, such as a pastor for example, will be hesitant to discipline their members because it will make them unpopular, raise strong emotions that cannot be dealt with, and alienate other members, especially the offender's family.²²⁴ In a shame-oriented culture, accepting help from a counsellor is an unattractive prospect because it makes internal problems known to "outsiders." In such cases the family unit becomes "a castle wall set to keep out intruders."²²⁵ Wiher discusses the difficulty of shame-oriented people having to adapt to the judicial system formulated for the most part for guilt-oriented cultures. He cites the example of human rights, which he says arises from an egalitarian view of society.²²⁶ Shame cultures, being highly stratified, find it hard to resonate with such a concept. In a similar way, since the central value of the group is harmony, some interpersonal offences, for example theft or adultery, that would be considered "wrong" or "evil" in a guilt-oriented society, are not considered important in a shame culture unless they disrupt the whole group.²²⁷

A group or collective is assumed to be characterized by certain traits and these traits are fixed and unchanging. Thus, people are stereotyped. No one is expected to stand out from the crowd or to display traits or behavior not normally associated with their group. People feel that their place in society

---

222. Wiher, *Shame and Guilt*, 337.
223. Ting-Toomey and Oetzel, *Managing Intercultural Conflict*, 31.
224. Yang, *Discipline or Shame?*, 32.
225. Augsburger, *Pastoral Counselling*, 133.
226. Wiher, *Shame and Guilt*, 362.
227. Wiher, 362.

is ordained by the gods from birth; a slave would always be a slave and a noble always a noble.[228]

Hiebert describes the Indian value of interdependence. Every person has certain roles to fulfill for the sake of the family, and each caste has a role to fulfill in society. Diversity and cooperation are values, rather than interdependence[229]; therefore, individual psychology or self-consciousness would be irrelevant and unnoticed.[230] People are typified by their race, family, place of origin, craft or trade, etc. Children would be expected to exhibit the character traits of their parents.[231]

In Mediterranean society people reserved close friendships for their kin group. With most people the honorable thing was to be closed, not revealing one's inner feelings, thoughts, dreams, or anxieties.[232]

Ting-Toomey, in her work on intercultural communication, proposes the motif of identity security-vulnerability as the base that effects intercultural encounters:

1. Individuals bring their sense of self-image or identity to their communicative encounters. The individual's self-identity is helped by cultural factors. It is culture that ascribes meaning to ethnicity, age, and gender, etc.
2. Individuals acquire their identities by their interactions with others in their culture. Culture is always evaluating our performance.
3. Individuals feel a sense of safety when communicating with people who they view as supportive and familiar to them.

Nobody develops a sense of self in a vacuum. Personal and social identity are linked and both are developed within the culture. In the identity negotiation perspective, identity is defined as "the reflective self-conception or self-image that we each derive from our cultural, ethnic, and gender socialization processes."[233] We might well be unconscious of these identities

---

228. Malina and Neyrey, "First Century Personality," 73–75.
229. Hiebert, *Cultural Anthropology*, 360.
230. Malina, *New Testament World*, 75.
231. Malina and Neyrey, "First Century Personality," 73–75.
232. Malina and Neyrey, 79.
233. Ting-Toomey, *Communicating across Cultures*, 28.

but they influence our interactions, and behavior. Identity is divided into two categories: primary and situational. Primary identities include cultural, ethnic, gender, and personal. Situational identities are role, relational, face work, and symbolic identity. Personal identity is the unique identity that results from our experiences and responses and the influence of others, especially role models. A person may have an actual personal identity as well as a desired personal identity. The actual identity is seen in their behavior.

Face work is the specific communicative behaviors we enter into to save face for others or ourselves. What constitutes skillful face work will differ from culture to culture (assertiveness versus tact).

Shame as social control

Shame, like guilt, operates as a mechanism of social control. Chinese parents teach their children that family scandals must not be discussed outside the family. Certain behavior is shameful and if carried out will bring ridicule and shame upon the child. A Chinese parent will not tend to tell the child why it is wrong to behave in a certain way but rather point to the consequences of that behavior for the child.[234] The Chinese child is taught to bring honor to the family, primarily through excelling in their studies and getting good jobs. They must not bring shame to the family, which will reflect also on their ancestors.[235]

As well as this public exposure, shaming can also be achieved by teasing, joking, gossiping, and direct accusation, in order of seriousness. Gossip is a powerful means of social control amongst the Daba society in North Cameroon.[236] For an Asian person, loss of face is a severe loss to be equated with death, separation, the loss of limb, and other losses. The intense feeling it evokes for the person and their family can even lead to suicide.[237] Yang cites Chen-Lou Chu, a well-known Chinese sociologist who postulates that the shame personality of the Chinese derives from two sources: Confucianism (with its emphasis on societal norms and ideal models) and humanism (with

---

234. Yang, *Discipline or Shame?*, 18.
235. Yang, 19.
236. Lienhard, *Restoring Relationships*, 169–170.
237. Yang, *Discipline or Shame?*, 6.

its concern for harmonious relationships).[238] According to Hu, a Chinese sociologist, there are two types of honor: there is *mien-tzu*, which is the reputation one has achieved through success in life; it is "social or positional face." The other is *lien*, which is the public perception of the person's moral integrity; it is a person's "moral face." A person can have good *mien-tzu* but be without *lien*. Concern about face might be universal but what the desirable face is, is culture specific.[239]

Maintaining social image

In shame-oriented cultures, people desire to maintain a positive social image, which is the impression others have of us. There is a difference between this and "face," a concept originally developed by E. Goffman in 1959. Face is the positive impression a person attempts to project to others and claims for themselves.[240] Face is thus about self-presentation, while social image is how others see us and the values they ascribe to us.[241] In collectivistic cultures there is a greater fusion between self-image and social image. In an experiment to discover the responses to insults among two groups it was found that the individualistic, or low honor, group reacted typically with either anger or shame, but those who felt shame withdrew. Among the collectivistic, or high honor, group there was anger but also shame. The desire to protect social image empowered these people to engage with the one who had insulted them, usually in the form of verbal disagreement.[242]

In Arab cultures, what society deems shameful is to be avoided. However, if an Arab were to find themselves in another culture, their behavior could change. Thus, to drink alcohol or engage in sexual promiscuity in a Western culture that does not see these things as shameful is quite acceptable to the Arab who is visiting that culture. Muller quotes an Arab proverb which says, "when you are not known, do whatever you like."[243]

---

238. Yang, 20.

239. Yang, 20–21; Ting-Toomey and Oetzel, *Managing Intercultural Conflict*.

240. Rodriguez et al., "Attack, Disapproval, or Withdrawal?," 1472; Ting-Toomey and Oetzel, *Managing Intercultural Conflict*, 36.

241. Rodriguez et al., "Attack, Disapproval, or Withdrawal?," 1473.

242. Rodriguez et al., 1476.

243. Muller, *Honor and Shame*, 82.

To have a shameful act discovered adds to one's shame. An Arab proverb says, "a concealed shame is two-thirds forgiven."[244] An Arab might avoid responsibilities and challenges because of the fear of failure within the Arab culture, but be a risk taker within another context.[245]

The Dynamics of Honor

As has been said, what is honorable varies from one period to another, one region to another, and one class to another.[246] The way that honor works is that "the sentiment of honor inspires conduct which is honorable, the conduct receives recognition and establishes reputation and reputation is finally sanctified by the bestowal of honors."[247] Since honor is a publicly acknowledged quality, honor that is not seen does not exist. Therefore, people ensured there were things they could do to demonstrate their honorable status.

Group honor

Honor is not only possessed by individuals but by groups and communities. The dishonorable conduct of one member will affect the honor of all, while each member shares in the honor of the whole group.[248] Honor resides in the head of the group; for example, a father of a family or the monarch of a nation.[249] In the Mediterranean, as well as in Arab cultures, the focal institution or central unit of organization is the family.[250] Beyond the family lie the clan, tribe, and ethnic group. The family is the "repository" of all the accumulated honor of generations past and as such bestows honor upon those who are born into it.[251] Thus, the organizing principle of life would be belonging, and success would be dependent on having the right relationships to the right people.[252] A person's honor was protected by the family, and in turn, a person must take

---

244. Muller, 82.
245. Muller, 82.
246. Pitt-Rivers, "Honor and Social Status," 21.
247. Pitt-Rivers, 25.
248. Muller, *Honor and Shame*, 50.
249. Pitt-Rivers, "Honor and Social Status," 35–36.
250. Pitt-Rivers; Muller, *Honor and Shame*.
251. Malina, *New Testament World*, 32.
252. Malina, 29. This is as opposed the focal institution being economics in the USA, which would make the organizing principle instrumental mastery (i.e. the ability to achieve and possess materialistic success).

responsibility for preserving the family honor, since what a person does will reflect on the family. In Arab cultures, a high degree of conformity is expected from family members but in return the person receives a stable position of belonging, a group who will act in their interests, and unquestioning defense from "outsiders."[253] A person "owes" loyalty, allegiance and honorable behavior to their family, not to others who are not kin. Moxnes defines these honor values as "exclusive and particularist" rather than "universal and inclusive" as in the West where a person might perceive they have a duty to behave in a certain way towards everyone, regardless of who they are.[254] Honesty, respect, and loyalty are key values within the group.[255] Moreover, the history of the family is important – a person "inherits" the honor of their ancestors.[256] A person is expected to maintain and contribute to the honor of one's kingroup. To insult or commit a crime against them would be scandalous, considered sacrilegious, and have serious repercussions for the group's continued stability. On the other hand, affronts against those outside this natural group are not considered sacrilegious and could well be meritorious.[257]

While the family, tribe, and ethnic group is the natural kin group into which a person would be born (or adopted), it is not the only "in-group" to which a person would belong. In-groups would be formed based on similar interests and values. The other "kin group" would be an optional group such as trade guilds, municipalities, or parties like the Pharisees, Sadducees etc. In general, voluntary associations of this nature would be relatively rare and come about through need.[258] In optional groups, those in elected posts of honor have authority over all dimensions of honor in the group. In both groups the head or leader (father, monarch, etc.) symbolizes honor in two senses – precedence (social status) and virtue. They decide what is honorable; they define the allegiance of the group. They cannot be dishonored. They are attributed ethical honor that goes with the position. A leader in such a group is above criticism. They can do no wrong since they define right and wrong. Any criticism levelled against them is seen as disloyalty. They (king, father,

---

253. Muller, *Honor and Shame*, 79–80.
254. Moxnes, "Honour and Shame," 28.
255. Campbell 2007, 96.
256. Moxnes, "Honour and Shame," 28.
257. Malina, *New Testament World*, 45.
258. Malina, 45.

religious leader; generally male) must be followed, obeyed and honored.[259] Rituals of honor, whether heartfelt or not, are obligatory and serve to reinforce the leader's authority and the members' obligations.

The patron-client relationship was formed between people of unequal social status, but such a relationship could also exist between social equals, in which case it was called "friendship."[260] In Indian society, there is an underlying belief that people are born into certain roles either to serve or to enjoy certain rights and privileges. The ideal is that there is a system of interdependence in patron-client bonds.[261]

The public court of reputation

As we have seen, honor is an individual claim that must be publicly acknowledged. For a person to be dishonored, strictly speaking the insult has to be offered in public because it is the public who form the "court of reputation."[262] This "public" realm becomes for the person the court of reputation, that "body of significant others whose 'opinion' about what is honorable and shameful, and whose evaluation of the individual, really matters."[263]

People act in accordance with the reputation they must maintain or avoid.[264] This emphasis on social acceptance and social censorship means that it would be too simplistic to assume that there can be an objective list of what is "right" and "wrong." Values might differ from practice. Norms are "manipulable." Some things that society deems "wrong" might be "right" if done by certain people in certain circumstances. As such, even having committed an action that appears shameful, people might defend their honor simply by vehemently claiming it.[265]

Where minority cultures exist within a dominant culture (e.g. the Jews, or the Christians in the Roman Empire), the composition of one's group of "significant others," or court of reputation, must be well defined. Behaving in such a way as to maintain the ideals of the dominant group or culture will

---

259. Malina, 46.
260. deSilva, "Patronage and Reciprocity," 34.
261. Hiebert, *Cultural Anthropology*, 360.
262. Pitt-Rivers, "Honor and Social Status," 27.
263. deSilva, *Honor, Patronage, Kinship*, 40.
264. Gosnell, "Honor and Shame Rhetoric," 107.
265. Gosnell, 108.

bring honor from the wider public but not from the minority culture. The court of reputation must comprise of individuals who uphold the group's values in their grants of honor and censure. "Including some supra social entity in this group (e.g. God, Reason, or Nature) offsets the minority (and therefore 'deviant') status of the group's opinion."[266]

Showing honor

Honor is often demonstrated through rituals which offer respect associated with the person's head. People may bow their heads before the honorable person, crown him, or be forbidden to touch his head. Conversely, slapping a person's face would be an insult. In Arab countries, three main ways of showing honor are through hospitality, flattery, and gift giving. Hospitality honors the guest. Urging food upon the guest, presenting them with something they admire in the house as a gift, where they sit, and what they are served will all express honor.[267] To keep someone on your doorstep will be shameful and the person who is treated this way will not visit that house again.[268]

The presence of the individual has an impact on their honor. An incident that is an insult or affront if carried out in a person's presence may not be an insult if carried out behind his back. "What is offensive is not the action in itself but the act of obliging the offended one to witness it."[269]

Shame-oriented cultures place great value on courtesy. It is one thing to be criticized behind one's back, but it is quite another to be shown contempt to one's face. It is quite acceptable that two people who have quarrelled and are not able to treat each other with courtesy should avoid being in one another's presence. Their acquaintances will understand that this is the acceptable alternative to courtesy and will do what they can to facilitate this kind of social avoidance without interfering.[270]

Intentions are very important when considering honor. To have dishonorable intentions is to be dishonorable whether or not one puts that intention into action. Similarly, the essence of an affront to honor is the desire or intent

---

266. deSilva, *Hope of Glory*, 6.
267. Muller, *Honor and Shame*, 89.
268. Muller, 89.
269. Pitt-Rivers, "Honor and Social Status," 25–26.
270. Pitt-Rivers, 41.

to dishonor. Therefore, if an apology is offered, in which it is made clear that there was no intent to insult, then the seriousness of the offence is mitigated. This has the effect of making the apology easier both to accept as well as to make, since the apologizer's humiliation is reduced.[271] "Thus one can see that while honor is established or impugned by physical behavior, this is because certain intentions are made manifest in it, are, as it were, made implicit."[272]

A person commits his honor only if he truly intends to do so. They can only be judged to be honorable or dishonorable based on their intentions. For example, when a person gives his word of honor, he is bound by it; but if he intends to deceive, then not delivering on a promise is not dishonorable. "It is lack of steadfastness in intention which is dishonoring, not misrepresentation of them."[273] Therefore, someone who is a liar, a deceiver, who by his actions humiliates and gets the advantage over others through trickery, might be validly considered honorable (e.g. Don Juan).

To swear an oath should reduce ambiguity since a person would be dishonored for refusing to submit to an oath. People were not obligated to tell the truth to everyone, only to kin. The right to truth belonged to kin and to superiors, not to equals or inferiors.[274]

As such, lying to someone implicitly defined their relationship to the speaker. Lying deprived them of honor, it implied they were inferior. It also marked them as an outsider, not part of one's kin group. To lie to someone was to deprive them of honor and respect. As such it was an implicit challenge. To be called a liar was a great public dishonor. "While to lie in order to deceive is quite honorable, to be called a liar in public is a grave affront."[275]

A person cannot take offence at an insult directed at him by his superior. Likewise, a person does not have to feel dishonored by an inferior, but only by social equals. He might still choose to punish an insult from an inferior as an impudence, but his honor is not impugned.[276] An "inferior" cannot cause damage to a superior's honor. Insults bring shame in Arab countries whether

---

271. Pitt-Rivers, 26–27.
272. Pitt-Rivers, 27.
273. Pitt-Rivers, 32.
274. Malina and Neyrey, "First Century Personality," 37.
275. Pitt-Rivers, "Honor and Social Status," 33.
276. Pitt-Rivers, 31.

addressed to the person or addressed to other members of the group such as parents or a spouse.[277]

Some actions are recognized as being offensive. Others may be offensive or not depending upon the interpretation put on the action. If the action is ambiguous, a person may get away with insulting another since no one can prove his intentions. The antagonist in such a case is left in a quandary: if he takes up the challenge and it is not proved he may be seen as quarrelsome and touchy; on the other hand if he does nothing, he may be seen as a coward.[278]

Precedence and virtue

There is a difference between honor that is derived from position or precedence and honor that is due to virtue. No individual would want to distinguish between the two when it pertains to them. Pitt-Rivers remarks that just as a healthy bank balance ensures credit, the possession of acquired honor guards against dishonor because the man with sufficient honor to his credit may not be challenged. So a king can do no wrong because he is king and as such is the arbiter of what is right.[279] "Thus thanks to its duality, honor does something which the philosophers say it cannot do; derive an *ought* from an *is*." Honors are heaped on those who have power, legitimizing the status quo.[280]

Satisfaction

If a person is insulted they require "satisfaction," which is an attempt to restore honor. This satisfaction may be through receiving an apology that is a "verbal act of self-humiliation" or it may require avenging, especially if there is no apology forthcoming.[281] "To leave an affront unavenged is to leave one's honor in a state of desecration and this is therefore equivalent to cowardice."[282] Satisfaction is not the same as winning or triumph. All it requires is that the offended party has the opportunity to restore honor and keeps to the rules

---

277. Muller, *Honor and Shame*, 84.

278. Pitt-Rivers, "Honor and Social Status," 28. The masculine pronoun is being used in this section since according to these sources, the situation could be different for a female, whose main sphere of operation was meant to be the home. It would be left to her male protector to defend her honor.

279. Pitt-Rivers, "Honor and Social Status," 37.

280. Pitt-Rivers, 38. See also the section "Defining honor."

281. Pitt-Rivers, 26.

282. Pitt-Rivers, 26.

of social engagement it requires. "Satisfaction then has the nature of an ordeal, implying a judgment of destiny or fate, or God's sanction."[283] In Arab countries, if shame cannot be hidden it must be avenged. Shame is feared because with it comes loss of status and power which could disempower one's whole group.[284]

A person is the guardian of their own honor, since it is they who must assess whether or not they have been insulted. Ideally, they will deal with the insult by demanding satisfaction (e.g. in a duel). A person would prefer not to seek redress in a court of law because to do so would be to acknowledge publicly that they have been wronged, and it would also imply their inability to deal with the matter themselves since they are seeking help from others. The one who has offered the insult may add to it by stalling the judicial process, calling attention to the matter, being insolent and so on. It is better to take matters into one's own hands.[285]

Competing for honor

Since Mediterranean society loved honor and since it was seen as a limited commodity, people competed for honor. Another's success posed a threat to one's own ambition and so envy, hostility, and conflict often followed suit. Histories of these times are replete with stories of wars, competition to gain office, competitive sports, competitions for drama and poetry, etc.[286] Plutarch mentions various fora in which conflict could erupt such as the marketplace, gym, politics, public beneficence, and friendship. Everything could become the object of competitiveness: houses, children, clothing, beauty, lovers, reputations, and respect.[287] In every city in the Roman Empire this relentless search for glory continued; thus, the erecting of public buildings like temples, baths, and theatres with the names of the glorious donors inscribed, the distribution of food, and holding of public games as members of the elite competed to outdo one another.[288]

---

283. Malina, *New Testament World*, 43.
284. Muller, *Honor and Shame*, 85.
285. Pitt-Rivers, "Honor and Social Status," 30.
286. Neyrey, *Honour and Shame*, 19.
287. Neyrey, 20.
288. Jewett, *Saint Paul Returns*.

Summary

From the discussion above, it emerges that cultures have several characteristics that may distinguish them from one another. There is wide acceptance for the existence of shame cultures and guilt cultures. However, there are also warnings against using the terms "honor" and "shame" without proper understanding of their meanings in different contexts. Herzfeld sounds a warning about the "massive generalizations" being made about this terminology.[289] Sri Lankan culture, being South Asian, collectivistic, and predominantly Buddhist, may be assumed to fall into the category of shame-oriented. However, we cannot therefore assume that any or all of the characteristics of other shame-oriented cultures are to be found in Sri Lankan culture.

Herzfeld argues that paradoxically, it is out of "ethnographic particularism," that "theoretical insights" must be gained, rather than from rather than generalizations.[290] It also seems clear that all cultures display aspects of both value orientations. Thus, rather than labelling a culture one or the other, we might say a culture is shame-oriented or guilt-oriented to show which value predominates. We also conclude that to say a culture is shame-oriented is not to say that this is a sign of the inferiority of a culture. Shame is a complex reaction to failure, whether it is seen by others or not.

However, in collectivistic cultures, the opinion of significant others matters greatly in one's estimation of oneself. What is considered honorable and shameful differs from culture to culture, and even where two cultures may agree on a certain value, like justice, the expression of that value may well differ in each culture. The values of a culture will affect its view of conflict, ways of dealing with conflict, and bringing about reconciliation.

The validity of distinguishing cultures as shame-oriented and guilt-oriented has been established in the literature. This review continues by highlighting the characteristics of shame-oriented cultures that specifically affect conflict and its resolution.

---

289. Herzfeld, "Honour and Shame," 349.
290. Herzfeld, 349.

Dynamics of Conflict in Guilt and Shame-Oriented Cultures

Conflict involves both perception and interaction. Conflict can be defined in many ways. It can be described as an intense disagreement process between two interdependent parties over incompatible goals and the interference each perceives from the other in their effort to achieve this goal.[291] Sande defines it as "a difference in opinion or purpose that frustrates someone's goals or desires."[292] Conflict does not always arise from sin. It might result from differences that are natural, from poor communication or from differing perspectives.[293] Conflict, even frequent conflict, does not necessarily mean relationships are weak. It is the "competency" with which those conflicts are dealt with that leads to relationships being built up or broken down.[294] Ting-Toomey and Oetzel call the interaction during a conflict a "conflict script" that proceeds according to cultural norms, making them visible, even if the underlying beliefs and values are unseen.[295]

Many books written on conflict resolution tend to follow the pattern laid out by Roger Fisher and William Ury in their influential book, *Getting to Yes* (1991). Fisher and Ury suggest a "principled negotiation method" rather than a "positional" method to successfully negotiate conflicts. The steps to this are to

1. Separate the people from the problem;
2. Focus on interests not positions;
3. Generate a variety of options;
4. Insist that the result be based on objective criteria.

However, in a shame-oriented culture, it is not so easy to separate the person from the problem; neither do people from such a culture find it easy to agree on objective criteria on which to base their resolution. In short, in a shame-oriented culture where honor is sought and shame is avoided, both the causes of conflict and the process of conflict management will be affected. Added

---

291. Ting-Toomey, *Communicating across Cultures*, 198.

292. Sande, *Peacemaker*, 29.

293. Sande lists four primary causes of conflict which are, first, misunderstandings; second, differences in values, goals, gifts, priorities, experiences, opinions, or interests; third, competition over limited resources; and fourth, sinful attitudes or habits (Sande, *Peacemaker*, 30).

294. Ting-Toomey and Oetzel, *Managing Intercultural Conflict*, 3.

295. Ting-Toomey and Oetzel, 11.

to that, since within a shame-oriented culture there may be social groups, subcultures, or individuals who espouse a guilt orientation, some conflicts will be exacerbated by the fact that the parties espouse these different worldviews although they might inhabit the same culture.[296] For this reason, along with the distinctive characteristics of shame-oriented cultures that might influence conflict and its resolution, the differences between shame-oriented cultures and guilt-oriented cultures are also highlighted below.

The desire for respect is universal and not confined to shame-oriented cultures. Face loss occurs when a person's claim to respect is ignored or challenged.[297] However, how that need is communicated and what constitutes those elements will differ.[298]

Conflict Resolution in Shame-Oriented Cultures

According to Ting-Toomey, differences between collectivistic (shame-oriented oriented) and individualist (guilt-oriented) cultures often center on goal issues. She identifies four main contenders:

1. Conflict-content goals: that is, the substantive issues involved. Although on the surface this goal seems to have objective criteria as a goal, there are usually underlying identity issues.
2. Identity-based goals: issues of identity always underlie the substantive issues; even in settling a material concern like where a meeting is held can affect how others view us and how our value and worth is affected. Face-saving is at stake. If the conflict is not resolved, it will have an impact on self-worth.
3. Relational-conflict goals: how we view the importance of the relationships involved, and how we communicate that.
4. Conflict-process goals: may be direct or indirect, linear or spiral.[299]

---

296. Ting-Toomey defines intercultural conflict as "the perceived or actual incompatibility of values, norms, processes or goals between a minimum of two cultural parties over content, identity, relational, and procedural issues" (*Communicating across Cultures*, 194).

297. Ting-Toomey and Oetzel, *Managing Intercultural Conflict*, 20.

298. Ting-Toomey, 197. Harinck et al. distinguish between "honor cultures" and "dignity cultures". They define a dignity culture as one in which people have "inalienable worth" which is neither conferred by, nor can it be taken away by, others ("Good News about Honor Culture"). This is an interesting view which is worth pursuing in the light of the rising interest in understanding shame in the West.

299. Ting-Toomey, *Communicating across Cultures*, 195–196.

For shame-oriented cultures, the goal of conflict resolution is to regain honor for individuals, and the restoration of relationships, harmony, and prestige in the group. That is, the goal is relational, whereas for guilt cultures, the goal is "judicial," that is, to receive the verdict of innocence and rightness.[300] For the person from the shame-oriented culture, harmony is more important than concepts of truth or justice. The substantive issues are secondary to relational issues.[301] In guilt-oriented societies, there is a strong desire to get to the truth of the matter and hold people accountable for their misdemeanors. In shame-oriented societies, the group will try to shield its members from personal accountability.

For shame-oriented cultures, the process of conflict resolution is as important as the outcome, whereas for guilt-oriented cultures, the outcome is what is important.[302] For collectivistic cultures, the conflict has to be dealt with appropriately, not just effectively. That is, each person must act according to the expectations due to their age, status, and so on, saving face for all concerned. It is only then that the conflict resolution is effective.[303]

Mennonite anthropologist Friedmann describes how many people groups in the Majority World are not interested in discovering the facts of a conflict or allocating blame and punishment. In the pursuit of group harmony, the process of reconciliation will be set up such that there will be an equal loss of face for all parties.[304] Friedmann, who was often called in as mediator to church quarrels in Africa and Asia, writes that during one such negotiation, one of the parties called him aside to strongly criticize his own behavior. This was, in fact, a way of allocating a certain element of loss of face to the mediator as well.[305] The traditional Chinese mode of conflict resolution is based on saving face for all concerned. Public announcements after secret negotiations will often present the solution in which neither party loses face, even if the reality is that one suffered more. There is an understanding that if one party is in a weaker position, it is dangerous to push them to the place where they

---

300. Wiher, *Shame and Guilt*, 402.
301. Ting-Toomey, *Communicating across Cultures*, 195.
302. Ting-Toomey, 210.
303. Ting-Toomey, 220.
304. Friedmann, *Helping People Resolve Conflict*, 15.
305. Friedmann, 61–62.

have lost face completely. When they have nothing left to lose, they are apt to react with an attack.[306]

Identity of Self and Group

As described above, shame-oriented cultures tend to be collectivistic cultures. In a collectivistic culture, people tend to have what Ting-Toomey calls an "interdependent self" as opposed to an "independent self." People with a strong sense of interdependence see themselves as group-bound and harmony seekers.[307] Those with an "independent self" will show themselves to be "autonomous, self-reliant, unencumbered, and as rational choice makers."[308] The way this will impact interpersonal conflict is that among interdependent self's, events that cause dishonor to one member of the group, affects all, especially in family or kin-groups.

In a collectivistic culture, there is a stronger sense of the "in-group" and "out-group" than in individualistic cultures.[309] There will be a tendency to treat more favorably those who belong to one's in-group and to treat others differently, a principle which Ting-Toomey calls the "in-group favoritism principle."[310] This technique adds to a person's "social identity," which in turn adds to their self-esteem and self-worth.[311] To belong to a prestigious group adds honor and status to all its members. As we have seen in our discussion on honor and shame in chapter 2, less is owed to those outside one's group. Honesty, loyalty, and trust for instance, are expected within the group but not necessarily extended to those outside the group. As Hofstede puts it, "in low individualism cultures one just does not trust a 'somebody' – one only trusts 'us.'"[312]

Research shows that in more collectivistic countries, people feel less of a need to make specific friendships. Their friendships will follow naturally

---

306. Augsburger, *Conflict Mediation across Cultures*, 95.
307. Ting-Toomey, *Communicating across Cultures*, 206.
308. Ting-Toomey, 206.
309. Ting-Toomey and Oetzel, *Managing Intercultural Conflict*, 38.
310. Ting-Toomey, *Communicating across Cultures*, 148.
311. Ting-Toomey, 147.
312. Hofstede, *Culture's Consequences*, 165. Hofstede does describe one of the characteristics of low individualistic countries is that employees have high expectations of their organisations. They expect to be cared for as if by a family and have their interests protected. If they are disappointed, they are easily alienated (*Culture's Consequences*, 173).

from prescribed relationships within the group. In cultures with more individualistic tendencies, making friends and maintaining a relationship with these friends is a significant factor in an individual's role in socialization.[313] Gudykunst, Ting-Toomey, and Chua cite research into Japanese culture which shows two types of friendship – one that arises from social obligation and another that arises from liking and shared interests and values. The latter type is usually comprised of same sex school friends, is limited in number, and endures for a lifetime.[314]

In collectivistic cultures, people tend to see the problem and person as related.[315] Chua and Gudykunst have carried out research on conflict resolution styles in high- and low-context cultures. Their research demonstrates that people from high-context cultures, where communication tends to be based on shared systems of meaning rather than verbal content, find it hard to separate the person from the conflict issue.[316] This means that criticism is taken personally even if aimed at a particular action. Mayers writes of his attempt to correct the superstition of a young man in a Central American village. He realized too late that "an attack on one aspect of life is seen as an attack on the whole; a criticism of a thought pattern is a criticism of the entire person."[317] Since shame is experienced as a "globalized negative evaluation of the self," the remedy for shame is not reparation or punishment, or even absolution and forgiveness, but must involve "a remaking or renovation of the self in some way."[318] As we have seen in our exploration of the concept of shame, shame affects the whole person. In connection with the sense of identity and the preservation of honor, we could include the sub-points below.

Desire to save face

In a shame-oriented culture to lose face, or to be shamed, is far worse than merely being embarrassed or humiliated is in a guilt-oriented culture. Elmer explains the violence it does to a person when he defines the term in certain cultures. In Thailand, the term for losing face literally means "to tear

---

313. Hofstede, 163.
314. Gudykunst, Ting-Toomey, and Chua, *Culture and Interpersonal Communication*, 41.
315. Augsburger, *Conflict Mediation across Cultures*, 91.
316. Chua and Gudykunst, "Conflict Resolution Styles."
317. Mayers, *Christianity Confronts Culture*, 43.
318. Flanders, "Shame," 814–815.

someone's face off so they appear ugly before their friends and community." In Shona, the language of Zimbabwe, it means "to wipe your feet on my name."[319] Lingenfelter and Mayers call the action "to save face," the "concealment of vulnerability."[320] Those who desire to conceal vulnerability and protect their self-image will tend to deny culpability if found out in an error. Their fear is that by admitting their fault they will be shamed. They will refuse to accept criticism and any suggestion that their actions, from a different perspective, could be construed as wanting in some way. This attitude can result in such people arguing to justify themselves and covering up mistakes rather than admitting their faults.[321]

Difficulty in confession and showing repentance

With a shame-oriented conscience, the person suffers from shame anxiety, anticipated punishment, and the fear that someone will discover their offence and bring shame on them (and their group). The offender will thus attempt to hide the offence and deny it. The fear of shame will make it impossible for them to disclose it.[322] Within leadership especially, there is a tendency to cover up, and resist admitting a mistake.[323] Repentance is harder in shame cultures because the call to repentance can increase feelings of shame.[324] Confession is seen as a "violation of conscience,"[325] "self-shaming,"[326] a "verbal act of self-humiliation."[327] While guilt confession can be therapeutic, with shame, the re-telling of the shameful episode adds to one's shame as the experience becomes known to another. Also, with every telling, the person relives the experience and feels its pain again.[328] Kraus, writing of the Japanese situation, says confession can turn to a form of groveling.[329]

---

319. Elmer, *Cross-Cultural Connections*, 175.
320. Lingenfelter and Mayers, *Ministering Cross-Culturally*, 104.
321. Lingenfelter and Mayers, 104.
322. Lienhard, *Restoring Relationships*, 33.
323. Wu, *Saving God's Face*, 18.
324. Wiher, *Shame and Guilt*, 403.
325. Lienhard, *Restoring Relationships*, 34.
326. Kraus, *Jesus Our Lord*, 212; Wiher, *Shame and Guilt*, 300, 405; Yang, *Discipline or Shame?*, 212.
327. Pitt-Rivers, "Honor and Social Status," 26.
328. Capps, *Depleted Self*, 82; Yang, *Discipline or Shame?*, 54.
329. Kraus, *Jesus Our Lord*, 212.

Repentance requires humility, which is harder for honor-conscious people in a hierarchical society as compared to those who live in an egalitarian society.[330] Shame-oriented people see vulnerability as weakness.[331] When asked directly, the shame-oriented person will attempt to avoid shame by denial of culpability, or by arguing to prove the rightness of their actions.[332] Protection of one's image is vital. Criticism, even when directed at a particular action will be taken as a personal attack.

Shame that arises from the discovery of one's transgression is experienced as a globalized feeling of "I am bad." The person will attempt to hide weaknesses and shortcomings by withdrawing. Because of the desire to save face, shame-oriented people would prefer to be approached by a mediator who will initiate reconciliation and who will be able to communicate the offender's repentance to the offended party.[333] The person feels swamped, trapped, and cannot see a way back. All the energy of the person goes into covering up since their whole identity is at stake.[334]

Even the act of conferring pardon on a person may be understood as affirming their badness and adding to their shame.[335] The difficulties of accepting an apology without adding to a person's shame makes it far easier to overlook, excuse, or forget than to confess and forgive.[336] It is common for people to protect intimate associates by tolerating or making excuses for them. This is because in these societies a respectful relationship has a higher moral value than legalities or objective truth. The web of inner relationships is protected by indulging the indiscretion. However, this does not lead to freedom and intimacy, but rather intrigue and manipulation. Where the wrongdoing is of such magnitude that it cannot be overlooked, the only other recourse is exclusion.[337] At the same time, shame anxiety will persist in the

---

330. Wiher, *Shame and Guilt*, 403.

331. Mayers, *Christianity Confronts Culture*, 160.

332. Mayers, 160.

333. Wiher, *Shame and Guilt*, 404.

334. Albers, *Shame*, 23.

335. Wiher, *Shame and Guilt*, 406; Yang, *Discipline or Shame?*, 212.

336. Yang, *Discipline or Shame?*, 212. Yang mentions that in Japanese the word for "forgive" means to excuse, indulge or permit.

337. Yang, 212.

offender until the action is disclosed. This pressure could lead to suicide, the ultimate act of exclusion.[338]

To the Western worldview, a verbal apology is the only way to show proper remorse or repentance for one's errors. In fact, many books on reconciliation will list specifics that must be included in a proper apology.[339] In a shame-oriented culture, apologizing does not come easily. If an apology is presented, the presentation will be as important as the words, for words are also actions and the way things are said is more important than the substance of the words.[340] In apologizing, one will usually deny the intention to cause offence because the intention is vital to the action. "By proclaiming it to be unintentional, the offender reduces the gravity of the affront; it makes the apology easier to accept while it also reduces the humiliation of the apologizer and therefore makes it easier to give."[341]

Shame as sanction must be used cautiously because there is little chance of reconciliation when one has shamed another. There is virtually no possibility of reconciliation. A person who seeks to make reparation by self-exclusion may atone, but only by exclusion, so there is again no possibility of reconciliation. This does not mean the guilt-oriented conscience will not feel shame, but the feeling of guilt will predominate and the person will find it easier to confess since confession brings relief.[342]

Pattison suggests that the ability to laugh at oneself is a sign that shame has been dealt with and signals the possibility of reconciliation. "At the very core of the process of reconciliation lies good humored laughter, especially laughter at oneself."[343] The admission of one's own faults and the ability to laugh with others at them signals the completion of the shame response cycle, and so signals the possibility of reconciliation not only with others but with oneself. The pretension, anger, bitterness, greed, and ambition are dissolved. However, laughter and jokes can also demonstrate self-hate. The

---

338. Lienhard, *Restoring Relationships*, 34.

339. Sande, *Peacemaker*, 126–134, lists the 7 A's of apology: Address everyone involved, avoid "if" and "but," admit specifically, acknowledge the hurt, accept the consequences, alter your behaviour, and ask for forgiveness.

340. Pitt-Rivers, "Honor and Social Status," 27.

341. Pitt-Rivers, 26–27.

342. Lienhard, *Restoring Relationships*, 34.

343. Pattison, *Shame*, 161.

use of laughter can also increase a person's shame if they are perceived as being directed at them.[344] James 5:16 commands us to confess our sins to one another. Bonhoeffer says that "he who is alone with his sins is utterly alone."[345]

Mayers describes conflict arising when a person feels rejected by the other. Acceptance reverses that rejection and sets the scene for reconciliation. Acceptance has to be shown and that is done by seeking out a bridge between the people involved. Mayers lists some of these bridging components as: information, clarification, an admission, an explanation, a gift, a favor, use of a metaphor, a show of power, correction, a counterstatement, verbal apology, action apology, approval, and a compliment, as well as flirtation, levity such as teasing, joking, heckling, a game, and acquiescence.[346]

Loewen perceptively remarks that even in the West, confession in a church context and the sense of receiving the assurance of forgiveness from the church is vanishing. He cites the example of the young girl writing to a newspaper columnist with the confession of her sexual encounter with a man. The columnist's advice to learn from it and move on is her "absolution" to the public confession she has made.[347] The role of the church as a healing community has been replaced by counsellors, psychiatrists, and third parties on the internet. Loewen says that with the Reformation, and the removal of the priest in favor of the priesthood of all believers, confession and forgiveness became even more removed from the church. As churches grew, urbanization, mobility, and social distance all added to the church's relinquishing of its role.[348]

Loewen advocates his use of "self-exposure" to help people in shame cultures come to a point of acknowledging their sin. He tells the story of a church leader who was reported by several people to have committed adultery. He himself denied the charge. Local leaders shrugged the matter off saying no one knew the truth of the matter. The missionaries were concerned but uncertain what to do. In an unexpected turn of events, the missionaries were put together for three days with the leader in question. After much prayer, they decided to speak to the local leaders of how they suffered from sexual

---

344. Pattison, 161.
345. Bonhoeffer, *Life Together*, 110.
346. Mayers, *Christianity Confronts Culture*, 267.
347. Loewen, *Culture and Human Values*, 332–333.
348. Loewen, 337.

temptation when away from their spouses. They asked the local leaders if this was a problem for the local believers too. Before too long, the leader suspected of adultery confessed. Loewen makes the point that we are trained from an early age, in all cultures, to wear masks, to hide our true self, our weaknesses, and pain. "The way of the mask, of course, is the compartmentalization, where we have a church life and an everyday life, a life of reality at home and the way of the façade in public."[349]

Reparation and forgiveness

According to Hiebert, in shame-oriented cultures, here is an emphasis on saving face but also on reconciliation. Wrongdoers may be punished but at the end of that process they must be restored to their status in the community. After a person has made restitution, some societies will incorporate a ritual of reconciliation which functions to signal the end of the rift and the reinstatement of the person into the community. If the person does not regain their dignity, resentment will build up.[350] Interestingly, Wiher suggests that in a shame culture reparation is not considered important. There is an assumption that forgiveness will be given and that forgiveness will mean the reaffirmation of relationship and restoration of harmony.[351] He gives the illustration of a driver whose behavior caused an accident. When he had sent a mediator to intervene on his behalf, with his apology, the missionaries for whom he worked accepted the apology but refused to give him his job back. The refusal to reinstate him to his original position was seen as withholding forgiveness.[352] Shame provokes people to defend themselves against it, often by maintaining a sense of power, such as the power to forgive or by an assertion of righteousness.[353] Some suggest that shame stands in the way of being able to offer forgiveness.

Loewen identifies four kinds of forgiveness: divine, social, self, and secular.[354] He states that the first three are essential for a person to be fully released from any lingering problems while the fourth has arisen due to the failure of

---

349. Loewen, "Self-Exposure," 53.
350. Hiebert, *Transforming Worldviews*, 111–112.
351. Wiher, *Shame and Guilt*, 401.
352. Wiher, 27–28.
353. Pattison, *Shame*, 198.
354. Loewen, "Four Kinds of Forgiveness," 153–168.

the church to help people deal with their guilt. His whole essay focuses on guilt and does not mention shame. However, his examples are drawn from societies that include shame-oriented societies. He shows that in small collectivistic societies, the community will often be involved in mediation and in hearing confessions and pronouncing absolution. However, as a society fragments, or with the influence of Western missionaries, the church becomes less able to function to offer social forgiveness. Increasing individualism, the distancing of clergy from laity isolates individuals with their guilt.[355] Loewen stresses three steps that must be included in true forgiveness: confession, expiation, and release. Once again, he does not distinguish between guilt and shame, but in his description, he explains that what causes guilt will vary from individual to individual and even more from culture to culture. His description of the need for individuals to confess to someone in order to restore their own self-image seems to relate to those from predominantly shame cultures. He says that the guilty person is aware that they have been operating under false pretenses and that society's acceptance and respect has been based on this false image. "However, if he can find at least one member of the human race who will listen to him sympathetically and who, while knowing the worst will still love and respect him, the culprit finds that his own self-respect can also be restored."[356]

Style of Communication

A person's culture affects the way they communicate, just as the way people communicate can change the culture they inhabit.[357] In shame-oriented cultures, communication is indirect. Elmer describes one organizational response to a staff member's inefficiency in an Asian context. The leaders brought the whole group together and urged everyone to work hard. This was seen as evasive and unfair by the Westerners, who were angry that they were being blamed for someone else's laziness. The Asians were unperturbed by the meeting, but slowly the work improved.[358] Augsburger writes of the Madagascan village in which there was a thief whose identity was unknown.

---

355. Loewen.
356. Loewen, "Social Context of Guilt," 88.
357. Gudykunst, Ting-Toomey, and Chua, *Culture and Interpersonal Communication*, 17.
358. Elmer, *Cross Cultural Conflict*, 45–46.

The villagers talked openly of the evils of thieving and of their disapproval of the recent act of thieving. This is a public shaming even though it is not addressed to anyone in particular.[359] Adeney gives the example of an American couple who felt their Egyptian landlady was continually invading their privacy. When an argument arose, they decided their best solution was to move. American friends urged them to confront the lady and not let the situation "fester." An Egyptian friend however advised them to let the situation heal by itself and avoid confrontation. Following his advice, they made a close friend of the lady because she saved face.[360]

While the guilt-oriented person will value direct speech, open confrontation, and clear presentation of the facts of the matter, the shame-oriented person will use verbal and nonverbal communication in a way that is as nonspecific as possible. In a guilt-oriented culture, people tackle the conflict directly with direct verbal assertions, questions, and clarifications.[361] The guilt-oriented person seeks to be impersonal and objective, being hard on the problem but soft on people while the shame-oriented person sees the problem as closely entwined with all the people involved, as well as the context.[362] In high-context, collectivistic cultures, even though a person might be experiencing the stress of conflict, they will try to conceal their emotions.[363] Vagueness and hiddenness characterize the response to stress.[364] It is believed that if something is not known to those outside the group (usually the family), then no shame attaches to it. "The belief that unknown things do not exist results in hiding the family secrets."[365] Non-verbal communication such as avoiding eye contact, spiral responses, and vagueness might give the impression to someone from outside the culture that the person is being deliberately evasive, underhanded, weak, or cowardly. Collectivistic cultures, in turn, will view the direct method as rude and lacking in taste and sensitivity.[366] In a shame-oriented culture, the listener is expected to decode the message being

---

359. Augsburger, *Conflict Mediation*, 78.
360. Adeney, *Strange Virtues*, 43.
361. Lingenfelter and Mayers, *Ministering Cross-Culturally*, 151–153.
362. Augsburger, *Conflict Mediation across Cultures*, 91.
363. Ting-Toomey, "Towards a Theory of Conflict," 80.
364. Ting-Toomey, 80.
365. Auli, "Shame, Guilt and Church," 64.
366. Augsburger, *Conflict Mediation across Cultures*, 91.

sent, or to read between the lines of this indirect communication.[367] For example, a request for help will be given in an indirect way and the listener who reads the subtext can choose to offer help or withhold it without either party losing face.[368] Within the Korean culture, a person would rather say "I agree with you in principle, but please understand that . . ." and explain any reservation, rather than saying "I do not agree with you."[369] Silence in a collectivistic culture may mean either disapproval or approval[370] which makes it harder for the outsider to interpret. Another way of describing this is using the terms "high-context" for cultures with a strong group orientation and "low-context" for more individualistic cultures. In low-context cultures, verbal abilities are important and valued. Logic and reasoning and detailed explanations are expressed verbally. High-context cultures however, rely far more on context, nonverbal messages, and shared meaning.[371] Jandt cites as an example of high-context communication, the elaborate tea drinking ritual of Japan. A low-context observer might want to hurry up and drink the tea because, for them, the communication between host and guest is in the words. For the Japanese however, the communication is in the process and context of the ceremony.[372] A high-context individual will talk around a problem and expect the listener to know what is bothering them, without having to be explicit. In a low-context culture, people might openly disagree, even shout and fight over a task-oriented issue and still remain friends. A subordinate whose report is queried will produce facts and figures and defend their position. In a high-context culture, the subordinate whose report is rejected will withdraw, take it as a personal attack or sign of lack of trust and probably resign. Openly disagreeing with someone is interpreted as an insult, resulting in loss of face for both parties.[373]

---

367. Lingenfelter and Mayers, *Ministering Cross-Culturally*, 15; Ting-Toomey, *Communicating across Cultures*, 104.

368. Ting-Toomey, *Communicating across Cultures*, 104–105.

369. Ting-Toomey, 105.

370. Ting-Toomey, 216.

371. Jandt, *Introduction to Intercultural Communication*, 62–63.

372. Jandt, 63–64.

373. Ting-Toomey, "Towards a Theory of Conflict," 77. Abu-Lughod, "Romance of Resistance," Abu-Lughod researched the life of the women of the Bedouin tribe Awlad 'Ali. She shows that there are different ways in which those who are disadvantaged by their place in

The Western mind-set assumes that people would like to know how to improve themselves. It is therefore right and helpful to allocate blame and advice on better performance. To the rest of the world it looks rude.[374] It is significant that directness might be acceptable if one is a member of the same group, that is, an "insider," for example a member of the family, team, or club.[375] Directness implies that you can address a problem and not offend the person, that you can separate the person from the problem. In fact that is one of the steps in a successful conflict management style, as laid out by Fisher and Ury, mentioned above.[376] Individualistic Westerners learn to critique ideas and to argue and debate without it getting personal, but in other cultures, the idea and the person are one.[377] Asian, African, and Latin American cultures prefer to approach conflict obliquely. So speech is not direct or pointed, as that would be considered harsh, disrespectful, and even cruel. Such cultures make use of passive and stative voice, saying for example "it fell" rather than "I dropped it," or "an accident happened to me," "it doesn't work. It needs to be fixed." Their words describe the situation without going into what caused it. The subject is unclear. The situation simply exists.[378]

Conflict Resolution Style and Process

While in a guilt-oriented society the conflict process is clear and well defined, in a shame context, it tends to be more diffuse. In a guilt-oriented culture, the process occurs step by step. People are good at looking at the facts, getting to the specifics of the problem, and brainstorming to come up with a variety of solutions. Ting-Toomey describes this as proceeding at a "monochromic" pace.[379] In a shame-oriented culture, the process proceeds at "a polychromic pace." The conversations are a spiral rather than direct. Elmer offers two metaphors to describe the mode of conversation: the onion, in which layers have to be slowly peeled to reveal the heart of the matter; and the spiral,

---

society offer resistance against those who seek to dominate them. Women use their seclusion, persuasive protests and irreverence to undermine the regulations governing their lives.

374. Elmer, *Cross Cultural Conflict*, 40.
375. Elmer, 49.
376. Fisher and Ury, *Getting to Yes*.
377. Elmer, *Cross Cultural Conflict*, 50.
378. Elmer, 50–51.
379. Ting-Toomey, *Communicating across Cultures*, 212–213.

which slowly winds its way to the center of the matter.[380] People look at the conflict within a larger whole, see the big picture and are good at analyzing what has occurred rather than at offering solutions.

Lingenfelter and Mayers distinguish between "analytical" thinking which occurs in guilt cultures, and "synthetic" thinking which occurs in shame-oriented cultures. Analytical thinking is expressed in judgments that are black and white and right or wrong according to specific criteria. Synthetic thinking tends to offer more open-ended judgments. It is more holistic, taking into account the whole person and all the circumstances. Shame-oriented culture people tend to offer an "and/and" rather than an "either/or" solution.[381] Duane Elmer gives as an example of holistic thinking, the tendency to view possessions as being available to whoever is in need, rather than belonging to the owner. "Borrowing" in such cultures might mean a permanent loan. "The category of yours and mine is not nearly so strong as the category of 'ours.'"[382]

Conflict style variations

A well-known analysis of conflict styles is listed as competing, accommodating, avoiding, compromising, and collaborating.[383] According to Ting-Toomey and others, cultures tend to prefer certain styles of conflict management to others.[384] These styles are learned as part of the enculturation process.[385] Research has shown that individualists tend to prefer controlling and competing styles while collectivists tend toward collaborative and compromising styles. In task-related conflicts, collectivists tend toward obliging/accommodating and avoiding styles.[386] Western writers tend to view avoiding and accommodating (or obliging) in a negative light whereas collectivistic cultures favor them as preserving relationships and saving face for all

---

380. Elmer, *Cross-Cultural Connections*, 151–152.
381. Lingenfelter and Mayers, *Ministering Cross-Culturally*.
382. Elmer, *Cross-Cultural Connections*, 146.
383. These styles were first suggested by R. R. Blake and J. S. Mounton in their *The Managerial Grid* (1964), and made popular by K. W. Thomas and R. H. Kilman, in their *Thomas-Kilman Conflict MODE Instrument* (1974).
384. Ting-Toomey, *Communicating across Cultures*, 216–228.
385. Ting-Toomey and Oetzel, *Managing Intercultural Conflict*, 46.
386. Ting-Toomey, *Communicating across Cultures*, 216; Ting-Toomey and Oetzel, *Managing Intercultural Conflict*, 49.

concerned.[387] Research carried out by Chua and Gudykunst on thirty-seven countries confirmed this premise. They found that high-context culture individuals preferred an indirect style of communication and sought to avoid admitting the presence of conflict. They chose what the researchers called "nonconfrontation" as opposed to "solution orientation." Nonconfrontation orientation included withdrawing, silence, concealed feelings, and glossing over differences.[388] These styles can be plotted on a graph in which the two axes are concern for self-interest and concern for the others' interest.[389]

Ting-Toomey and Oetzel add three more conflict styles, "emotional expression," the use of one's emotions to guide one through the process; "third-party help," which makes use of a mediator; and "neglect" which they define as the "passive-aggressive responses to side-step the conflict but at the same time getting an indirect response from the other conflict party."[390] Based on studies that have been carried out across several cultures, Ting-Toomey and Oetzel make the following assertions.[391]

1. Emotional expression: cultural norms exist that regulate the display of emotion during conflict. Studies show that in many Western cultures, open expressions of emotion are considered a sign of honesty and openness, which is appreciated and accepted. In many Asian countries on the other hand, displaying self-control and a calm outward demeanor is a sign of maturity. The use of silence, even a smile, can mean different things in different cultures. In some Asian countries, like Japan and China, a smile can hide disapproval, and silence can denote shame. Members of the same culture will be able to decode such communication.[392]

2. Neglect style: can be a destructive conflict style where one party uses avoidance or passive-aggressive techniques to ignore the other party's demands. For example, in family quarrels, a wife from a collectivistic culture might react in a neglect style to her

---

387. Ting-Toomey and Oetzel, *Managing Intercultural Conflict*, 46.
388. Chua and Gudykunst, "Conflict Resolution Styles," 33–36.
389. Ting-Toomey and Oetzel, *Managing Intercultural Conflict*, 46.
390. Ting-Toomey and Oetzel, 47.
391. Ting-Toomey and Oetzel, 54.
392. Ting-Toomey and Oetzel, 82–83.

individualistic husband's more aggressive, open conflict style, by withdrawing. A strategic neglect style will be when one party retreats (neglects) to gain time to think of a helpful response.[393]

3. Third-party help: individualists would find it helpful to seek help from an independent neutral third party, for example with a marital conflict, since they feel the person has expertise to help them. Collectivists would think of that as airing their problems in a public space and bringing shame on the family.[394] They would prefer to ask for help informally from relatives, wise advisors like teachers, whom they trust and respect.[395] Chua and Gudykunst, who carried out research into conflict management styles, affirmed that their findings were consistent with other research that found, in high-context cultures, a mediator would prefer to meet each party separately to avoid them having to confront each other.[396] Hannes Wiher stresses the importance of mediation in shame-oriented cultures.[397] Research has shown that people from high-power-distance societies like Japan or China will be more likely to look to a "high status" mediator to help them in a conflict. Researchers studying intercultural conflict among twenty-three national groups found that low power-distance culture workers would seek help from peers or subordinates in a workplace-related conflict, while high-power distance culture workers would be more likely to seek help from their superiors.[398] In Arab countries, a wise third party who can skillfully negotiate an end to conflict is honored. The only other way to end conflict is through force.[399]

---

393. Ting-Toomey and Oetzel, *Managing Intercultural Conflict*, 84–85.
394. Ting-Toomey and Oetzel, 88; Augsburger, *Pastoral Counselling*, 132–133.
395. Ting-Toomey, *Communicating across Cultures*, 218.
396. Chua and Gudykunst, "Conflict Resolution Styles," 34.
397. Wiher, *Shame and Guilt*, 362. Wiher says a lack of recognition of the shame element of a person's personality will result in a lack of success in the methods used to rehabilitate someone who has offended. The judicial system that seeks acknowledgment in a law court and then sends the offender through a prison system which reinforces feelings of shame, will let loose the shame-anger-rage spirals. This will be evidenced in aggressive behavior which limits the chances of the person being reintegrated into society. It is interesting to note, he says, that the Old Testament law which lays down severe penalties for law-breakers, never resorted to imprisonment as a penalty.
398. Morris et al., "Conflict Management Style," 729–747.
399. Muller, *Honor and Shame*, 50.

Research into shame-oriented oriented groups has shown that in the absence of insult, people from shame-oriented communities tend to demonstrate greater willingness and ability to react more constructively than those from a "dignity" culture, as they describe the individualistic culture. They give two main reasons for this. First, the shame-oriented culture's politeness norms lead to an initial avoidance or appeasing style. People will tend to ignore minor annoyances and try not to offend others or provoke a reaction that could be violent. Second, the risk involved in responding with an aggressive conflict style in an honor culture is greater. The potential to lose more than what is the substantive issue at stake leads people to try to avoid engaging with the other party.[400] If, however, a person from a shame-oriented culture perceived the conflict as bearing a personal insult, the reaction would be more aggressive than from a person from a dignity culture.[401]

Crisis (declarative) versus non-crisis (interrogative)

Lingenfelter and Mayers distinguish between the crisis orientation of the individualistic culture versus the non-crisis orientation of the collectivistic culture.[402] Lingenfelter found that the Yapese "downplay the likelihood of a crisis and avoid taking action on an issue as long as possible" and when they can no longer avoid taking action, choose from whatever options are now open to them.[403] In some cases this inaction is because they perceive the complexity of the crisis that is looming, and the disastrous consequences that could come upon them, and their fear leads them to do nothing and hope the crisis will either be averted or work itself out.

For example, since a child will feel great shame if confronted about poor school work, even to the point where they might commit suicide, Yapese parents will tend to ignore warning signs until there is some crisis,[404] while the crisis-oriented person (Mayers calls them "declarative persons") will anticipate problems, put systems in place, follow procedure, and seek expert help. When the crisis is upon them, they work single-mindedly according to planned procedures to eliminate the crisis. People who do not fit in or

---

400. Harinck et al., "Good News about Honor Culture," 69.
401. Harinck et al., 70.
402. Lingenfelter and Mayers, *Ministering Cross-Culturally*, 67–69.
403. Lingenfelter and Mayers, 67.
404. Lingenfelter and Mayers, 68–69.

adhere to the plan might get hurt in the process. Crisis-oriented persons will actively look for flaws in systems, so as to minimize the unexpected crisis. A non-crisis-oriented person will take life as it comes, with an optimistic outlook that keeps them from looking too closely at potential problems. They deal with each crisis as it emerges, based on their own experience and expertise, judging for themselves when the time is right to act. They are able to tolerate a high level of ambiguity in their lives and do not push for early resolution to conflict.[405]

Status and Power Distance

As noted above, honor is both ascribed (from identification with family and other in-groups) and achieved through noble acts. In collectivistic cultures, status is derived primarily from birth and social rank.[406] In such cultures people tend to associate primarily with those from their own peer group. In individualistic cultures, people tend to gain prestige or status through their individual performance. People have to prove themselves and not rely on their family name or titles.[407] They may achieve their own status through advancement in their career, through the accumulation of wealth, or through the quality of their life. They may have to keep achieving in order to maintain their status or others may overtake them, as happens in the arena of sports or Hollywood.[408] However, in collectivistic cultures, once status has been ascribed, it cannot easily be taken away. In many Asian societies people enjoy being addressed by their titles.[409]

A person who has honor or status through birth or impressive connections will be honorable whatever their behavior or assets.[410] In China, the ideal is a leader who leads by example.[411] That is, they have ascribed honor as well as "honor virtue." Collectivistic cultures tend to be high power-distance

---

405. Lingenfelter and Mayers, 70–71.
406. Lingenfelter and Mayers, 91–92.
407. Lingenfelter and Mayers, 94.
408. Lingenfelter and Mayers, 94.
409. You, "Shame and Guilt Mechanisms," 61. It is not unknown for someone to feel insulted and even formally protest that their title has been omitted in a written communication, or that they have been addressed as "Pastor" instead of "Reverend."
410. Lingenfelter and Mayers, *Ministering Cross-Culturally*, 95.
411. Wu, "Biblical Theology," 6.

societies, in which members give priority treatment and respect to people in high status positions.[412] Benedict refers to the Japanese language as it has a "respect language" to ensure that a person is addressed according to their status. The method of greeting would indicate whether the person being addressed is superior or inferior.[413]

Social status directly impacts the practice of conflict management. Those in high positions cannot be questioned. Hofstede in his research into high and low power-distance characteristics, enumerates the following. In high power-distance communities, the societal norm is that these levels of inequality are right and serve to protect people who know where they belong, and how to relate to those around them. Superiors and subordinates perceive each other as of a different order. Powerholders are entitled to privileges, there is a stress on coercive power, and there is a high level of distrust between people. The powerful are distrustful of anyone who might be a threat to their power and the less powerful distrust one another.[414]

Jackson Wu, writing about Chinese culture, says that it is a principle of social interaction that the subordinate defers to the superior. "Authority is central to ethics, value and identity."[415] Pitt-Rivers illustrates it by saying that the king cannot be dishonored. He is above criticism.[416] Although there is a difference between honor that derives from virtue and that which derives from status, (what Pitt-Rivers calls "precedence"), in practice, those of high status, or honor precedence claim honor virtue. "Hence, just as capital assures credit, so the possession of honor guarantees against dishonor, for the simple reason that it places a man (if he has enough of it) in a position in which he cannot be challenged or judged."[417]

In conflicts that arise between people of different statuses, the views or woes of someone of a lower rank or lower status in society (e.g. children and women) may go unaddressed. Those low in power will fear retaliation from

---

412. Ting-Toomey and Oetzel, *Managing Intercultural Conflict*, 31. Hofstede, *Culture's Consequences*, 70–71, defines power distance as the "measure of the interpersonal power or influence between B and S as perceived by the least powerful of the two."

413. Benedict, *Chrysanthemum and the Sword*, 47.

414. Hofstede, *Culture's Consequences*, 94.

415. Wu, "Biblical Theology," 2.

416. Pitt-Rivers, "Honor and Social Status," 37.

417. Pitt-Rivers, 37.

those high in power and are not wrong to do so. The amount of respect that is given to someone of a high status is fixed, regardless of their personal failings. People favor autocratic decision-making processes, though ideally through a benevolent autocrat.[418] Leadership is linked with authority rather than competence.[419] Leaders expect subordinates to be loyal, are sparse in communicating details to them, and tend to micromanage.[420] Rewards and punishments will be based on a person's status arising from age, rank, seniority, and title.[421]

On the other hand, a grievance channel may be used by someone in a low power position for personal revenge against a superior.[422] High power-distance communities tend to work through their network of connections to resolve conflict rather than depend on independent action.[423]

Relativistic Morality

Every culture has its own system of values and morals. Vahakangas, examining the attitude of Chagga men in a Tanzanian diocese to excommunication, discovered that the men felt little guilt or shame at being excommunicated for fathering a child outside of marriage. However, they felt great shame at being childless.[424] His conclusion was that they felt shame because childlessness was a matter of identity formation. There was a nexus of cultural tradition, Lutheran theology and modernization, which together contributed to a man's social identity. Why is excommunication a lesser shame than childlessness? In this case, the traditional cultural force that insists that a man's fertility is part of his social identity is stronger than either the Christian or the modern moral codes.[425]

---

418. Hofstede, *Culture's Consequences*, 259; Wu, *Saving God's Face*, 6.
419. Wu, "Biblical Theology," 6.
420. Wu, 6.
421. Ting-Toomey and Oetzel, *Managing Intercultural Conflict*, 31; Wu, *Saving God's Face*, 7.
422. Hofstede, *Culture's Consequence*, 260.
423. Ting-Toomey and Oetzel, *Managing Intercultural Conflict*, 33.
424. Vahakangas, "Shame, Guilt, and Church," 53–69.
425. Vahakangas, 67.

Augsburger notes, "Human existence is moral existence. Moral values, moral choices, and moral responsibilities are human universals."[426] Just as it is true that each person is in some ways like all others – in some ways like some others, and in some ways like no other – so it is with morals too. Some are universal, some are shared with one's culture, and some are unique to families or persons. "In every culture there is a sense of ought."[427] The "oughts" arise from a complex web of sometimes complementary and sometimes competing groups, such as family, faith, state laws, and peer groups. What a person chooses to practice as their ethic will be culturally informed, arising out of the worldview embraced.

Stackhouse, on whose work Augsburger builds, distinguishes between three ethical orders: cultures appeal to categories of "right," "good," or "fit."[428] The first is the deontological approach that asks if an action is "right" or "wrong," with reference to laws or principles that are considered universally valid. The second "teleological" ethic of "good" or "evil," makes decisions based on goals, ideals, or ends, whereby an action produces good for the greatest number of people. The third option is the ethic of responsibility in which each situation must be weighed on its own merits and a decision made that suits, or is morally "fitting" to the situation at hand.[429]

As with the concepts of shame and guilt, these three views on ethics are all present in all cultures, though some suggest that there is a greater tendency towards one or the other in particular cultural traditions. Augsburger, using Stackhouse's categorizations, identifies an ethic of "fit or unfit" as predominant in Indian, African, and Indonesian systems. The ethic of "good or evil" is most prevalent in Chinese ethical systems. The ethic of "right and wrong" is predominant in most Western cultures.[430]

This fits with the model of basic values produced by Lingenfelter and Mayers, in which they identified shame cultures with an ethic that seeks harmony, and virtue, and may rely on the traditions, customs, and morals that fit the group. This links in with the tendency of collectivistic people to

---

426. Augsburger, *Pastoral Counselling*, 245.
427. Augsburger, 245.
428. Stackhouse, "Social Ethics," 248.
429. Stackhouse, 328–329; Augsburger, *Pastoral Counselling*, 248.
430. Augsburger, *Pastoral Counselling*, 250.

be holistic rather than dichotomistic in their thinking. Augsburger gives the example of a case in which a North American pastor lends a motorbike to a fellow church member, a Haitian, on the understanding that it would be returned within a stipulated time. He shows how in the pastor's mind (an ethics of "right and wrong"), truth and integrity demanded the bike be returned on time. For the borrower, (an ethic of "fit"), his needs, the shame he would feel if he was late at the event he was attending and the pleasure of being able to arrive on the bike, outweighed other considerations. The bottom line was that the bike would be returned, but not on time.[431]

Hiebert writes that in most collectivist, tribal, and peasant groups, morality is based on duty and ethical judgment in relation to right relationships, which form the basis of morality. Morality is violated when relationships are broken.[432] Benedict writes of the Japanese value of "taking one's proper station" that refers to conformity to what is appropriate for a particular person, in a particular situation, not to abstract principles.[433] Young Gweon You writes of Korean culture that, because it is a "sociocultic" culture with a belief in ancestral spirits who reinforce societal values, the concept of morality is different to that of a monotheistic culture.[434] He illustrates this with the story of a murderer who confessed to the crime, when he believed that ancestral spirits were causing various misfortunes in his life.[435]

Collectivistic groups also tend to be holistic thinkers.[436] This means they will tend to view the offence of a person in the context of their entire life. This leads them to be slow in making their minds up about someone, whereas a dichotomistic thinker will tend to label people according to specific criteria, thinking in terms of black and white, and pigeonhole people. They find security in systems and categories and in finding their place within a role or category in society.[437] Lingenfelter and Mayers contrast American and Yapese in their evaluation of others. Americans tend to evaluate on the basis of performance. For example, a good teacher is one who teaches well, while

---

431. Augsburger, 255.
432. Hiebert, *Transforming Worldviews*, 61.
433. Benedict, *Chrysanthemum and the Sword*, 71.
434. You, "Shame and Guilt Mechanisms," 61.
435. You, 61.
436. Lingenfelter and Mayers, *Ministering Cross-Culturally*, 53–67.
437. Lingenfelter and Mayers, 56.

Yapese will need time to know the person and evaluate them on the basis of the total person.[438] Dichotomists will regard holistic thinkers as soft, inconsistent, and unprincipled while holistic thinkers will regard dichotomistic thinkers as callous, rigid legalists.[439]

Western thought from Greek times to the enlightenment took truth as its central value, and since then has chosen justice as central.[440] Because of this, guilt-based cultures tend to be good at analyzing situations into categories of right and wrong and looking for and allocating blame. Everything is expected to fit into categories of right and wrong.[441] The principles that underlie guilt might be a sacred text, or what is prescribed by the authorities, public opinion, or political correctness.[442] Based on the understanding that the world is orderly, that right will win out against wrong and that problems that arise need to be fixed, the guilt-oriented person will want to know who did what, assign blame, and fix the problem. In a guilt-oriented culture, there is a desire to be found innocent, to be "okay," and to exercise one's rights.[443]

Many of the world's cultures see the world as more complex, incomprehensible, and unalterable.[444] Shame-oriented cultures tend to have relative morality rather than a universal, absolute morality. Restoring harmony will be the goal of personal interaction and right and wrong are not absolute categories. Right is what is appropriate to the situation.[445] Citing the Indian worldview as an example, Hiebert states that actions cannot be easily labelled good and evil and even the distinction between offender and offended is blurred.[446] Right and wrong depends on who one is and the situation being faced.[447] Muller writes that in Middle Eastern Islamic cultures, what is important is what is honorable, and what is honorable will depend on what

---

438. Lingenfelter and Mayers, 64.
439. Lingenfelter and Mayers, 64.
440. Augsburger, *Pastoral Counselling*, 247.
441. Hiebert, *Anthropological Insights*, 117; Muller, *Honor and Shame*, 22–25.
442. Muller, *Honor and Shame*, 22–23. Muller points out that the younger generation in previously guilt-based cultures are drifting towards a shame-based culture in which right and wrong is being replaced by "cool" and "uncool".
443. Muller, *Honor and Shame*, 23.
444. Hiebert, *Anthropological Insights*, 117; Muller, *Honor and Shame*, 22–23.
445. Hiebert, *Transforming Worldviews*, 342.
446. Hiebert, *Cultural Anthropology*, 361.
447. Hiebert, *Transforming Worldviews*, 342.

society finds acceptable.[448] Hsu states that the core of Chinese ethics is "filial piety." The principles by which a person charts their way in public life will be different from the way things are within "his human group."

Principles that are correct for one set of circumstances may not be appropriate for another, but the principles in each case are equally honorable. Thus, for all practical purposes, a person will have multiple standards.

> Since double or multiple standards of morality and conduct are normal, they present the individual with no inner conflict. . . . He may be taught charity as a personal virtue, to improve his fate and that of his ancestors and descendants, but he will have no necessary compunction or desire to champion the cause of the oppressed as a whole or to overthrow the privileged position of all oppressors. The primary guide for his behavior is his place.[449]

Law and absolute truth have to take relationship into account so "morality cannot be separated from relationships that exist in concrete situations."[450] Creighton distinguishes between American and Japanese morality thus. Americans are more likely to evaluate an act based on a prescribed notion of right and wrong that exists independent of the situation. Whereas the Japanese are more likely to judge an act depending on the situation and based on the impact it has on significant relationships.[451] A Japanese will not speak of sin but apologize for *machigai*, meaning, "a misplacement in context." Sin is what violates the harmony of the group and offends honor.[452] Values are relational not intrinsic. Thus, a deed is "good" when it meets with parental approval. There is no perceived intrinsic goodness or otherwise in the deed itself.[453] In Asia, says Yang, what people think is more important than what is right or wrong. The question to ask before doing something is not "what is what?" but "who is who?"[454]

---

448. Muller, *Honor and Shame*, 47.
449. Hsu, *Clan, Caste and Club*, 2.
450. Wu, *Saving God's Face*, 7.
451. Creighton, "Revisiting Shame," 297.
452. Wiher, *Shame and Guilt*, 302.
453. Augsburger, *Pastoral Counselling*, 129.
454. Yang, *Discipline or Shame?*, 20.

Adeney gives the example of an American who was asked by an Egyptian if he played ping-pong. In the characteristic of the American's culture, he downplayed his expertise and said, "a little." The Egyptian from a culture where being open about one's accomplishment gained one honor, said he was an excellent player. When the game was played, the American won. The Egyptian believed the American had lied to shame him, while the American considered the Egyptian's claim an empty boast.[455]

According to Wiher, in a shame-oriented culture, sin can be defined as a "diminution of salvation and life force." In communal cultures, what is sin will be defined by the community and will usually involve an offence against the community.[456] Wiher cites African theologians who state that in traditional society, although the community believes that sin is committed against God, in daily life sin is seen as that which is offensive to the community, one's family, and one's ancestors. A person's awareness of the shame and disappointment felt by significant others overrides fear of God's wrath.[457] Wiher states that regardless of intention, the outcome will decide whether or not a sin has been committed.[458] When honor has been affronted, the discovery of this disruption discloses a sinner. Interestingly, in African culture, it is not necessarily the perpetrator who is the sinner. It could be the person who discovers the wrongdoing who is considered to be the sinner.[459]

Wiher describes the problem of corruption as being a typical issue for shame cultures. A person, say a foreigner, might be taken advantage of by being charged the wrong amount but the person doing this feels no shame only an element of anxiety that they might be found out. "The legal norms do not have the same priority for them as for guilt-oriented individuals. They are considered flexible."[460] Interdependence, with its mutual obligations, is a stronger force than laws or codes. A person who has received goods or favors from someone feels obligated to reciprocate and keep the relationship mutual.[461]

---

455. Adeney, *Strange Virtues*, 14.
456. Wiher, *Shame and Guilt*, 302.
457. Wiher, 302.
458. Contrary to Pitt-Rivers' analysis of Mediterranean cultures ("Honor and Social Status," 27) discussed in this study in chapter 2.
459. Wiher, *Shame and Guilt*, 303.
460. Wiher, 359.
461. Wiher, 359–360.

> Moral choice in every society is founded in the cultural character of a person and the way he or she sees the world. We are cultural creatures who make sense of our lives by a narrative that distinguishes between the good and the evil, the important and the insignificant. What we pay attention to shapes our ability to choose . . . Neither relativism nor absolutism is an adequate approach to moral choice. . . . to cooperate with good while exposing the evil is a task that requires character, sensitivity, and knowledge.[462]

Envy

Scholars like Malina and Neyrey have observed how among peasantry in the Mediterranean, there is a perception of limited good.[463] Hiebert lists this phenomenon as part of the Indian worldview.[464] All of their environment, all the desired things in life – status, wealth, friendships, security, and land – are all considered to exist in limited supply. An increase in one person's share means another person has suffered loss. This means that if one person in a community is seen to be improving their lot and gaining in status, their neighbors will see them as a threat since the increase means their own decrease. As a result, in shame cultures, people are reluctant to improve themselves because they are well aware of the reactions of their neighbors and the animosity and envy that will be directed towards them.[465] To give honor to someone else is to rob oneself of it, their success is our loss and we envy them.[466] Crook suggests that perception of limited good is what distinguishes a shame-oriented culture from a non-shame-oriented culture, which might well include aspects of shame-oriented values but does not have to defend honor quite so intensely since it is not limited.[467] This perception of limited good means envy plays a large part in shame cultures.[468] In an individualistic, capitalist culture, people

---

462. Adeney, *Strange Virtues*, 160–161.
463. Neyrey, *Honour and Shame*, 19; Malina, *New Testament World*, 18.
464. Hiebert, *Cultural Anthropology*, 361.
465. Hiebert, *Transforming Worldviews*, 343.
466. Neyrey, *Honour and Shame*, 18.
467. Crook, "Honour, Shame and Social Status," 593.
468. Malina, *New Testament World*, 108–133; Neyrey, *Honour and Shame*, 19.

are free to choose among many options and envy will not be as widespread or potent. People can easily rise to a higher status than the one they were born with, and most people would be considered one's social equals. In the Mediterranean, people stayed in the status they received when they were born. There was little, if any, social mobility upwards or downwards. There would be little reason to envy someone who, by birth or acts, was socially entitled to more than one had. That was just the way things were. So envy would be displayed primarily towards people of the same status, who have attempted to breach the boundaries set by birth.[469] In order to avert others' envy, those who have something to be envied might resort to (1) concealment, (2) denial, (3) bribe, and (4) sharing.[470]

"Envy was a value that directed a person to begrudge another the possession of some singular quality, object, or relationship that gave or expressed honor."[471] Thus, action would be taken against the other to reverse the status quo so that honor is once more balanced in one's own favor. Envy towards kin is denounced but envy towards others is quite acceptable. By possessing something that causes envy, the person envied has disturbed the status quo and it is fair game for those who wish to restore the status quo and the stability of the community.[472] Envious people display their internal feelings in many ways: from gossip, ostracism, and slander, to feuding, litigation, and even homicide.[473] By these means the honor of the offending party is lowered, their reputation could be ruined, they might be publicly shamed (for example in the case of litigation), and of course, in the case of homicide, they would be removed from their position permanently.[474] In Filipino culture, people speak of the "crab mentality" based on the nature of crabs, which, if left in an open basket or container, will pull down a crab that manages to succeed in climbing to the top of the container. People will pull down anyone who seems to be succeeding in their field.

Muller says that in shame-based cultures people will tend to criticize sooner than encourage others. This is meant to keep them from becoming too

---

469. Malina, *New Testament World*, 131.
470. Malina, 125.
471. Malina, 114.
472. Malina, 118.
473. Malina, 118.
474. Malina, 119–120.

proud. He describes how in Arab cultures people will often criticize and even shame a leader or pastor who is perceived as being too ambitious or proud.[475] Because of this tendency towards envy, the people of the Mediterranean feared what others could do to them arising from envy. They believed that certain people, animals, demons, or gods had the power to cause harm to something or somebody by looking at them. This they called "the evil eye."[476] Evil eyes could work whether voluntarily or involuntarily. This effect was caused by the condition of the heart, which might be filled with envy, and worked out through the power of the eyes to which the heart was thought to be closely connected.[477]

Lying

Pitt-Rivers explains that while honesty is considered honorable, to lie is not dishonorable if the intention was to deceive. Truth is not owed to everyone. "To lie is to deny the truth to someone who has the right to be told it and this right only exists where respect is due."[478] This means, for example, a child would be expected to tell the truth to their parents but the parents do not have a duty to reciprocate.[479] A person's honor is at stake only if they are not true to their intentions. For example, if a man gives his word, and is found to be false, it is not dishonorable if he meant to be false. If, however, he swore an oath, he declared an intention to be truthful and so his lie dishonors him. Intentions are paramount.[480] "The anomaly therefore is this: while to lie in order to deceive is quite honorable, to be called a liar in public is a grave affront."[481] Muller says of Middle Eastern Islamic cultures that a lie, if it is uttered for honorable reasons, such as to protect the honor of the tribe or family, is acceptable. If told for selfish reasons, then it is dishonorable.[482]

---

475. Muller, *Honor and Shame*, 54.
476. Malina, *New Testament World*, 120.
477. Malina, 120.
478. Pitt-Rivers, "Honor and Social Status," 33.
479. Pitt-Rivers, 33.
480. Esler, "Making and Breaking an Agreement," 291–292.
481. Pitt-Rivers, "Honor and Social Status," 33.
482. Muller, *Honor and Shame*, 51.

Extreme Reactions to Being Shamed

The desire to save face and preserve identity also leads to extreme reactions when people perceive themselves as under threat. Myers identifies four main responses to conflict when a person recognizes that they have transgressed cultural norms.[483]

1. Escape or withdrawal, with suicide being the extreme reaction.
2. Conformity, sometimes purely in order to please the other, with no conviction that one's actions are right or pleasing to the self, but simply to gain approval. In this case, a person may violate their own principles and feel a loss of self-respect. If, however, conformity is born of acceptance that change is required, say to fit into a new culture, then self-respect is preserved.[484]
3. Projection (seeking a scapegoat), which is projecting the blame onto something or someone else.
4. Forming a new group centered around the conflict. This new group will support and encourage the person, relieving some of the tension for them. Sometimes this new group will be the source of new conflict.

Shame, understood psychologically, is experienced as exposure of self, evoking strong emotions. The normal response is to run and hide. It makes it difficult to face oneself or others. A culture that values harmony will try as far as possible to avoid conflict. In their sensitivity to conflict, their first reaction will be to internalize it, to try non-confrontational strategies.

Takie Lebra lists seven common non-confrontational approaches in Japan, though not restricted to that country:[485]

1. Anticipatory management. If one foresees that an action might lead to a situation of unavoidable conflict, one may take precautionary measures by adapting one's behavior or actions. For example, not being able to reciprocate, one might refuse a favor.
2. Negative communication. Silence, avoidance, or evasion to show disagreement or anger.

---

483. Mayers, *Christianity Confronts Culture*, 186–188.
484. Mayers, 187–190.
485. Cited in Augsburger, *Conflict Mediation across Cultures*, 109–111.

3. Situational friendliness. One might interact with politeness at certain social gatherings or compulsory meetings, but then avoid the other at other times.
4. Triadic mediation. A powerful third party may mediate, urging people to come to an agreement using the threat of losing their own face, to bring about compliance.
5. Displacement. Anger or disapproval of one person is projected onto another, usually less threatening, person. This can also be done by gossiping, or by shifting the blame to another. For example, saying "my husband can't sleep" to the neighbor whose piano playing is keeping one up at night.
6. Self-aggression. Anger is expressed through exaggerated compliance, apology, or self-sacrifice.
7. Acceptance and resignation as destiny.

Being shamed may also cause rage and hate toward the one who has shamed us.[486] Violence can be an acceptable way to restore a person's honor and to send a message to others that they are able to protect their reputation and interests.[487] In Japan *giri* to one's name is the duty to act to keep one's reputation intact. This action can include both acts of violent revenge, or at the other extreme, suicide, as well as any intermediate steps in between these two extremes.[488] "Humiliation is a fertile breeding ground for hatred and for revenge-seeking."[489] To leave an insult unavenged will be interpreted as cowardice.[490] Rage becomes an insulator. The one who has been shamed must deal with the exposure of self in the present and the fear of future shame. When one party in the conflict reacts with rage the other might retaliate with the same and this gives rise to a shame-rage spiral.[491] As finite beings, we create our identity with the help of and against the world. A person put to shame is forced to confront himself in their weakness as well as the world. This can create a deep resentment, even hate towards the one who has shamed them.[492]

---

486. Chiu, Tsang, and Yang, "Role of Face Situation," 173–180.
487. Harinck et al., "Good News about Honor Culture," 68.
488. Benedict, *Chrysanthemum and the Sword*, 145.
489. Kaufman, *Shame*, 26.
490. Pitt-Rivers, "Honor and Social Status," 26.
491. Kaufman, *Shame*, 85–87.
492. Riezler, "Comment on the Social Psychology," 459.

Other extreme reactions to shame include:

1. Perfectionism. Developed early in life when a person is being told they are not good enough, that acceptance is based on performance.
2. Transfer of blame to others. The cause of the shame is assigned to others, often those who cannot defend themselves. Along with this, anger, violence, and resentments might be focused outward.[493] In some shame cultures though, like Japan, shame is directed inwards and the shamed person could commit suicide.[494]
3. Envy and competitiveness. The shamed person cannot be happy at success of others. They will attempt to bolster their own self-confidence by comparing themselves favorably with others.
4. Self-righteousness. This is shown in judgmentalism and contempt.[495] Shame is projected onto others so that the self is insulated (Luke 18:9–14). The person may come across as arrogant or smug.
5. Power and control through disguised manipulation. The rationale is that one is less vulnerable when in control. Power can be gained through hierarchical position or through money.
6. Passive-aggressive behavior. Typically, silence, withholding support, staying out of communal activities, and secretiveness are all designed to cause anxiety, fear, or concern among the community. The community will react by conforming to what the person wants in which case the person will resume their place and their support.[496]
7. Being seen to be right. Such a person will go to any lengths to prove they are right, especially if in a public arena. Power becomes useful in two ways: to compensate for shame already felt and also protect from future shame.

---

493. Muller, *Honor and Shame*, 82; Capps, *Depleted Self*, 95.
494. Muller, *Honor and Shame*, 82.
495. Capps, *Depleted Self*, 96.
496. Albers, *Shame*, 76.

8. Scapegoating. The inability to process or acknowledge one's own shame will make it imperative to externalize it and pin it on others.
9. Martyr complex. The attempt to protect from the shaming of others by self-shaming, self-deprecation, and self-effacement. This position is justified by a misinterpretation of the scriptural concept of servant hood and often receives commendation from others. It soon becomes a way of life. Others may take advantage because of the image projected.
10. Withdrawal and isolation, where the isolation can become a place of safety. Not necessarily physical but emotional isolation. Lebra lists this amongst seven strategies common in Japan. Silence, avoidance, or absence may be used to show disagreement or anger without threat. If confronted the person may deny that they intended their action to be interpreted thus.[497]

This is not to say that those from a guilt-oriented culture will not react in similar ways. Research carried out among a group of both shame-oriented and guilt-oriented people shows that both groups felt anger and shame at being insulted. The anger reactions were similar: wanting to punish, aggression, verbal and physical assaults. By contrast, people differed in their shame reactions. In non-honor cultures, shame was closely linked to self-esteem or self-image. Shame thus diminishes a person in their eyes and causes them to withdraw. Subjects from honor cultures needed to act to protect their social image. One way to do this was to express verbal disapproval that rejected or condemned what the other said. As a deterrent, this is satisfactory because it is less antagonistic than more aggressive behavior. It reduces the risk of escalating the conflict, acts as a deterrent, as well as offering an alternative social image.[498]

Summary

Ting-Toomey provides a helpful comparative analysis of conflict resolution styles and process in individualistic (guilt-oriented) cultures and collectivist (shame-oriented) cultures.

---

497. Lebra cited in Augsburger, *Conflict Mediation across Cultures*, 110.
498. Rodriguez, et al., "Attack, Disapproval, or Withdrawal?," 1471–1498.

Table 2.6. Comparative Analysis of Conflict Resolution Style and Process

Individualists (Guilt-Oriented)	Collectivists (Shame-Oriented)
Identity goals. Need face saving, face respect, face consideration and face competence.	Identity goals. Need face saving, face respect, face consideration and face competence.
Outcome focused.	Process focused.
Emphasis on factual detail, evidence.	Emphasis on holistic picture, experience, intuition.
Face saving is through direct mode.	Through indirect mode.
Substantive issues must be resolved before relational issues can be addressed. Content goal oriented.	Unless relational issues are solved, substantive issues neither are nor fully resolved. Relational goal oriented.
Conflict process is step by step, linear; brainstorming, offering options, good at generating solutions. Monochromic pace.	Spiral, holistic, looks at big picture. Context driven; good at analyzing. Polychromic pace.
Handle conflict directly with direct verbal assertions, questions, clarifications.	Indirect ("Should we? Perhaps we could finish this together? If it's not too much trouble, could you?").
Independent concept of self: independent, autonomous, verbally direct.	Interdependent concept of self: cautious, reflective, responsive communication.
Outcome oriented: move rapidly through process, assert individual "I-identity" interests.	Process oriented: preservation of group face through the process before coming to outcomes.
Use of personal resources, initiative.	Use of communal resources, like high status intervention, status-based norms.
Competitive/controlling style.	Avoiding/accommodating style.
Goal is effectiveness.	Emphasis on appropriateness.

Source: Ting-Toomey, *Communicating across Cultures*.

Ting-Toomey also distinguishes between low and high power-distance cultures. High power-distance cultures tend to be shame-oriented cultures.[499]

Table 2.7. High and Low Power Distance Distinctives

Low power distance	High power distance
Individualistic: tendency to value individual identity over group identity, individual rights over group responsibility. Strong personal opinion, importance of personal accountability, display of personal emotions. Desire to get to the truth. Hold person accountable. Openness and honesty valued.	Collectivistic: suppression of emotions, values group opinions, protection of member from accountability.
In low power distance (Scandinavia, Australia, New Zealand etc.) subordinates expect to be treated with respect, people valued for personal attributes more than titles.	In high power distance (Philippines, Korea, Malaysia, Japan, Guatemala, Arab countries) members give priority treatment and respect to people in high status positions.
Self-construal: (strongly affects how we communicate) independent; autonomous, self-reliant, entitled to make their own choices.	Self-construal: self is interdependent, seeking harmony, bound to group, responsible to group.
Low-context communication: straight talk, sender oriented, (speaker must be clear).	High-context communication: ambiguous, nonverbal, recipient centered/interpreter sensitive. Listener must read between the lines.

Source: Ting-Toomey, *Communicating across Cultures*.

Missiologists Lingenfelter and Myers produced a model of basic values that identifies various sources of tension between different cultures. This was first developed by Mayers, based on his experience in Guatemala, then validated by Lingenfelter using it to explain social interactions experienced in the Pacific Islands. See table 2.8.

---

499. Ting-Toomey, *Communicating across Cultures*.

Table 2.8. Comparing Individualist and Collectivist Values[500]

Individualistic	Collectivist
Time oriented	Event oriented
Task-oriented	Person oriented
Dichotomistic	Holistic
Status oriented	Achievement focused
Crisis	Non-crisis
Willingness to expose vulnerability	Unwillingness to expose vulnerability

Wiher, further developing this research, came up with a more developed model of values that shows specific characteristics that work to exacerbate conflict within a shame-oriented culture, and also between individuals within the culture who have embraced different value systems. The Lingenfelter and Mayers and Wiher models are integrated and presented in appendix A.[501]

Positive Aspects of Shame-Oriented Cultures

The above analysis shows several cultural complexities that tend to hinder reconciliation in shame-oriented cultures. However, these cultures also have positive aspects that can be harnessed to motivate and move toward reconciliation in the church.

Catalyst for Transformation

Lynd, in her exploration on identity, states that the experience of shame reveals something about a person, not only to others but to themselves. If that experience is confronted by the self, instead of being covered up, it can reveal something deep about one's own desires, and allow for more holistic growth than for those on the guilt axis, where guilt is an isolated act.[502] The experience of shame can motivate people to face up to weaknesses or failure and move towards their ideals.

---

500. Lingenfelter and Mayers, *Ministering Cross-Culturally*, 9–10.
501. Lingenfelter and Mayers, 156–177; Wiher, *Shame and Guilt*, 428.
502. Lynd, *On Shame*, 231.

Noble retells the experience of a Christian family counsellor who was ashamed of his failure to answer the questions raised by his student who was about to be married and had come to him for answers. This experience of being shamed motivated the professor to study further to be better prepared.[503] Noble cites the work of Christian psychiatrist E. Mansell Pattison, who questioned the adequacy of a super-ego-based morality. While a necessary part of the moral aspect of personality, an over-reliance on the super-ego as internal sanction can lead to legalism. Morality, says Pattison, has not merely to do with prohibitions "but rather the values and definitions of appropriate behavior by which man governs his behavior."[504] It is not the super-ego but the ego-ideal which is the seat of morality.[505]

Noble argues that at its deepest level, guilt (existential guilt as Pattison calls it) is almost identical to a state of shame.[506] Existential guilt is guilt over broken relationships. It is a person's denial of their values. Too much emphasis has been placed on dealing with punishing or forgiving specific acts, which, while necessary, does not deal with "the sort of person that one is," which is existential guilt.[507] Merely satisfying the super-ego leads to a superficial repentance which ignores the challenge to change the kind of person we are.[508] Instead of a punishment model which satisfies the outer layers of guilt, we need a "reconciliation model." Noble says,

> I believe that one important reason for the low quality of Christian life among evangelicals is their overuse of the guilt approach and their neglect of the shame dimension in their proclamation of the gospel. The guilt approach which is essentially negative does have some success in preventing sins of commission but it has limited success in preventing sins of omission. Sins of omission are failures, not transgressions.[509]

---

503. Noble, *Naked and Not Ashamed*, 10.
504. Pattison cited in Noble, 79.
505. Nobel, 79.
506. Noble, 79–80. Pattison lists four types of guilt: civil guilt, which is impersonal and arises at the violation of objective rules. Psychological guilt feelings related to the superego, existential guilt, and ontological guilt (original sin).
507. Nobel, 80.
508. Noble, 80.
509. Noble, 81.

Noble further comments, "shame demands transformation for a solution. Being cannot be forgiven. It can only be changed."[510]

Schmidt asks his readers to imagine themselves involved in a clandestine meeting that turns into an act of betrayal of one's true love. Imagine that the light is turned on and at the door stands the one who could most be hurt by your act. There is nowhere to hide and no denials to be made. "The moment that one is faced with one's own essential badness is an awful moment, but it is also a precious moment. For if in that instant a person is reduced, it is not the reduction from the normal to something abnormal, but a reduction to true humanness."[511]

Desire for Harmony

We have seen that shame-oriented people desire harmony. Community is critically important for group-oriented, shared identity cultures. We can capitalize on this desire to reinforce the value of reconciliation. As we shall see later, this will involve reinterpreting the community's perception of "harmony" to be more than the absence of open conflict. The rich biblical concepts of community and relational harmony are rooted in the theological understanding of shalom.

Conceptual Framework

In this chapter, the researcher has uncovered several elements of shame-oriented cultures that impact interpersonal conflict. The contributions of Lingenfelter and Mayers,[512] Wiher,[513] Ting-Toomey,[514] and Ting-Toomey and Oetzel[515] have proved to be especially helpful.

The following list of shame-oriented culture characteristics is not exhaustive. Yet the features listed appear with sufficient regularity in the literature to suggest that they are the predominant characteristics that broadly dominate the shame-oriented culture spectrum. Just how these impact the experience

---

510. Noble, 83.
511. Schmidt, *Trying to be Good*, 24–25.
512. Lingenfelter and Mayers, *Ministering Cross-Culturally*, 156–177.
513. Wiher, *Shame and Guilt*, 428.
514. Ting-Toomey, *Communicating across Cultures*.
515. Ting-Toomey and Oetzel, *Managing Intercultural Conflict*.

of conflict, and attempts at conflict resolution in Sri Lankan urban church culture, is the focus of this research study. For the subsequent field research, the following seven elements will be used as a conceptual framework with which to analyze case studies and interviews.

Table 2.9. Conceptual Framework Elements and Explanation

Element	Explanation
Goal of conflict resolution	Do parties seek substantive or relational goals? How does the desire for harmony help or hinder conflict resolution?
Identity of self and group	To what extent does the collectivistic identity help or hinder conflict resolution? Who forms Public Court of Reputation (PCR)? How do parties save face for themselves and others? How difficult is confession, repentance and forgiveness?
Style of communication	Is communication direct or indirect?
Conflict resolution style	Which style prevails? (competing, accommodating, avoiding, compromising or collaborative) How important is mediation?
Status and power distance	How does status affect the relational dynamic and sense of entitlement?
Relativistic morality	Are there culturally accepted practices in the conflict script which transgress Biblical morality? To what extent do identified traits of envy and lying occur?
Extreme reactions	To what extremes will conflicting parties go to achieve their goals? What are typical reactions to the perception of being shamed?

CHAPTER 3

Field Research Design and Implementation

The research problem lends itself to qualitative research using the case study design for ethnographic research. Data collection was primarily accomplished through individual interviews followed by a questionnaire.

Qualitative research methods answer the "how" and "why" questions of human behavior, where quantitative research focuses on the "what," "when," and "where" questions.[1] Instead of the researcher putting forward a hypothesis arising from theory and then testing it though empirical enquiry, the researcher's enquiry gives rise to the theories and concepts.[2] Also, data collection and analysis in qualitative research can be cyclical rather than linear and rigidly separated.[3] Data collected from interviews may give rise to further investigation.

The present study began in the libraries of Sri Lanka. Advice was sought from a leading sociologist who confirmed that little had been written on the topic of conflict within a shame culture, or about the characteristics of Sri Lankan culture through the lens of honor-shame. The researcher found literature in the fields of missiology and cultural anthropology dealing with people groups from other shame-oriented cultures especially helpful. Most helpful was the work of Wiher in his research on shame and guilt for cross-cultural

---

1. Sheperis, Young, and Daniels, *Counselling Research*, 115.
2. Robson, *Real World Research*, 19.
3. Robson, 19.

mission.[4] This is built on the work of Lingenfelter and Mayers.[5] Although their work was not specifically aimed at understanding conflict resolution, several of the characteristics that Lingenfelter and Mayers identified as cultural values in collectivistic cultures resonated with what the researcher had experienced in Sri Lanka.

Research Design Rationale

The nature of the study's ethnographic purpose and conceptual framework suggest using interviews and case studies as the primary research approach. Data were collected from seven complementary data sources consisting of pastors and leaders, each with over ten years ministry experience with believers from a cross section of the church in Sri Lanka. Data collection methods included interviews, questionnaires, and participant observation. The design utilizing complementary data sources and multiple methods intentionally enhanced validity through triangulation.

Toward the end of the interview, interviewees were asked to share one or two cases that illustrate what they have revealed about their experience of conflict amongst believers. This provided the researcher the opportunity to analyze actual situations. It allowed the researcher to perceive nuances that might have been missed in the interview. All shame-oriented cultures are not alike, and within a culture people and sub-groups can think and act differently than the rest of the culture. This multi-pronged approach was intended to minimize unfounded generalizations thus enhancing the validity of the study.

Hiebert affirms case studies as "one of the most powerful methods of ethnographic research."[6] According to Colin Robson, "Case study is a strategy for doing research which involves an empirical investigation of a particular contemporary phenomenon within its real-life context using multiple sources of evidence."[7] Yin adds that this research is especially apt when the context is essential, as he puts it, "the boundaries between phenomenon and context

---

4. Wiher, *Shame and Guilt*.
5. Lingenfelter and Mayers, *Ministering Cross-Culturally*.
6. Hiebert, *Gospel in Human Contexts*, 170.
7. Robson, *Real World Research*, 5.

are not clearly evident."[8] Case studies may be confirmatory, descriptive, explanatory or exploratory, or a combination of all or some of these.[9] In this study, use of cases at the end of each interview was confirmatory. The analysis of the interview and case data is descriptive and explanatory, based on the conceptual framework. Ethnography answers "how" and "why" questions.[10] In seeking to understand "why" Christians behave this way, the key question is: "How does the Sri Lankan shame-oriented culture impact Christians' actions and reactions?"

The purpose of using multiple cases in this research was to provide cross-case analysis to both describe and explain the contribution of honor-shame culture characteristics to conflict resolution in Sri Lanka. What took place in this study is what Robson would consider ethnographic study: a study carried out by an ethnographer, who, through involvement with a group, seeks to provide "a written description of the implicit rules and traditions of a group."[11] This study was ethnographic research on a subgroup or microlevel. "Micro-research seeks to understand the situation from the point of view of the humans involved."[12] Hiebert calls this the "street level" approach to studying people from within the culture (emic studies).[13] This research seeks to provide a rich or "thick" description of the subgroup.[14]

The use of more than one case study introduces the possibility of achieving results that corroborate the research carried out through participant observations and interviews, but this is not certain. Yin argues that multiple case studies may be "generalizable to theoretical propositions," even if they may not be universally applicable.

Hiebert suggests two levels of analysis – description and explanation.[15] In analyzing and presenting this study's research findings, a mixture of strategies

---

8. Yin, *Case Study Research*, 18.
9. Yin, 4–5; Robson, *Real World Research*, 43.
10. Yin, 4–5; Robson, 43.
11. Robson, *Real World Research*, 148.
12. Hiebert, *Gospel in Human Contexts*, 163.
13. Hiebert, 163. Hiebert suggests various ways of ethnographic research including participant observation, conversations, interviews, ethnosemantics, case studies, grounded theory, and participatory action research (Hiebert, 164–173).
14. Robson, *Real World Research*, 148.
15. Hiebert, *Gospel in Human Contexts*, 170.

is used, as described by Yin.[16] First, the conceptual framework provides an explanation of conflict behavior in shame-oriented cultures based on the literature review. Second, there is a rich descriptive element inductively formulated from the interviews and cases in the specific Sri Lankan culture studied.[17] Third, interview data and cases were analyzed using the pattern-matching technique, with explanation building comparing the findings to the characteristics identified in the literature research.[18] Fourth, the final discussion and conclusion follow what Yin terms "cross-case synthesis." The findings from each case were compared, then aggregated.

Instrument Design Rationale

As developed in chapter 2, the conceptual framework for the field research integrates a model of shame-oriented cultural values (collectivist cultures) that relate to conflict resolution. As noted, the contributions of Lingenfelter and Mayers,[19] Wiher,[20] and Ting-Toomey[21] proved to be especially helpful. The following characteristics/values of shame-oriented cultures relate closely to the processing of interpersonal conflict (see table 3.1). These were used as a back drop to the development of the interview protocol (see appendix B), and more explicitly to the culture rating grid used at the end of the interview (see appendix C).

Collectivistic societies tend to be those that are also described as shame-oriented. From within this grid, all the values described have an impact on interpersonal conflict to a lesser (time orientation) or greater (unwillingness to expose vulnerability) degree. In addition, Ting-Toomey's intercultural conflict model complements Lingenfelter and Mayers's grid. It shows several features in common with Lingenfelter and Mayers but also includes other aspects of culture which affect conflict resolution styles. This can be summarized in table 3.2

---

16. Yin, *Case Study Research*, 127–162.
17. Yin, 131–132.
18. Yin, 141.
19. Lingenfelter and Mayers, *Ministering Cross-Culturally*, 156–177.
20. Wiher, *Shame and Guilt*, 428.
21. Ting-Toomey, *Communicating across Cultures*.

Table 3.1. Summary of the Basic Values of Mayers

Individualistic	Collectivist
Time oriented	Event oriented
Task oriented	Person oriented
Dichotomistic	Holistic
Achievement focused	Status oriented
Crisis	Non crisis
Willingness to expose vulnerability	Unwillingness to expose vulnerability

Table 3.2. The Intercultural Conflict Model of Ting-Toomey

Individualists (Guilt-Oriented)	Collectivists (Shame-Oriented)
Outcome focused.	Process focused.
Content goal oriented: substantive issues must be resolved before relational issues can be addressed.	Relational goal oriented: unless relational issues are solved, substantive issues are not fully resolved.
Conflict process is step by step, linear; brainstorming, offering options, good at generating solutions. Monochromic pace.	Conflict process is spiral, holistic, looks at big picture. Context driven; good at analyzing. Polychromic pace.
Outcome oriented: move rapidly through process, assert individual "identity" interests.	Process oriented: preservation of group "face" through the process before coming to outcomes.
Competitive/controlling conflict style.	Avoiding/accommodating conflict style.
Goal is effectiveness.	Goal is appropriateness.

The researcher used a combination of these two grids to understand the dynamics of conflict within a shame-oriented culture.

For this study's field research, the following seven elements form a conceptual framework with which to analyze case studies and interviews:

1. Goal of conflict resolution
2. Identity of self and other
3. Style of communication

4. Conflict resolution style
5. Status orientation (Power distance)
6. Relativistic morality
7. Extreme reactions

Ethical Considerations

Care was taken that ethical standards were maintained when obtaining information through interviews and surveys. Interviewees were told the purpose of the interview and asked permission before recording the interview. Names of people in case studies were changed and specific details were suppressed to maintain confidentiality. A copy of the script of the transcribed interview and case study were sent to the interviewee for checking and approval.

Data Collection Procedures

Data collection procedures were influenced by the nature of the research problem, the conceptual framework, and the research design. This section will look at sampling rationale and data collection procedures.

Sampling Rationale

Criterion sampling was used to choose seven Christian leaders for the purposes of generating information about the typical processes of conflict resolution within the church. The seven chosen were leaders in the church or in Christian organizations, and included some professional counsellors. All of them had wide-ranging experience observing conflict between believers in various parts of the Sri Lankan church. They were also known for their involvement in conflict resolution

They were chosen from one region, the city of Colombo. This does mean that they represent an urban culture, which is more globalized than the rest of the country. However, many of these leaders had been ministering among believers from a variety of backgrounds. The leaders were also people who understood the teaching and expectations of the church since they were involved in preaching, teaching, counselling, and discipling significant numbers of Christians.

Interview Protocol

Because there is little documented research into interpersonal conflict in the Sri Lankan culture from an honor-shame perspective, interviews formed the primary data collection method. In these interviews, the primary objective was to discover the main causes of interpersonal conflict, how believers react to such conflict, and how the wider church responds to conflict in its midst.

The interviews were semi-structured using a list of questions prepared to form a guide. This guide formed the first part of the interview questionnaire (see appendix B). Consistent use of similar questions drawn from the literature review provided the ability to compare responses. However, in order to take advantage of fresh discoveries and to pursue different nuances, the interviews were not restricted to the prepared question format.

This kind of interview has been termed as "in-depth, semi-structured or loosely structured form of interviewing."[22] While Mason suggests that qualitative interviewers rarely have a complete script of questions, the questionnaire used was designed to ensure confidence that the main themes were covered. The questionnaire, which in some cases was sent in advance to the interviewees, was meant to be a prompt for the interviewer while allowing the conversation to flow into other relevant areas. These interview questions formed the first part of the questionnaire (see appendix B).

If the discussion in one interview raised other topics to be investigated, they were added on. This allowed the researcher to direct questions towards significant areas of disagreement with other reports, or to build on the results of previous interviews. Mason notes, if the researcher is interested in "a social process which operates situationally, then you will need to ask situational rather than abstract questions."[23]

All those being interviewed were informed of the purpose of the interview. Since interviewees were answering questions about their experience over a period of years, it was expected that their answers would be the outcome of long-term observation and reflection, thus generally accurate and insightful. At the start of the interview, the researcher did not impose the grid of shame-oriented cultures onto the discussion. Of course, since the purpose

---

22. Mason, *Qualitative Researching*, 62.
23. Mason, 64.

of the interview had been explained to them, interviewees were aware of the researcher's general area of interest.

Each interview lasted a minimum of one and a half hours. The interviews were conducted at the place of work of the interviewees, or in two cases, at their homes. During interviews, notes were taken and audio recorded when possible. The transcribed interview was sent to the interviewees so that they could approve them as accurate representation of what they said. This precaution helped to ensure objectivity in recording and presenting data since any bias on the part of the recorder could be noticed and eliminated. Interviews were collated and salient points prepared according to the format of the interview.

Case Studies

In addition to the interview question, each lead interviewee was asked to share a story or two illustrating the typical patterns of people experiencing conflict. The transcripts of the case studies are summarized in appendix E.

Table of Characteristics

Finally, after the interview and case study, interviewees were provided with the second part of the questionnaire. This consisted of a table of characteristics related to handling conflict in shame-oriented cultures. Using a Likert scale, interviewees are asked to assign a value between one and seven to indicate to what extent they saw those characteristics present in the culture outside the church, as well as within the church. Here, for the first time in the interview, the researcher set out what the preliminary literature review seemed to suggest were the defining characteristics of a shame-oriented culture. (See appendix C the table of characteristics, part 2 of the interview questionnaire.)

Data Analysis Procedures

Data analysis procedures were influenced by the nature of the research problem, the conceptual framework, and the research design. The conceptual framework helped form the core analysis grid for the study.

Interviews and cases shared were analyzed according to the categories developed in the conceptual framework. Data were coded to identify correspondence to and variations from the conceptual framework. The resulting elements were compared between cases, as well as between cases and interviews. The diagram below represents the process for analyzing the data from the field research.

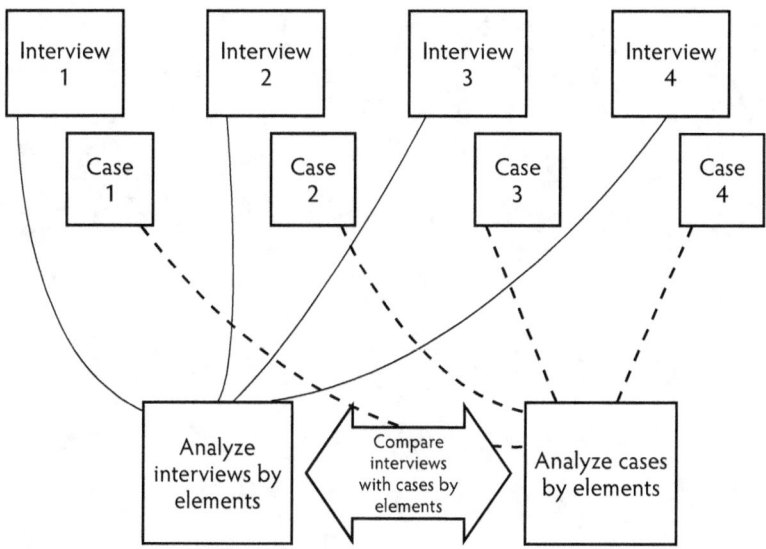

Figure 3.1. Data Analysis.

CHAPTER 4

Field Research Findings

This chapter sets out the field research findings from three major sources. First, certain broad characteristics of Sri Lankan culture are presented drawing from ethnographic observations by the researcher (participant observation) collected over decades of living in Sri Lanka. This allows the researcher to compare and contrast general features of the culture with the subgroup of the urban Colombo church. Second, the data received from the interviews are organized using the conceptual framework. Third, the case data received from the interviewees are presented. Finally, new insights gleaned from the field research conclude the chapter.

Cultural Characterization

This section seeks to identify cultural characteristics that impact conflict and reconciliation. The researcher's years of observation and conversation about local culture are aided by her having been born and raised in Sri Lanka, having lived in England for fifteen years, then returning to Sri Lanka (with new eyes to see the culture) and completing fifteen years of seminary teaching in Colombo with students from around the country.

Sri Lanka's People, History, and Religions

Sri Lankan culture, like any other culture, is not monolithic. The country's two main ethnic groups, the Tamil and the Sinhalese, each have a distinct culture, though there are many commonalities. Tamil culture can be further subdivided into subcultures arising from being "Jaffna Tamils" and "up-country Tamils," just as Sinhalese "from the deep South" might have distinctives not seen in Sinhalese from the Central District.[1] The Burghers, descended from the Portuguese and Dutch who successively colonized the island in the fifteenth and sixteenth centuries, have their own culture, while young city people display a different culture influenced by globalization. Local churches may display the flavor of these different cultures depending on where they are situated, their history and composition.

The people of Sri Lanka are deeply religious and atheism is still a rare phenomenon, nominalism being more common. A person's identity is closely entwined with their religion. Sinhalese are traditionally Buddhist, following Theravada Buddhism, mixed in with folk religion. Tamils are traditionally Hindus, with a pantheon of gods. People of all religions throng to religious shrines, to make vows and offer prayers. Folk religion includes a lot of superstition with lucky days, auspicious times, omens, and horoscopes. Ethnicity is also an important identity marker, made more prominent by the thirty-year civil war not long ended leaving a legacy of division, suspicion, and fear.

Both Buddhism and Hinduism subscribe to a caste system. Ascribed honor derives from the caste one is born into, and the education and wealth which tend to be attached to caste. Christians are drawn from the Sinhalese and Tamil ethnic groups as well as from the Burgers, making the church the most diverse community in the country.

Basic Collectivistic Values

We begin by using a broad-based set of characteristics first proposed by Mayers,[2] which was built on by successive missiologists in collectivistic cultures (e.g. Lingenfelter and Myers, and Wiher).[3] These values have implications for conflict situations as will be shown.

Holistic

A holistic (as opposed to a dichotomous) view of life accepts that many things are happening at any one time, which all have to be held together. One rash action will jeopardize harmony, so much thought needs to go into

---

1. Jaffna is located in the north of the island where the population has been majority Tamils for many years. The country is divided into nine provinces and twenty-five districts. The "up country" refers to the hills in the center of the island where the tea plantations have been worked by Tamil workers, many of whom are of Indian descent.
2. Mayers, *Christianity Confronts Culture*, 159–160.
3. See chapter 2 for a discussion.

any action. When things are working as a whole, even if certain parts of the process are questionable, society tends to accept it for what it is. Sri Lankans are slow to protest, whether it be at broken promises of politicians or poor working conditions in their workplace. They appear to turn a blind eye to what obviously needs changing. Any change has to be gradual and must not upset the equilibrium. As holistic thinkers, they are slow to pass judgment on someone since they want to take into account all aspects of their character. On the other hand, they are slow to admire or praise people since they balance the good with what they believe are negative qualities. If asked, for example, if they would recommend an applicant for a job, they might do so, even if they have grave doubts, because they feel that the person should not be judged based on their past performance.

Non-crisis orientation

A non-crisis orientation leads people to react to a crisis rather than prepare for it. Sri Lankans tend to have a short-sighted view of the future. For example, a person who has been given a job at a house to paint the walls may carry out the job faithfully and so be called back the next year. However, this time, they may decide to steal from the homeowner or borrow money and leave without finishing the job. They do not consider it detrimental to their business to sabotage their reputation with one customer. As long as there is money coming in to cover the day's expenses they will not worry. People are thus vulnerable to the expanding credit market, which offers them the possibility of possessing items which they cannot afford, and paying later. Assets are re-possessed from these naïve consumers who soon find out they cannot sustain repayments. In organizations and churches, it is rare to have budgets and strategic plans, which means that clashes occur when resources are limited. This non-crisis approach means that problems are usually not tackled when they first appear. They are ignored in the hope that with time things will settle and no awkward intervention will be necessary. Little forward planning is put into place to prevent conflict or to teach people to deal with it in a satisfactory manner.

Event orientation

Sri Lankan culture tends to be event oriented rather than time oriented. The important thing is that the task is accomplished and people are accommodated rather than that there should be excessive planning. People are not expected to be on time and it is common for events to begin late because the organizers are waiting for the caterers, the sound system or the most important guests to arrive. Events might take several hours longer than anticipated, because no one would have thought of timing the activities to be able to tell guests when the ceremony would end. Just as guests will be patient at delays in the events they go to, they do not expect to have to tell their hosts if they will be attending. People seldom reply to invitations even if asked to RSVP. Church services in many rural churches may go on for several hours and people might be disappointed if the preacher were to time their talk to finish in half an hour. In city churches and organizations, more effort is made to keep to time and often there are limits placed on numbers invited, which can cause some disappointment. In Christian organizations that attempt to be professional and thus have to be more time oriented, conflicts can arise when the two values clash.

Relationship oriented

In a relationship-oriented culture, people are more important than goals. One obvious area of conflict is when those with this orientation are expected to become goal oriented and keep to deadlines and meet targets. It is also very difficult to separate task and person. Criticism of the way a task was done is interpreted as criticism of the person, and therefore a kind of shaming. This makes organizational procedures like year-end appraisals fraught with potential conflict. This is complicated by the fact that people find it hard to maintain the boundary between professional responsibility and personal relationships. For example, in some organizations, especially Christian ones, people address each other in familial terms like "akka" (elder sister), "aiya" (elder brother), "aunty" and so on. These terms are meant to convey respect for those older, but also the intimacy of a family. Employees expect to be treated as family, with personal matters and family concerns being brought into the work place. A younger manager might have difficulty dealing with discipline issues with an older person under their supervision. In some corporate settings, strict boundaries are maintained between different status groups, for example executives and manual laborers. If, however, those boundaries are broken down by a progressive employer, those who now mingle at the dining table find it hard to maintain the chain of command since in their eyes, they are now equal.

Prestige ascribed

Prestige is primarily ascribed, rather than achieved. That is, the aristocracy and those considered to be of high status will expect to be treated with deference because of who they are rather than because of what they have done. Government officials, religious leaders, and teachers are among those who also receive honor in the community.

It is sometimes surprising to see those who are well-educated and from upper- or middle-class families passing on this sense of entitlement to their children. An example would be the sight of a child throwing a used carton out of the window of a large expensive car. Those from high positions expect that they will not have to undergo the inconveniences that lesser mortals have to undergo. That car might then park in an unauthorized spot or stop in the middle of the road to drop its passengers off as near to their destination as possible. Another example of this is seen when important officials are driven through the city either in motorcades or with their police protection. Vehicles are waved off the road so that these people do not have to negotiate the heavy traffic. When standing in a queue it is routine to see people ignore the line of people patiently waiting and walk to the head of the queue to demand instant service because of perceived status.

Vulnerability as weakness

Communities with this value resist revealing their weaknesses to others. Image is important and this is shown, for example, in leaders who fear the giftedness of those beneath them. Conflict arises when people find it impossible to discuss concerns and have their grievances heard by those in authority. This orientation also means that people will rarely admit to making a mistake and will lie or be evasive in order to hide their vulnerability. Confession is rare. This value fits in with the shame-oriented culture's desire to save face. As one leader described it, "Ego is everything." He was bemoaning the fact that companies do not progress because senior leaders are unwilling to listen to those who have newer better ideas, and instead feel threatened by these younger leaders.

Values Directly Related to Conflict Resolution

Shame-oriented cultural values directly related to conflict (conceptual framework) are now discussed. Connections are also seen with the foregoing discussion.

Goal of conflict resolution

Sri Lanka has had a long history of violent ethnic conflict. It has demonstrated that society avoided contentious issues until violence erupted. It is inevitable that the protracted civil war has affected society and the study of its effects is outside the scope of this paper. In general, the goal of conflict resolution is relational. People attempt to maintain group harmony. Harmony is not however, the same as peace, with its attendant requirements for true reconciliation based on repentance and forgiveness. Harmony is to do with maintaining the status quo, avoiding awkward questions, and possible ruptured relationships.

Identity

Sri Lankan culture is collectivistic rather than individualistic. The extended family is typically the closest and most important group or collective. When inviting one member of the family to an event, it would be expected that the whole family, along with any relatives who happen to be visiting will attend. A young person being introduced to an older person, will often be asked "Whose son/daughter are you?," "Are you related to X, Y or Z (some well-known person of the same name)?" This would give the inquirer some idea of the young person's credentials. Again, on meeting for the first time, people will often search for some connection between themselves, like a mutual friend or distant relationship. Other questions to establish a proper identity would be "Where does your father work?," "Where do your parents come from?" and "What school do you/did you attend?" The answers will all provide clues to the background of the person being questioned. Honor resides in the family name and heritage, employment status of the head of the family and educational background. In both Sinhala and Tamil cultures there is a caste system and this will also contribute to whether one comes from a "good family" or not. Children are encouraged to marry within the same caste and ethnic group as well as religion where possible. Although, with the relative independence of young women and the opportunities for education, some young people may find a partner at university or at work, arranged marriages are still the norm. Although many young women have the opportunity to have a career, they may be warned not to become too educated or it will be difficult to find a husband, since a man will not want to marry a girl more qualified than himself. If a young person is determined to marry someone their parents disapprove of, they might find themselves expelled from the house. A parent, especially a father, might show his disapproval by refusing to attend the wedding. Although many married women now go to work, unlike in previous generations, and may aspire to almost any career they choose, male and female roles continue to be strictly defined in the home. Girls are usually expected to help around the house but not boys. Wives will do most of the housework as well as taking responsibility for the care of children. If money is scarce, it will be the boys of the family who will be educated, since they are expected to be providers while girls will be expected to marry and be provided for.

Children learn to call friends of the family or anyone who is not in a formal relationship, like teacher or employer, by family terms. Those who are a few years older than them are called *akki/acca* "big sister" and *aiya/anna* "big brother" or if they are older than that, "aunty" and "uncle" or "grandfather" and "grandmother." Even in offices, it is not uncommon for employees to address their peers with the title *akki* (older sister) *aiya* (older brother), *malli* (younger brother) or *nangi* (younger sister).

In child rearing, parents will warn children against misbehaving with the admonition "what will people think?," or "see everyone is watching." A person engaging in inappropriate behavior will be asked "have you no shame?" (*Ladja nedda?*). The honor or shame of one member of the family will affect all the others. If a girl earns an unsavory reputation, she will be warned that not only will she make herself unmarriageable, she risks making all her sisters ineligible too. Women are expected to be chaste and not give rise to any speculation about their unblemished reputation. To be pregnant and unwed is perhaps the most shaming thing for a girl. Sexual misdemeanors bring shame on a family, but especially on the woman involved. Any sexual irregularity such as homosexuality, pre-marital sex, or even infertility would be something to hide from others.

Extended family will form a person's in-group. People are protective of the honor of those in their in-group. If there is an argument between children, whereas in the West a parent might be more inclined to attribute some blame to their own child, shame-oriented people will tend to defend their own child and blame the others. In a typical extended family grandparents, aunts, and uncles will all play a part in a child's upbringing. This intimacy is reflected, for example, in the titles given to the mother's sisters. They are called "small mother" (*podi amma/chinnama*) and "big mother" (*loku amma/periamma*). It is their instruction that informs the ego ideal. Respect is given to the aged, rather than to youth. It is not unknown for a child to be brought up by a grandmother or aunt if the parents have to go overseas to work, or if there are too many mouths to feed or, in some cases, when a horoscope reveals that a child is "unlucky" for a family.

In order to protect the honor of the family or in-group, shameful aspects discovered will have to be hushed up. Abuse of children and spousal abuse is rarely brought to light because it would bring shame on the family. The child or woman may be told not to tell anyone about it, rather than be encouraged to speak up and indict the culprit.

Within the family, relationships between parent and child tend to be stronger than between husband and wife. It is not unknown for husbands and wives to sleep separately, with the wife sleeping with the children. Siblings are meant to take responsibility for one another. Quarrels between siblings tend to be over matters of property, especially houses or land passed down from parents. The role of the male in the household is provider and defender. Thus, a man's honor is impinged if he cannot provide for his family or if his wife becomes the main breadwinner. Care of children and domestic chores are usually the province of the women and girls, even when, as it is now, women usually need to find paid employment to help family finances.

Scholars suggest that in collectivistic cultures, collaboration rather than competition is favored, and there is a fear of standing out. In the researcher's experience, children are introduced to the idea of competition in schools where getting into a good school, and getting places at university both depend on outdoing others.

Achieved honor

As we have seen, ascribed honor is received through birth. The family name, caste, positions held by the head of the family all contribute to the honor one receives through birth. Through the choice of an appropriate spouse that honor is carried on.

Achieved honor can be gained through wealth. A rich father will offer a generous dowry to enable his daughter to get the best possible bridegroom. Education also brings honor. It is debatable if education brings more honor than wealth. The ideal would be to have a prestigious lineage as well as education and wealth. There is not much social mobility between class groups, though with education there is a chance to better oneself. Parents would prefer their children to marry into their own class, educational background, and ethnic group. Girls may be told not to study too much since no man will want to marry a woman who is more qualified than him. Competition is fierce for places in prestigious schools and universities. Children are put under a lot of pressure to perform and most children in the cities are sent for private tuition so that they can outperform the other children. Achievements that bring honor to the country also increase a person's honor. In recent years the achievements of the Sri Lankan cricket team have made these players national heroes, overriding their antecedents and educational achievements. Someone who makes us feel good about ourselves is a hero.

Education and learning also brings honor. Traditionally teachers are highly respected in the community. Religious leaders of all communities have also been honored. Special seats for clergy are reserved in public transport and certain establishments such as airports. Open questioning or arguing with respected elders, teachers, or religious leaders would be a shameful matter. A teacher will generally not admit to not knowing something, for that would lead them to lose face before the student. In the church too, honor is often given to those who are rich, well-educated and gifted. Ministry becomes a way of achieving honor in the church.

Looking after one's parents is honorable behavior. Faithfulness and loyalty to one's friends would be expected of honorable people. Loyalty to leaders is expected and commended. Leaders are seen in a paternal role, rather than public servants, and are therefore to be obeyed and honored. Patriotism in such a context means unswerving loyalty to those who lead the country. For example, the international call for investigations into war crimes in Sri Lanka has been met with outrage and with accusations of foreign conspiracies, which is all part of the collectivistic response to what is perceived as an attack on the communal identity. Those who challenge or question the leadership are denounced as traitors. Bringing shame on your country is a terrible crime, rather than as public servants.

Getting caught in a crime or shameful act is shameful, but honorable people are considered to be above the law. Public figures may be known to be unfaithful to their marriage vows but they will still be held in high esteem. On the other hand, the vulnerable can be easily put to shame. Sri Lanka has a very high rate of suicide. Many suicides among young people are due to their being chastised by parents or teachers. The misdemeanors, usually an inappropriate relationship with a member of the opposite sex, or failing an exam, would be considered minor in many cultures, but the resulting shame can lead to a young person taking their own life.

In both secular society and in the church, abuse of power is a prevalent issue. This fits in with a culture in which those who have status do not expect to explain themselves or be accountable to external standards or live up to the expectations of those they consider inferior to them.

Patron-client relationships

In Sri Lanka, the family is the closest kin group. People also form connections such as the patron-client relationship. The most common example of a patron-client relationship would be between those who used to be called "servants" and are now called "domestics" or "menial workers" and those for whom they work. Such an employee would expect certain favorable treatment from their employers, even after they had left their jobs. Employers might find jobs for the children of such employees, help them with their education, assist them in times of sickness, and occasionally find them a place to live when they are unable to work any longer. In some situations, tenants on a large plantation, such as a tea estate, would qualify as the clients of the landowner. The client would show loyalty by inviting their patrons to important events, defending their reputation to others, and so on. However, as one senior Sri Lankan historian remarked "loyalty is a value but betrayal is common."[4]

Other more informal relationships exist between relatives and extended family. What most Westerners would call "nepotism" would merely be considered looking after one's own in Sri Lanka. One's network of connections is expected to smooth the path by providing "insider" help for their contacts. For example, "do you know someone at the . . . office" would be a prelude to

---

4. Professor G. P. V. Somaratna in a private conversation with the researcher.

being granted a job interview, be given a job, have traffic fines waived, etc. It is not what you know or do but who you know that matters.[5]

A crowd can easily be manipulated. It is a standing joke that at the elections, a bus load of voters can be persuaded to vote for the person who gives them a packet of rice and curry. Similarly, a crowd can be incited to violence by extremists, even against their neighbors, as many minorities have experienced.

Desire to save face

This trait is seen in Sri Lankan culture in the way people struggle to hold on to their self-image in the face of competition and in the context of their own weaknesses. It is rare to see someone in a position of prestige being willing to admit to a fault. It is noticeable that even when bumping into someone on the road, if a person were to apologize, they would most likely use the English word "sorry" rather than an equivalent word in their vernacular. In some way that distances them from the act for which they have apologized.

Indirect communication

In some ways, Sri Lankan communication may seem overly direct to someone from the West because subjects that are considered private in the West are openly addressed. For example, a young woman recently married may have to face constant questions about why she is not yet pregnant, or if she has one child why she is not trying for another. Jokes about someone's weight are common and meant to be borne with good humor. A single person may be asked why they have not married. A person who is hurt by these remarks will learn to mask their emotions. However, emotions are rarely communicated directly. A person will hesitate to tell a neighbor or friend that they have been offended or hurt by something they did or said. In the same way, rarely will love be openly declared. Whereas children in the West grow up being told they are loved and are used to the phrase "I love you," it is assumed that actions can be interpreted as love in most contexts in Sri Lanka.

---

5. Evelyn Miranda-Feliciano discusses the same phenomena in her *Filipino Values and our Christian Faith* (3–5). She discusses the fact that bribery and corruption is part of the system that can be justified by the fact of the low wages public officials get paid, and the inordinate waste of time together with the frustration of legitimate business, if one does not work with the system.

Indirect communication is used so as not to offend. Anyone who is asked for directions will promptly assist, even if they are not sure or are completely wrong. Repairmen or gardeners, if asked to call round promptly to carry out some emergency work, will reply in the affirmative even though they have no intention of turning up until it is convenient to them. Invitations to weddings or other events will seldom receive a response if there is a possibility of that response being interpreted wrongly. Junior employees may well not explain or defend themselves if blamed for a lapse at work, but remain silent and seem to accept the rebuke, at least in front of their superiors. What they tell others is often a different story.

Raising the issue if one is offended does not come easily. Harmony is highly valued. Confronting, is feared since it might bring about argument and hostility and cause the offender to lose face or be shamed. Harmony will be destroyed and the relationship might be irrevocably broken. A person who has been offended might prefer to send a message through a third party, raise the issue in a roundabout way without specifying to whom they are referring, withdraw, or show by body language that they are offended. Alternatively, if they are in a position to, they might choose to get even by sabotaging the offender's job or ministry by disagreeing with decisions they make, by refusing to cooperate with them, or picking a quarrel over a completely different issue.

Silence must sometimes also be interpreted as communicating something that cannot be directly expressed. One example can be drawn from the response of students to an anonymous student evaluation of the classes they attend. The leadership of the school assumes that since the evaluation forms are not signed students will freely express their concerns about their classes and the feedback can be acted upon by the school. However, it has been discovered that students will not give negative feedback on those forms. When asked why, the reasons given included the fear that the lecturer or the school would penalize them for criticizing the lecturer, a lack of trust that leaders would listen to the voice of lowly students, and a desire to save face for the lecturer. What a student might do to signify disapproval or complaint is either refrain from completing an evaluation form, or leave a question blank.

Conflict resolution style

Sri Lankan people are generally easy going, hospitable, and kindly people. But crowds are volatile and easily roused. When the international community, primarily from the West, called for an investigation into war crimes, mobs reacted by burning effigies and attacking foreign embassies. Vigilante justice is not uncommon. If a vehicle runs over a pedestrian the local community will beat the driver and burn the vehicle.

In general, people value harmony and small grievances are ignored. Issues related to more irksome conflicts will be confided to friends or family but rarely to the person concerned. The prevalence of the accommodating or avoiding mode of conflict resolution might explain why people tend to be situated more towards the ends of the spectrum of fight and flight than in the middle (see figure 4.1). It seems like Sri Lankans will generally fall into one or the other end of the slippery slope. When the injury is minor, or perpetrated by someone with higher status, or when the other party in the conflict is showing anger, displaying intimidating behavior, or has the power to harm them in some way people tend to the avoidance, or flight mode. This is evidenced, for example, in the very high rate of suicide in the country. When the injury is severe like a public insult, or if the perpetrator is of lower status, the reaction is to fight. Violence is displayed in disputes over land, revenge attacks and vigilante style justice meted out to criminals of various types.

Figure 4.1. The Slippery Slope[6]

---

6. Based on "The Slippery Slope" illustration by Ken Sande (1991). Escape responses are suicide, flight, and denial; while attack responses are assault, litigation and murder. The Slippery Slope is used courtesy of Ken Sande and originally appeared in his book *The Peacemaker*, published by Baker Books, USA. All rights reserved. For more information on Ken and his

Power distance

Although education might provide a way to overcome the disadvantages of caste or poverty, so that a child of a white-collar worker might become a doctor, there is little mobility between classes and even education will not completely eradicate the status of being "one of those" from a certain class or caste. To that extent there is a level of stereotyping. For example, those who offer themselves as domestic helps in a household will generally be held to be of a lower class and caste from their employers. They will not generally be expected to sit with their employers or eat with them. There is a fear that if such leniency is exercised the "servant" will forget their place. Certain jobs are reserved for the "lower classes."

Expressions like "what cheek!" or "do they realize who they are talking to?" are indications that someone has breached the boundaries of power distance. Those who consider themselves of high status will not wait in line, whether it is at the bank, at the traffic line, or the bakers. There seems to be something within the psyche that demands that one at least tries to outdo others by getting in there first. It is an interesting observation that even those who do not have an entitlement to high status will attempt to assert themselves over others when possible. So, waiting in line is something very few feel obliged to do. There is an element of competitiveness where a person demands attention first, simply because they feel their need is urgent. Similarly, the researcher observed that if a motorist does stop for pedestrians on the pedestrian crossing, pedestrians will not acknowledge the courtesy and will slow down to take as much time as possible. It leads one to wonder if, in the absence of actual position and power, people strive to take control and exercise power if they find an opportunity to grasp it. One leader described it in this way, "everything is such a struggle that people get used to being aggressive."

People enjoy titles and public acknowledgment. For example, being on the board of a company, being conferred with an honorary doctorate, or being a chief guest is a reflection of one's status. People who consider themselves of high status will have difficulty dealing with people whose role or designation gives them an authority that high status people do not recognize. For example, a senior pastor who is being contacted about something by a seminary would

---

ministry, please visit www.rw360.org. © Ken Sande and Relational Wisdom®360. Used by permission.

expect to hear from and meet with the principal even if another staff member has special responsibility for that particular work. A student at a seminary who is also a senior pastor might find it difficult to be called to task for his late assignments by a young member of faculty, especially a woman. A retired director of the electronics company will expect to be invited into the new CEO's office to discuss the purchase of a microwave, rather than deal with a salesperson.

In churches, the fact that attitudes have not completely been transformed by the gospel will be revealed when parents are arranging a marriage for their child, or if a young person has chosen a partner for themselves but wants parental approval. Caste, class, and even ethnicity are often factors in their selection. Since most churches have congregations based on language, those who worship in English will generally be economically, and sometimes educationally, of higher status than those who worship in Sinhala or Tamil. There is a certain amount of elitism associated with the ability to converse in English and churches are not immune from this.

Since honor is closely bound up with lineage, adoption has traditionally been unpopular. While a relative might unofficially "bring up" the child of a poor or overburdened relative, adopted children are usually not considered to have the same honor as legitimate children of the family line, though this attitude is slowly changing.

Age is respected. Children in the Sinhala-Buddhist culture will show respect for their parents and elders by bending to touch their feet and receiving their blessing. Elderly parents are looked after in the home of their son or daughter and not expected to be independent or to be placed in the care of strangers, unless completely unavoidable.

People receive honor from their association with other honorable people. For example, to have honorable people (rich, middle class, senior) attending a funeral of a poor person lends honor to the family of the deceased. Nepotism is widely practiced.

In churches, the title "pastor" or "reverend" is important. Leadership brings status and power. It is rare that a pastor will be called by their first name. Many who are leaders in the church have not come from high status families. There is a noticeable problem with abuse of power in some churches. Members of the church will refer to one another in the same "family" terms that are used outside (sister, brother, uncle, aunty), as a sign of respect for those who are older, but showing that they are not strangers but part of the inner circle. Having said that, in city churches at least, there is rarely a congregation that would describe itself as a family (even if the term might be used).

Somehow it seems that the Christian gospel has brought an individualizing impact on a collectivistic culture. There is an emphasis on personal conversion within evangelicalism that emphasizes the value of the individual along with it. The result is that in most local churches, there is, instead of close personal family-like friendships, a collection of individuals and families for whom church is one among many voluntary associations to which they belong. Biological family ties are generally strong, as is often remarked on by those from Western cultures, but the willingness to befriend and invest in those from outside the family is low.

In the light of successive communal conflicts in the island, it would be remiss to avoid mentioning the strong nationalistic fervor that has been stirred up in the Sri Lankan people. Ethnicity and religion play a large part in perceived honor. To that end many in public life have forsworn their Christian heritage to take on the majority Buddhist identity to ensure their advancement is not hindered by their religious heritage.

Relativistic morality

People act according to the need of the situation rather than according to abstract principles. Take the example of a person who parks their car across the gates of another person's house. The one who parks does not consider it a general principle that the gate way should be left accessible for the house owner. Instead they observe that there is no car in the drive (that is, no one needs to drive away), or that the car arrives back after a certain time of day. They then feel justified in parking there when they considers it not in use. People will pick flowers from gardens in their neighborhood without permission, for use in the temple. The rationale being that if it is used for worship, there is no need to consider this someone's personal property. A church that built an illegal structure on a neighbor's boundary wall gave as their explanation, "we thought no one was living in that house."

People will try to resolve a potential problem by changing what they say to match the hearer's expectations. For example, a taxi company may say "I will call you back in ten minutes." If the customer was to say, "Ten minutes – I cannot wait that long!" they would reply "I will call you back immediately."

They finally call back in fifteen minutes, which was quite probably what they intended all along. However, the unwary listener who thinks they negotiated a better response is appalled at this seeming deception.

Telling a lie is not considered wrong if it is done with the motivation of doing good or avoiding shame, either for the self or the other. A Tamil proverb says that it is acceptable to tell a thousand lies in order to arrange a wedding. That is to say, that the good of an arranged marriage makes up for certain lies that have been told, perhaps about the groom's employment or the bride's dowry. Workmen will regularly assent to deadlines they do not expect to keep because it is more respectful to agree with their customers. Sometimes, lies are made up to protect a reputation, but at other times, a lie may be told for which there seems to be no real reason. One example that an interviewee shared was of a shopkeeper who asked the maid why the lady of the house had not been to the shop recently. While the lady was quite willing to reply that the reason was that she did not need anything, the maid interrupted to say that the lady had been unwell. Presumably the maid perceived some reason to be evasive in her reply.

Corruption is endemic. Poorly paid government officials have made taking bribes a part of the system. Getting a driver's license, having one's building plans passed, building illegal structures, getting job contracts are all known to be facilitated by the paying of bribes. The church discourages the practice of paying bribes and it is not unknown for Christians to suffer for this since their refusal to pay for reasons of conscience is not understood or appreciated.

Envy is rife. There is also a belief that envious people can direct the evil eye to you. Children may be told not to tell others that they have succeeded at something, for fear of attracting the evil eye. A family may keep secret the fact that their daughter has got engaged or that proposals are being received, just in case other mothers become envious and cast the evil eye. An envious parent might even sabotage the delicate negotiations around the marriage brokering. There is a delicate balance between displaying what you have achieved in order to receive status and honor, and playing down your accomplishments to prevent envy and competition.

Envy is tied to the concept of limited good. The behavior of people at a buffet, a doctor's office or a queue demonstrates the outworking of the perception of limited good. People will push their way to the front, even if appointment numbers, seats, or food is sufficient and allocated to them. When boarding an aircraft, people will form or join a queue to board and ignore calls to remain seated and allow certain passengers or rows to come forward first.

Revenge is common. A trishaw driver who is told that a customer has complained about him will ignore calls from the customer after that. He explains that the customer is the one who loses by complaining because the company does not dismiss the driver concerned; but the driver will avoid picking up the customer again. Furthermore, the driver says, when he asked the customer why he had complained, the customer denies it. A legitimate customer service technique is sabotaged by the complex relationship between identity, saving face, and reactions to shame.

Extreme reactions

As mentioned before, children are brought up with the understanding that they should avoid bringing shame on their families and on themselves. However, discretionary shame is an important aspect of character development. *Ladja baya* is literally "fear of shame." People are meant to have this fear of shame, which is a healthy respect for one's own reputation. To court censure is to be shameless. "*Ladja nedda*?" means "have you no shame?" Having said that, to be shamed by another can give rise to extreme reactions. While in many cases, the one who has been shamed will react by avoiding or escaping the relationship, if the offence is a great insult, revenge is the chosen option.

In Western countries public figures, especially political figures, are fair game for the general public's satire or comment. In Sri Lankan culture, pointing out a leader's faults or making fun of them would cause great humiliation to the leader and usually result in the punishment of the offender in some way. For example, a popular theatrical comedy based on the life of a minister of parliament was recently banned. The ability to laugh at oneself is something that is difficult in a shame culture where image and honor are entwined.

It is considered wrong not to restore the honor that was affronted. Insults must be avenged. For example, if a young woman spurns the advances of a man, he might well lie in wait for her and throw acid in her face. More subtle ways are also available. A workman who feels he has been wronged by the house-owner may get his revenge by driving a nail through a water pipe, and then plastering over the pipe, leaving the leak to be discovered long after he has left the premises. At the other extreme, a young person who has been scolded by a parent over an illicit love affair is likely to commit suicide rather than face the shame of being labelled as promiscuous.

Field Research Findings: Interviews

What follows is the analysis of interviews with influential leaders in the Colombo church. Transcripts of the interviews were coded and examined in light of the conceptual framework of the study. This section presents a brief description of the leaders interviewed, a summary of causes of church conflict cited by them, data from the interviews, and suggestions related to the church's role in dealing with conflict.

Source Demographics

The Christian leaders interviewed were well experienced, evangelical practitioners with ten or more years of ministry experience with a wide range of Sri Lankans. The group was composed of three women and four men; three Sinhala and four Tamil. One was a pastor, three were heads of Christian organizations, one was a counsellor, and two were lay leaders in the church who held leadership roles in secular institutions.

Main Causes of Conflict in the Church

From the interviewees' responses, it appears that the main causes of conflict in the church are related to rejection of some sort, envy, issues of status, and confusion over leadership roles. Conflicts arise over feelings of rejection when someone, or a member of their family, is not selected for prominence. This could be, for example, when a child is not selected to sing a solo in the Christmas play, or if someone who has been working hard in some ministry is not selected to be on a committee, or some recognized leadership position. If a person's opinion or advice is rejected in favor of another, this could be taken personally and cause conflict. This feeling of rejection is further aggravated when it is realized that someone else, perhaps a friend, or someone considered less deserving has received the accolades or prominence that the person had sought. Feelings of anger can be directed at the person who seems to have succeeded where one has failed, and they might be unaware of it. People tend to be very critical of their Christian brothers and sisters, especially those who are most involved and active in the church. They are also very sensitive to what is said about them. "People take anything that has been said about an issue they are involved in as a personal attack," said one of the interviewees. There is no such thing as criticism that is constructive in this scenario. So, suggestions that we separate the person from the problem are not easy to implement in a culture where the person and the role are virtually indistinguishable and a criticism or questioning of a procedure or action is perceived as a personal insult. A suggestion that the accounts should be audited will be interpreted by those involved in administering finances as an allegation of dishonesty on their part, rather than as a suggestion for improved financial accountability. A debate over a proposal made by a member of the church resulting in their suggestion being laid aside in favor of another will often result in the proposer being angry that they were ignored. An impatient or insensitive remark, especially if made by a leader to a member of the congregation will cause great hurt and bitterness.

Conflict between leaders also arose because of differing views of ministry, said one interviewee. A leader who felt that they were being led by God to do something also felt that the way to do it was a given. To question or critique the method was to oppose the vision. Another source of conflict seems to be over material goods like property and finances (it was noted that there are few conflicts over doctrine). One interviewee mentioned that church members sometimes entered into business transactions with a great deal of optimism and faith in each other. They failed to take the normal precautions they would do in business deals and if the business hit problems, the parties seem to be totally unprepared for dealing with it.

From the three female interviewees, two felt that men were less likely to want to reconcile because there was more at stake for them, in terms of their honor. One interviewee also added that people are taken aback and completely surprised that conflict is possible in the church. This is probably especially true for those who have been converted from other faiths and whose expectations of this new community are high. The surprise increases the element of hurt.

Shame-Oriented Dynamics of Interpersonal Conflict

The data from the interviews were organized according to insights from the conceptual framework. The following subsections develop those categories.

Goal of conflict resolution

It was difficult to identify this goal from the interviews and case studies because conflict resolution was so rarely sought. However, it seems clear that the goal of those involved in conflict was to maintain the appearance of harmony rather than to strengthen relationships. While some sought the resolution of substantive issues or sought justice or fairness, most did not seek resolution in terms of reconciliation and restored relationships.

Identity of self and other

"In a conflict, the first thing a person will do is to question the other person's relationship with God," said one interviewee. They make value judgments about the other person. They bring up the past, they might say "this is the way they have always been." Suddenly, the offender becomes an outsider. Their caste or ethnicity are brought up and stereotypes are invoked. The past is recalled. "They have not changed. Do you remember what they did five years ago?"

Most interviewees felt that family and friends of the parties in a conflict have to get involved and choose sides. Occasionally, friends might say they do not want to be involved, but usually a conflict becomes a test of a friend's loyalty. That loyalty is meant to be unquestioning. Sometimes the spouses of quarrelling parties will attempt to carry on their relationships aside from the conflict. One interviewee said that the children of the parties involved were slower to take sides, which could mean that the younger generation shows signs of a different subculture from their elders.

Most friends and family will feel uncomfortable to associate with the "opposite side." The "opposite side" will assume that their opponent's friends are being influenced by their opponent and may automatically disassociate themselves even if the friends are trying to be neutral. The offended party, with their family and friends will form a clique against the offender. Loyalty to one party will keep a person from intervening to promote the other party's interests.

When asked about the potential for small groups to help in conflict resolution, one interviewee said that if the conflicting parties are members of small groups, those groups tend to get caught up in taking sides. However, the small group, in their experience, though not necessarily engaging in peace-making, could be the place where the person in conflict was enabled to be open about their problem and get to a place where they were ready to hear the challenge to be reconciled.

Face saving techniques
A way in which this concept plays out is in the ability to confess. All those interviewed said that conflicting parties resist verbalizing an apology. It was said by one interviewee that people would need some urging from a leader in order to do so. Generally, people would rather wait and hope the issue will sort itself out. Another one said that people do not want to be vulnerable, neither do they want to accept they could be wrong. Admitting wrong is shameful. Shame is seen as a greater evil than guilt, said one interviewee. It is better to avoid shame than to avoid guilt. Therefore, it is better not to own up, to bear the guilt of a wrongdoing rather than bear the shame of confessing to a fault. Since society is hierarchical, it would be even more unthinkable to admit wrong to someone who is lower than oneself, either in rank or age. A parent would not normally consider it necessary to admit that they have been wrong to their children. Similarly, it would be rare to find a leader admitting a fault to an employee or church member.

Honor is maintained by ensuring no mention is made of any wrongdoing. For example, no one will talk about the evils of an honored institution in society (e.g. the Buddhist *Sanga* [leadership], the government, or the family). This is considered very important for the stability of society. If, for example, there is an instance of physical or sexual abuse within a family, the wrongness of the action fades into insignificance in the face of the need to protect the honor of the family. The victim of the abuse, often a child or a woman, will be urged to say nothing so as to "protect" the honor of the family and in so doing, protect the perpetrator. If there is corruption or abuse of power in an institution, it might be an open secret but it will not be publicly denounced. Those who expose evil in an institution, family, or church may find themselves the targets of anger and hatred. It will not be uncommon for such people to receive anonymous phone calls or death threats and be ostracized by the very people they were trying to help.

For example, a leader in the province was jailed. His son, who had the seat in the provincial council, waited for his father to be released and gave the seat to him. The fact that the man was jailed was explained away. Obviously, it was claimed, he was innocent and his enemies framed him for a crime he did not commit. He might even become a hero in the area, as long as the people want him. Although he had done something criminal, that is not considered shameful. That kind of shame does not stain the politician's reputation for long. It will be forgotten and he is restored to honor. Similarly, in the church, someone who has been found guilty of stealing funds may simply leave the church and join another one, but they will feel no qualms about applying for the same post in the new church. They may rationalize their actions by claiming that God has forgiven them. They decide for themselves that they ought to be restored.

Signs of repentance

It was noted by one interviewee that within a church context, people who are worshipping get a sense that something is wrong that they need to fix. They feel a sense of discomfort with unresolved conflict. It is the process that they have to go through that is not straightforward. Typically, repentance is shown through actions. Verbal communication, in any case, will be last. As said previously, to admit a wrongdoing is to shame oneself and is especially hard for men.

In Sinhala culture, visiting is very important. Therefore, someone who is trying to show their desire to be reconciled will visit. No words are necessary. No mention will be made of the events that have caused the conflict. Other nonverbal ways of communicating apology will be an increased friendliness, displayed in smiles, closer physical proximity, words of praise, even flattery, and plenty of eye contact. Another way to show repentance is to try to show favor to the person, encouraging or cheering them on in some other area of the relationship.

An interviewee gave the example of a Bible study leader who has a conflict with a member of their Bible study group, who subsequently leaves the group. The leader now regrets what happened, but does not ask the member to come back, or speak of what is past. Instead they might be very effusive in their commendation of their ex-Bible study group member for leading the church camp. Usually, the other party can read between the lines and understands what is happening.

Another example given by an interviewee, is of a person who made serious accusations against a leader. The leader responded to the allegations made against them. They received a response that the one accusing was satisfied with this explanation. No apology was ever made for the accusations and for the discomfort the leader had felt at being not welcome in certain venues. Suddenly, there was an increased level of communication through email from the one who had been the accuser. They were vociferous in encouraging the leader's participation in events to which they had not been welcome before. When asked by the researcher if this was true repentance, the interviewee responded that it is hard to call it genuine repentance, but there was a personal recognition and acceptance that they had done wrong.

In Sinhala culture, certain gestures can connote a request for forgiveness or reconciliation. For example, bowing down and touching the feet of the person whose goodwill is sought could be interpreted as a request for forgiveness. This could be either accompanied by the offender's verbal explanation and/or apology, or accompanied by a mediator's explanation and plea. Another example of indirect communication would be for the offender to send a mediator to let it be known that they regret what has happened and want to make peace. Or the offender can make it known to others so that word gets back to the offended party. The one receiving the message will tend to accept it and carry on the relationship.

In churches, people may attempt to spiritualize and privatize their repentance by saying, for example, "I have repented before the Lord and he has forgiven me." Thus, the onus for reconciliation is placed on the one who was offended. There is a Sinhala word *samawenna* (literally "forgive me") but this is not the same as asking a person for forgiveness in the Christian understanding of the term. It is a request for another to "cancel my debt." There is no element of contrition in it as there is with "sorry," neither is there a sense of ownership. Rather the onus is on the offended party to forgive. This was highlighted by one interviewee who pointed out that when someone has done something wrong, they take a long time to get to the point that they can accept they are wrong, but when they make some move to make amends, they expect the other person to immediately be ready to forgive.

The offender who is sorry expects to be welcomed cordially by the one they have offended, such as by receiving a welcome kiss when visiting. The idea of offering some kind of restitution or going through some kind of discipline is seen as a lack of forgiveness. For example, when an employee/volunteer in a Christian organization is told that as part of their restoration they will need to undergo discipline, they will ask "is there no forgiveness in this organization?" For some Christians, repentance must be met with immediate restoration of honor that was lost, with everything else forgotten.

Willingness to forgive
Forgiveness is not a clear concept in secular society. When people are hurt, they often cannot see beyond that pain. When one has been dishonored, it is "almost a sin" to forgive the one who sinned against you, or your family, said one interviewee. By forgiving you dishonor your family because they too have been dishonored by the offender. An interviewee disagreed with the general view on the difficulty of forgiving. They argued that believers have a high view of forgiveness. They want to forgive and will but they need to be helped to get there.

This kind of forgiveness is not asked for in other religions even if the religion lists forgiveness as a virtue. This was illustrated by one interviewee who described an incident in which a lady in the congregation, who had a Buddhist background, was in a conflict with another believer and was asked to reconcile. Her response was "it's easier to be a Buddhist." When asked under what circumstances people find it easier to forgive, one interviewee said that if a person makes some kind of direct apology, the other party will generally be ready to forgive, but if there is no direct contact, it will not happen.

Usually an apology is met with, "that's alright." There are no right formulae for apologies or an acceptance of an apology. If a person has been previously hurt by someone and they offend again, the hurt party might say "last time this happened I forgave, but this time I am going to make sure everyone knows what they did."

Sometimes people will say they forgive but emotionally they have not. They still harbor anger and resentment. They lack someone who will patiently go through the process of showing why and how to forgive. To them, forgiveness means "I won't take revenge," it does not mean "I will not hold animosity against them."

There is a saying in the culture that a situation can be "shape." That usually means some kind of manipulative behavior that has resulted in a good result for the main protagonist. Interviewees suggested that that is what happens with conflict in the church. People "shape" the relationship, so that it continues, but damage has been done which is not addressed. One interviewee said that what people want is for the relationships to be smoothed over, and the appearance of reconciliation is more important than true reconciliation. They suggested that people were "accommodating" rather than forgiving, in that people were willing to blame the situation rather than the person.

Style of communication

Every person interviewed agreed that one of the main causes of the prolonging of conflict was the fact that offended parties would not talk to those who had offended them. As one interviewee said, "Neither Matthew 5, nor Matthew 18 is put into practice." Another interviewee commented that this is not part of the typical Sri Lankan's upbringing. Children are not encouraged to express their negative feelings openly, especially if this is in the form of criticism of elders. Thus, Sri Lankans do not learn to express criticism or any kind of negative feeling in a constructive way. They do not learn "the rules of engagement."

Indirect communication

Indirect communication is manifested in various ways. One way is to avoid being vocal in the appropriate forum. If there is going to be a meeting in which a contentious issue is to be raised, a person who disagrees with one of the speakers or decisions to be made, will be out, lobbying, gossiping, and spreading innuendo designed to dishonor their opponent. "They must be getting a cut" (benefitting from this financially), someone might say, or "they want to be the next president/treasurer." Thus, a faction is formed over an issue before the meeting convenes. When the issue is being discussed the dissenting person will be silent or raise some aspect of the issue which is, as one interviewee described it, "the tip of the iceberg." After that, the issue is taken up in other informal groups, so that the contentious issue is being discussed but not with or among those members of the group who are now in conflict over it.

Alternatively, if person A is in conflict with person B over something B has done, rather than tell B that they are offended, A will disagree with whatever B proposes at the meeting, as a way of venting their frustration and anger. B could well be left wondering why A seems so angry over the issue they brought up at the meeting. Since there is a discrepancy between what is *expressed* as the problem and what the problem *is*, there needs to be a lot more talking, to get to the root of the matter, but this does not happen.

Indirect communication means that nonverbal actions communicate a person's feelings and attitudes and must be looked for and interpreted that way. If a person is dissatisfied with the actions of another, since they will not openly discuss the matter with the person concerned, they will instead show their displeasure by what one interviewee called "benign neglect." That is, they will just not do what might have been assigned to them by the person who has offended them. They might also react with aggressive behavior in another forum, perhaps a meeting on a completely different issue. The pent-up emotions aroused by their grievance are given vent to in this way.

This reluctance to speak to the offender means that there are misunderstandings that grow into conflict because the offended party was not willing to clarify the matter with the person concerned. This unwillingness to speak openly to the person concerned can result in pent-up anger and frustration, which when it finally erupts is so virulent that it destroys the chance of reconciliation that there could have been when the conflict first began. Since conflict management and reconciliation is not a skill that is learned in childhood, people tend to be unskilled in conciliatory speech. If grievances are aired, people often lack even the vocabulary with which to engage another person without adding fuel to the fire. As one interviewee said, by choosing the wrong words, for example, "your behavior disgusts me!" instead of "your behavior disappoints me" parties prolong the conflict situation.

Instead of going to speak to the party involved, offended people will often turn to another in whom they confide. Their reason for confiding is rarely to ask for help with reconciling. In fact, they will usually be disappointed or even offended if the person they turned to was to speak up for the other party, or criticize their friend's behavior. One interviewee said that if advice was offered the response would be "you are a mature person, you can act that way. We can't." Instead the offended party seeks empathy. They want help "at an emotional level," one interviewee said. They expect the person they have chosen to support them and to see the incident from their perspective, allowing them the freedom to ascribe right and wrong to the parties involved. Often it is not just the issue at hand, but past injustices that are remembered and added to the current grievances.

Another consequence of the indirect style of communication is that there is a great deal of suspicion with which people interpret another's words and actions. People are not used to taking words at face value. They look for a hidden agenda. It means, as one interviewee said, "when you confront a personal issue, it always becomes political." In Sri Lankan culture, debates are not part of the traditional method of discussion.[7]

Third-party help

All the interviewees agreed that the church lacked a concept of mediation. People who knew there was a conflict situation that involved a friend, did not feel the necessity to intervene to bring people together. As one interviewee said, "everyone watches but no one intentionally tries to bring the parties together." Occasionally someone might advise their friend to do things differently or warn them not to overreact, but generally there will be no attempt to bring the two conflicted parties together. People lack close friends or confidantes to whom they can speak openly and who might help them get perspective and stop the escalation. This is surprising since most collectivistic cultures tend to have a tradition of elders or respected leaders taking the initiative to bring parties in a conflict together. When asked why this was missing in the church the reply was that even if such a tradition existed in the culture it was missing from the church. The conclusion was that the church might be especially prone to individualism because of the individualizing effect of the way the gospel is presented, especially within evangelicalism. As one interviewee said, the Sri Lankan church has produced a "hybrid community," which in terms of conflict resolution has the worst of both worlds – an inability to speak directly and openly (Asian orientation) coupled with an individualistic attitude (Western orientation) that does not seek advice, or appeal to the wider community for help. The church in that sense has "produced misfits."

The offended will talk to people they trust who will also share their anger. Sometimes, they may even go to someone with whom they were previously angry because they know that person also has a grievance against the offender. They tend to choose people who they are confident will see things their way,

---

7. Parliamentary discussions are infamous for name-calling, personal insults, and even violence.

even though they might be quite unconnected to the conflict. They want a chance to tell their story. The story tends to change with the re-telling; sometimes the situation is twisted and becomes much bigger with the re-telling. The person sharing their story will expect sympathy, prayer, and empathy but rarely mediation. The person they go to will usually be a friend rather than a church leader. The friend might then take it to a leader. One interviewee said that there is a general feeling that leaders are too busy to be bothered with these problems. It is interesting that none of the interviewees made much of the role of the pastor in mediation or conflict resolution.

All those interviewed agreed that the need for genuine mediators was great, and that one key aspect towards helping someone deal Christianly with conflict was that there should be people to listen, comfort, and aid in the healing process. It is in this context of acceptance that the person will be challenged to go and reconcile. They have to sense someone has listened and evil has been acknowledged. Until then you cannot tell them to forgive. As one interviewee said, there must be personal ministry offered to people in conflict. Interviewees acknowledged that in this process, the mediator will often be misunderstood and even hurt by the ones they are trying to help. It may be difficult and time consuming and others in the church may also misunderstand. Sometimes people turn on a mediator assuming they have been primed and sent by their opponent. Some listen but then accuse mediators of being biased towards their opponent.

An example given by one interviewee was a time when a couple in the church tried to counsel and comfort a rather troublesome person in the church. Others in the church, including their friends, suggested that this couple were being too soft on this person and condoning sin, but there was success with the person and eventually other relationships were also healed. The process of counselling and mediating in conflict is messy and protracted and not many people in the church are willing to participate in it.

A reason for the role of the mediator was that people were unsure what to do even if they talked together. Sometimes a person may say they have spoken to the one who has something against them, and so has fulfilled what was required of them but there has been no resolution. The situation may even be worse. An interviewee cited a case where a church worker was made aware that a member of the congregation had something against them. The church worker called the person and spoke to them and then said everything was all right, but the other party did not think so. Another reason for the importance of mediators is that although culturally Sri Lankans are group oriented, spiritual accountability is very difficult because of the potential for loss of honor. Therefore, the church needs "elders" who will act as mediators, who can maintain everyone's honor and still bring about reconciliation. One interviewee suggested that it would be best for the church to have a reconciliation team or board to eliminate any suggestion of bias.

Conflict style

When there is a conflict with another party, often at first there is a tendency to ignore what is happening. People feel angry, even outraged when they are offended. But people tend to shy away from saying they are angry, and will generally say they are hurt or upset, rather than angry. They see what has been done to them as an insult. They are aware only of the fact that they have been wronged. They feel an injustice has been done to them. There is a certain amount of self-pity.

There is a general reluctance to seek reconciliation. People prefer to wait and hope the situation sorts itself out. It was suggested by one interviewee that even an internal resolution within themselves is not affected since the person does not face the reality that there is a conflict. There is also often denial; when asked if something is wrong, people will deny there is a problem. Each person will expect the other person to take the initiative. If someone is told they have offended another, the alleged offender will trivialize the matter and say everything is fine.

A way in which people display the avoidance style of conflict management is to deny the existence of any conflict. "I don't have a problem with them" a person might say or "if they have a problem with me, let them come to me." People see confrontation as aggression, said another interviewee. There is no desire to meet the offender, there is a fear of losing face. There is a high probability that if there is a meeting, we could be insulted or humiliated, even publicly. The risk of being shamed is too great to allow parties to meet. A way to deal with this is to ignore the offender, or smile and greet them but keep one's distance. Other ways people show they have been offended is to avoid the person altogether, either by leaving the church or by stopping their attendance at meetings and events or places the other party was likely to be.

Conflict may be prolonged simply because people do not deal with the problem as it arises. One interviewee described this as "not very efficient in our relationships." Sri Lankans will delay small gestures that could have nipped a problem in the bud, like making a telephone call or writing a letter. This adds to the feeling of hurt or anger felt by the person who has been offended by us.

Churches typically take the fight or flight approaches when it comes to addressing sin in the church. Some may be happy to go and point out someone's fault, but do it in a manner and spirit far removed from Jesus's intention. If, as seems common, people interpret "go" only as "confront" they go unwilling to listen, defensive, and determined to get their pound of flesh. For others, the option of flight, ignoring the offender, or leaving the church altogether, seems an easier and sometimes more "Christian" thing to do, rather than rock the boat. However, leaving just shows the world that sin has the final say, and its power to separate is greater than the gospel's power to reconcile.[8]

Status and power distance

Sri Lanka would qualify as a high power-distance community.[9] There is a deep desire for status recognition. Honor seems to be bound up with position and prominence in the church. This might be exacerbated by the fact that many who are chosen as leaders in the growing free churches are those who have not had much recognition in the past. Some might not have been educated beyond secondary school, or might come from a poor background. It might be for the first time that their opinions are sought, or that they are addressed by a title and have the responsibility for supervising others. Although "servant leadership" is talked about and has become a buzzword, it is debatable if those chosen for leadership always understand what that means in practical terms. Thus, leadership once gained is hard to let go.

A member of the church who has been in charge of the youth group for a decade will likely be upset if the pastor suggests asking for new leaders to

---

8. Lewis, *Resolving Church Conflicts*, 44.

9. A low power-distance culture emphasizes equality, democratic decision making, equitable rewards based on performance etc., while high power-distance cultures emphasizes status-based credibility, asymmetrical role relations, rewards and punishments based on status, rank etc. (Ting-Toomey and Oetzel, *Managing Intercultural Conflict*, 31).

come forward to be ready to take over. People find it hard to let go of positions they hold. If there is any trespassing on their territory, if there have been instructions that have been unclear or lack of clear leadership, there is potential for conflict. People are particularly sensitive to the words and actions of leaders. A perceived slight or offhand attitude of a leader can cause anger or hurt. Conflict also arises between members of the congregation who have been appointed to carry out responsibilities in the church, whether those responsibilities carry official leadership titles or not. If there is any confusion over the role, if it is insufficiently defined, or if it seems to overlap with another's role, there is bound to be conflict. Conflict occurs when there is weak leadership in the church, but equally, there is a problem with authoritarian leadership. "Leaders assume they must be obeyed without question," said one interviewee. Such leaders assume they cannot be held accountable but must be trusted completely as God's representatives. Leadership seems to "breed arrogance" in Christian leaders, was this interviewee's conclusion.

One interviewee said that when we resolve conflict, Sri Lankans try to make decisions that would be favorable to the leaders of the church or the rich or influential rather than taking an unbiased view of what really happened. Occasionally, the entire leadership of a church might be composed of the senior pastor's family. Then, if a member of the church has a conflict with one of the leaders, they will say, "it's not worth telling pastor because this is his family member."

Sometimes what is called reconciliation is the stronger person forcing their views on a weaker person. The weaker person has to accept the resolution. Sometimes Scripture is used to coerce another person. One interviewee said that generally, leaders have to get involved to move a conflict situation towards resolution. Ordinary members will not get involved since they do not feel it is their responsibility.

Relativistic morality

The desire for honor, which as Julian Pitt-Rivers defined, involves both a claim to honor as well as public recognition of that honor, means that what other people think of us is very important. A person carries the honor of their family identity but also must uphold it when challenged. Sin is that which destroys the harmony that your group is meant to experience. For this reason, what the Bible labels sins may not be sin according to the culture, or subculture. If a kin group, for instance, knows that a sin has been committed, the normal action is to protect and cover up for the person since they are the group's responsibility. To accuse them or even worse to tell others about it would be seen as an act of treachery. However, one interviewee said, if someone, say a leader, does something to arouse his peoples' hatred, then all the wrongs they have committed in the past, to which people turned a blind eye, will be dragged up. In Sri Lanka, reputation is more important than morality.[10]

Certain instructions will usually be observed by those in a guilt-oriented culture (e.g. stopping at a pedestrian crossing, only going to an express checkout if one has five items or less). In a shame-oriented culture, these will be routinely flouted. Thus, police are deployed to stand at pedestrian crossings and stop the traffic. In the express checkout for five items or less, the staff of the shop would not want to shame the person blatantly flouting the rules but will intervene if another customer complains.

Lying is not considered wrong. It is worse to make someone feel small or shamed. It is not wrong to say that you will do something that you have no intention of doing, because it is an insult to say "no" to a request. In a sense, the end justifies the means. It is not that either Buddhism or Hinduism promote lying or deception. In fact, abstinence from false speech is one of the five precepts of Buddhism[11] and one of the four conditions of spiritual progress for laymen and women.[12] Ajith Fernando, Director of Youth for Christ for over twenty-five years, who has worked closely with new believers from many backgrounds says,

> Though there have been a lot of people who have entered the church from other faiths, developing Christian values among new believers has been a challenge for all churches doing evangelism among people of other faiths. For example, though Christianity teaches that believers do not lie, many do! This is a carry-over from their previous life where, even though they would daily recite that they will abstain from lying, lying is very much part of the Sri Lankan culture. This has forged an attitude

---

10. See Evelyn Miranda-Feliciano, *Filipino Values*, 42 for a similar analysis of *hiya* in the Philipino culture.
11. Weerasingha, *Cross and the Bo-Tree*, 98.
12. De Silva, *Buddhism*, 115.

that, though the holy books should be revered and defended, they cannot be practiced. Therefore, converts come to the church with a worldview that says that one does not have to practice all the ethical teachings of the Scriptures.[13]

Extreme reactions

The evidence from the interviewees suggest that within the church extreme reactions, in the form of violence or suicide are uncommon. However, a comparison of the field research with the literature review in chapter 3 reveals several non-confrontational approaches that are typical for the start of a conflict, such as avoidance, silence, scape-goating, and gossiping.

Application of Christian Faith to Conflict

Interviewees were asked to what extent conflicting parties consciously applied their faith to their situation. Sometimes people will resolve a conflictual situation in their own mind by saying they are justified because they are right. Some might say that because they are Christians, they are able to bear what has happened to them, or that because of their faith they will forgive if asked. One interviewee confessed that he was surprised at how peoples' feelings managed to override their convictions.

In the first instance, it seems, few people ask themselves what their faith expects of them. One interviewee said that at some point in the conflict people might be open to what the Bible says about their situation, but initially their desire is for what they see as justice, that they be treated as they feel they deserve. Another interviewee said that he had noticed that there are some who are patient, give others the benefit of the doubt, and are even willing to suffer loss, rather than act against their principles.

When asked what made the difference to those who were able to handle conflict well and follow biblical principles, one interviewee said it was not necessarily the length of time the person had been a Christian but "a spiritual sensitivity," that gave rise to a hunger for God. Another felt that it was the fact that some believers had developed "the lifestyle and disciplines of being a peacemaker." Asked how this came about, he replied that this lifestyle was

---

13. "Proclaiming the Gospel in Sri Lanka: Some Lessons from the Methodist Heritage" in email communication.

forged through biblical teaching, personal discipleship, and the experience of handling situations of conflict biblically, usually with the help of a spiritual parent. "They have learned what obedience in such situations is and have developed the determination to override cultural and personal hindrances to the path of obedience when hurt or in a conflict." This interviewee felt strongly that teaching and personal mentoring was essential to developing this lifestyle. While many believers might know the Scriptures, leaders need to invest time in helping congregations apply those Scriptures consistently until, as the same interviewee said "it becomes second nature and overcomes natural inclinations," including the desire for revenge or escalation of conflict.

One interviewee said that if people were already struggling in some area of their lives, perhaps financial strains, they were less able to deal well with conflict that erupted. There was a feeling however, that people's Christian faith kept them from taking the kinds of extreme actions that they might otherwise have done, though one interviewee did mention that he had evidenced an occasion in the church where people had come to blows.

The Role of the Church

Those who were interviewed felt that the church did not do as much as it should to help people prepare for and deal well with conflict. One interviewee said that church discipline is a huge lacuna. He suggested that when the community sees there is no mechanism for dealing with conflict, anarchy sets in. There is a lack of openness in church leadership that leaves people dissatisfied. Another interviewee felt that in their church there was an increasing awareness within the congregation that people cannot truly enter into corporate worship or experience the presence of God, unless there was reconciliation and unity practiced in the church. This led to a sense of discomfort when a person knew they had unresolved issues with another believer. The importance of interpersonal reconciliation for the believer was explicitly mentioned at communion services.

The data point to several related areas of church weaknesses that need to be addressed. The follow summary suggests paths for improvement as well.

Lack of teaching on conflict resolution

There is a lack of teaching and equipping for everyday life. One interviewee said that there is no teaching in the church about Christian life, family life, holiness, and forgiveness. We preach about the usual catalogue of sin but "we don't give people resources to deal with daily life. So, the church cannot really be church." Even pastors who face conflict within their own team are not equipped to deal with it. Christians must be trained in conflict resolution. Peace making must be talked about in ordinary discourse. What is preached and taught must be lived out and become a habit. Then others can learn from what they see around them, not just be expected to listen to what a preacher says.

Program vs pastoral care/discipling

Churches tend to be program oriented, with little emphasis on pastoral care. The picture of the pastor as someone who nurtures his people has gone. Now counselling has replaced pastoral care. A situation is left until it becomes so serious that professional help has to be sought. There is no place for the informal chatting that can treat this aspect of discipleship as an ordinary part of life. There are systems but no real pastoral, biblical discipling. One interviewee said that knowing Bible verses about reconciliation was not enough. They had to become part of the peoples' world view. "Worldview is imbibed," he said, and cannot be taught in a few sermons.

People who are able to deal with conflict in a mature Christian fashion are those who have been properly discipled. For example, one interviewee gave the example of someone who was brought up in a difficult family situation and was typically angry and violent, through constant discipling has come to a place that whenever they feel angry they will come to their spiritual father and talk about what has made them angry. When in a conflict situation, they constantly refer all their behavior to this "elder." It is this type of person, who, when Christianity clashes with culture will do what makes for peace. The same interviewee went on to say, "and then there are others who even though we try to disciple will not open up. They will 'shape' things, that is, they will do just enough to make the situation tenable but they will not be open even to their spiritual parent."

No real community

Although Sri Lankans are collectivistic people, there is no real community in the church. This was the conclusion of the interviewees. One said that community has been replaced with a corporate structure. The church is not equipped to deal with conflict, because conflict has to be dealt with pastorally. "Although we have a culture, which is meant to be group oriented, we do not deal with conflict in the Church as a family." The offended is not treated as a member of the family who must be cared for through this time of conflict. People do not respect a confidence and even counsellors are known to disclose personal information to others about their clients.

On the other hand, where a person is nurtured and mentored, especially by parent figures, they can look for affirmation and honor to those people. As one interviewee said, "when people know they have their father's support, they know they are not acting alone." Their spiritual parents become their kin group. Then the person has the confidence to act in what they have learned is a Christian way. That action is an action of honor because it is backed by the community. Christians know that the Bible gives new criteria for honor, but unless they see it and experience it they will go back to their old ways of understanding honor. One interviewee suggested that people be taught to come back to their community and discuss what has happened before they respond to someone who has offended them.

Accountability is ineffective

The process for dealing with accountability and discipline does not achieve its objectives. For example, a church might have a good system for discipline in its constitution. Then, someone is found to have done something wrong and a committee is set up. The process takes time, during which the person who is being disciplined continues to hold leadership and ministry positions. Sometimes, the way a leader is disciplined is to transfer them to a different church where their sin is not known. The message sent to those who know, including the offender, is that sin is to be treated lightly.

On the other hand, there is no pastoral care for the person. There is no sense among church leaders that pastoral care for the offender is a priority and that, as one interviewee said, "they must drop everything to care for this person." So, a church may be strong on one aspect – for example, in ensuring that accusations against leaders are not entertained without investigation, but weak in another aspect, like following through on disciplining and restoring someone who is found to have fallen.

Lack of understanding shame

There is a general lack of understanding and sensitivity to the dynamics of shame. One interviewee said that the church's method of dealing with conflict was to make every effort to get to the truth and settle truth and falsehood issues with very little emphasis on feelings or saving face. "Overemphasis on truth, in our culture frustrates the process of reconciliation" said one interviewee. The whole context and the feelings of the "offender" are disregarded. "We only want to know 'did you do this?'" Another interviewee said the weakness of this method was that truth was abstracted from feelings, and from relationships. Although relationality was a strength of shame-oriented cultures, this was being disregarded. One interviewee said "truth is more than a statement of fact. It must take other things into account."

False façades are encouraged

One interviewee suggested that the church encourages believers to present a façade of a virtuous moral life, in line with a list of virtues or values the church considered important. It left believers unwilling to expose vulnerability since that would be seen as shameful. People who were struggling with any sin or conflict tended to hide it because they wanted to fit in. "Truth is inconvenient," said one interviewee. Confession is seen as weakness. A person who has confessed to a weakness or failure, like a marital breakdown, will be gossiped about, looked down on, and even laughed at, rather than being supported.

Slow to act and no mediators

When an issue arises, several interviewees felt the church drags its feet. It is slow to take action. This might be due to a lack of planned response to interpersonal conflict, the fear of getting involved in a complicated relationship issue, or sometimes a sheer lack of awareness of what is happening in the lives of the congregation.

Although the concept of mediators is common in most shame-oriented cultures, there is a dearth of mediators in the church. As we have seen, friends see it as their role to support one another, whether they are right or wrong. People who are able to keep a confidence, who are wise and impartial are badly needed in the church.

Field Research Findings: Case Studies

Each interviewee was asked to share a story (case) illustrating how conflict is handled in the Sri Lankan church. An analytical comparison of the cases is found in appendix D, and the full summaries of each case are found in appendix E. The following analysis synthesizes the findings into the conceptual framework.

Goal of Conflict Resolution

Although research shows that collectivistic cultures value relationships and seek to maintain those even at the expense of attributing responsibility and seeking reparation, in the case studies this was seen generally only when the conflict was beginning. In many of the cases, the goal of resolution was the maintenance of harmony but only at a superficial level. For example, people only sought to be able to continue working together or worshipping in the same church. In some cases, relationships clearly were secondary to the restoration of personal honor, and/or substantive issues. It would seem that maintaining harmony is not the same as maintaining or preserving relationships. In some cases, at least one party would have liked to have resumed a relationship with the other party but generally that desire waned as the conflict escalated.

Identity of Self and Group

In almost all the cases discussed, honor and identity were closely entwined. At least one person in the conflict was shamed because they perceived that their identity was being attacked or threatened. Issues that touch on a person's core identity include a challenge to an idea they proposed; a rebuke that was perceived to have been communicated to others of lower status; a criticism of the role that was a large part of their identity; and a perceived disloyalty. This pattern is consistent with the collectivistic worldview that is more holistic – a person and their deeds are all of a piece. It also ties in with the understanding of shame as being a global effect rather than a discrete event.

In spite of the collectivistic nature of the culture, in one case, one party to the conflict acted against the advice of family, church and ministry leader

(C1CODaAm).[14] It seems that when the sense of shame is very great and revenge is sought, the individual is prepared to act alone, and even their in-group becomes the enemy. At that point values and norms are discarded.

None of the cases studied included a scenario where a verbal apology was offered or accepted. The avoidance of explicitly taking responsibility for one's part in a conflict seems to be the most common face-saving technique. We also see that the intervention of a mediator helps conflicting parties to move from indirect to direct communication (C2COYo and C3ChGiSu). Criticism and even vilification of others also constitute face saving techniques (C1CODaAm, C3ChGiSu, and C4ChRam).

Style of Communication

At the start of the conflicts, indirect communication was common (all cases begin that way). The injured person did not go to the one who had offended to discuss the issue. People often made assumptions about the other person and their motives and did not bother to clarify. In one case, the offended party went to the leadership of the organization their opponent belonged to, writing letters and making phone calls to influential parties. Their motive seemed to be partly to damage the opponent's reputation (C1CODaAm). Others who were deeply hurt went to friends to share their pain while the offender was oblivious (C5ChMaSa). Others absorbed the pain (C6ChHaJo) though their view of leadership was soured. It was significant though, that in the conflict cases, some parties did prefer direct communication (C1CODaAm), though they were in a minority.

Conflict Resolution Style

Though at the start of a situation, people tend to avoid the issue and continue a fragile relationship (C3ChGiSu, C5ChMaSa, and C6ChHaJo), as time goes on, if the situation continues, the shame-rage cycle takes precedence at which point relationships appear to be easily discarded. It does mean that in many of these cases, if the conflicting parties had raised the issues that troubled them earlier, it may not have escalated to the proportions it did. Although this study did not focus on gender issues, it does appear that women tend to be more prone to the conflict avoidance style while men are more confrontational.

---

14. Alpha-numeric codes refer to specific cases. See appendix E for summaries.

Although Ting-Toomey's studies suggested that in collectivistic cultures people are concerned to save face for others, this did not appear to be a prominent motivation in the cases cited by interviewees. In cases involving leaders, the avoidance style which those around them favored, allowed leaders to continue in their destructive behavior.

Status and Power Distance

In two of the conflicts there was a power distance between conflicting parties. In both case studies where there was a high power distance between parties in the conflict, the power distance was due to leadership status. Leaders generally expected to receive loyalty and acquiescence from followers. Also, there was a case of patron-client relationship where the disgruntled client obviously expected favorable treatment from their patron and was enraged when that support was withdrawn (C1CODaAm).

Relativistic Morality

It was found that even among this sample, which was constituted from Christians, several cultural sins emerged. Examples included lying, gossip, apathy or lack of love shown in watching relationships deteriorate and doing nothing. In one extreme case, there was a focused attempt at revenge, which included lying, malicious letters and phone calls, and attempts to destroy the reputation of an opponent. In this case, it appears that conversion had not altered the person's worldview. Virtues needing to be cultivated are: humility in leadership; an attitude of stewardship in ministry that allows a person to separate their identity from their ministry; and speaking the truth in love, which seeks to uphold the honor of all.

The necessity for a ministry of mediation is also demonstrated. Third-party intervention tended to be destructive, but where mediation was used, it provided opportunities for greater openness (C3ChGiSu and C5ChMaSa). However, an awareness that those who are most closely involved in ministry are very likely to be in conflict with others, perhaps purely out of a passion for the furtherance of the kingdom, needs to be recognized. This recognition should lead to viewing conflict as a necessary and potentially healthy way of growing as a family, with Christian "rules of engagement" learned early in Christian discipleship. Just as providing counsel in times of trouble used to be part of the church's natural ministry of nurture, peace-making should also be so. Unfortunately, both have become the province of "professionals."[15]

Extreme Reactions

The case studies show that except in one instance, parties did not exhibit extreme reactions. The one exception was where the offended party resorted to litigation (C1CODaAm). In that case, we also see that they were willing to resort to bribes and corrupt practices and to disassociate themselves from the wider Christian community to do so.

New Insights from Field Research

Case studies were primarily analyzed using the conceptual framework. As seen above, the evidence shows that urban Sri Lankan church culture largely corresponds to the seven features of a shame-oriented culture identified in the conceptual framework. In addition, the following new insights were gleaned.

The Fragile Nature of Identity

In most of the conflicts analyzed, the issue of identity emerged. This is in line with research that states that the person and problem are closely related in collectivistic cultures.[16] It also is inferred in Ting-Toomey's explanation of goal issues. She states that identity issues underlie any substantive issue.[17] It also fits in well with the implications of the desire to save face because the loss of face is far deeper and more painful than mere humiliation.[18]

The field research highlights the seeming fragility of many believers' confidence in their core identity. Also evident is that close identification with the church is a potential cause of pain. Coser provides some useful insights. He defines social conflict as "a struggle over values and claims to scarce status, power and resources in which the aims of the opponents are to neutralize,

---

15. While professional counsellors are needed for certain types of problems, many other difficulties in the Christian life ought to be part of the church's ongoing pastoral care.

16. Augsburger, *Conflict Mediation across Cultures*, 91; Chua and Gudykunst, "Conflict Resolution Styles," 32–37.

17. Ting-Toomey, *Communicating across Cultures*, 195.

18. Elmer, *Cross-Cultural Connections*, 175.

injure or eliminate their rivals."[19] One of his theses is that the greater engagement of the whole person in a group, the greater the likelihood of conflicts being "sharp." In a group like a church where, in Coser's terms, relationships are "diffuse" and 'affective," that is people relate on many levels, not just functionally, the investment of each person is greater.[20]

In case C2ChGiSu, Suraj's[21] involvement in the church is total. His whole family is involved in the ministry. His identity is closely wrapped up in his ministry. Because of his deep involvement, there is a greater likelihood that there will be conflict with others who are similarly involved. Coser says "individuals who participate intensely in the life of such groups are concerned with the group's continuance. If they witness the breaking away of one with whom they have shared cares and responsibilities of group life, they are likely to react in a more violent way against such 'disloyalty' than less involved members."[22]

This tendency to intense reactions could be mitigated if there was system whereby there was a "safety valve" method for expressing emotions. However, in most church settings believers are not taught how to "fight clean." Since churches tend to act as if they do not expect conflict, they do not prepare members for dealing with it. However, what Coser says is that close, intense, personal involvement in a group is likely to result in conflicts, which need not be destructive, if handled well.[23]

Trust Can Be Fostered with Time and Intentionality

It seems that where progress was made, or the conflict ended well, time to talk, a safe environment, and attitude of acceptance were key elements in the process (C2COYo). This is compatible with the psychological understanding of shame as a sense of inferiority or exposure.[24] It could also mean that some believers develop an excessive sense of responsibility in terms of their ministry that drives them to take on shame that is undeserved.[25]

---

19. Coser, *Functions of Social Conflict*, 8.
20. Coser, 68.
21. All the participant names have been changed to protect the identity of those involved.
22. Coser, 69.
23. Coser.
24. Pattison, *Shame*, 40, 53; Lynd, *On Shame*, 23–24.
25. Smedes, *Shame and Grace*, 16–27.

In all the cases that ended badly, one party attempted to bring in a more guilt-oriented approach. That is, they expected a confession, reparation, and used a "shaming" process, such as open confrontation. In the one case that ended well, the youth organization invested a great deal of time in persuading, listening, and giving people space to dissent. That culture of openness was fostered intentionally and over a period of time. In a culture where success, even in Christian ministry is increasingly measured in numbers and projects, such time is rarely given to foster true community which can be familial. Conflict resolution becomes much more likely in contexts where time is invested in relationship building. This is after all, the heritage of collectivistic cultures such as Sri Lanka. It is to the church's loss that busyness has become the badge of the successful Christian.

Low Value of Relationships

Cases included conflicts between friends, some with many years of relationship behind them (C3ChGiSu and C5ChMaSa). It appears that friendships have a relatively low value considering that many perceive collectivistic cultures to be "friendly" people. This coheres with Hofstede's research findings that people in collectivistic cultures show less inclination to make specific friendships.[26] At first sight, this seems to be contrary to the general impression one gets about the importance of community for collectivistic people. However, it is the kin group, or public court of reputation, that is important, and from within which friendships are made, not community at large.[27]

In these cases, it was observed that analyze friendships, or patron-client relationships that were long standing did not stand the test of conflict. In some cases, the relationship carried on with a lowered level of trust. In other cases, there was estrangement. This leads us to suggest that apart from family relationships, other relationships are treated pragmatically. When such relationships no longer benefit a person, they are discarded.

Differing Cultural Norms

In all the cases under consideration, at least one party seemed to act more in line with a guilt-oriented individualistic style, while the other acted more

---

26. Hofstede, *Culture's Consequence*, 163.
27. Malina and Neyrey, "First Century Personality," 79.

in line with the shame-oriented cultural attributes we have analyzed. This is in line with the insights provided by Opler, Mayers, and Augsburger noted in chapter 2, that cultures are better viewed as lying on a spectrum between shame and guilt rather than fully one or the other.[28] Also, it is expected that individuals within the culture may have their own unique cultural traits.[29]

A reason for this could be, as one interviewee said, that in Colombo city churches, the gospel has had an individualizing effect. It could also be that individuals who rise to leadership in the capital city have had access to Western education systems, which has the effect of strengthening the guilt-orientation of a person.[30] Part of the reason why the conflicts in these cases ended badly was that the two conflicting parties proceeded with different expectations and assumptions based on their cultural orientation. This is in accordance with our initial conclusion that cultures are not monolithic. People within a shame-oriented culture may appear on a spectrum of more, or less shame orientation, or even be more guilt oriented.

A Neglected Topic in Church

An encouraging note was that believers generally do desire to forgive and are aware that lack of reconciliation does affect their relationship with God. But there seems to be an overwhelming feeling that the church has not helped believers understand how to deal with conflict. There is a lack of clear teaching about the inevitability of conflict between people, including believers. This leads to a level of shock and disillusionment when a conflict arises which leaves conflicting parties confused and defensive. Believers are unaware of how to deal with differences in a respectful way that allows for vulnerability and grace. As one interviewee put it, "there is a whole vocabulary of conflict that needs to be learned."

---

28. Opler, "Themes as Dynamic Forces"; Mayers, *Christianity Confronts Culture*, 165; and Augsburger, *Pastoral Counselling*, 52–53.

29. Augsburger, *Pastoral Counselling*, 49; Muller, *Honor and Shame*, 22.

30. Suggested by Dr. Hannes Wiher in his class on "Ministry in Shame and Guilt contexts" held in Sri Lanka in May 2015. Wiher suggests that a system of education which is primarily individualistic, competitive, and assesses its pupils in linear thinking and analytical skills has the effect of moving people along the spectrum from shame – oriented (which he now calls "relational") to guilt oriented.

Lack of Recourse to Bible or Prayer

At the point of conflict, according to the data sources, very few sought help through prayer or searched the Scriptures for a biblical response. This suggests that believers are not being trained to inhabit a truly biblical worldview. There is a dichotomy between the sacred and the secular, with conflictual situations being treated as outside the domain of spiritual life.

CHAPTER 5

Interpersonal Conflict in the New Testament

Anthropological literature and field research have so far shown us the distinctive attributes of shame-oriented cultures such as Sri Lanka that impact conflict and reconciliation in society. We have seen that the church in Sri Lanka still reflects society in many ways (except in the area of extreme reactions such as murder, violence, and suicide). This chapter examines the culture of the New Testament era, focusing on its collectivist and shame-oriented aspects. Then biblical material dealing with conflict (direct commands, narrative passages, virtues, and values) will be interpreted with that social context in mind. This contributes to providing biblically based and culturally sensitive applications and recommendations for the church. Whereas the research so far has revealed the state of the Colombo church, this chapter points to the way the early church, itself located in a shame-oriented culture, learned to obey the dictates of the gospel, especially in reconciling interpersonal conflicts.

The New Testament does not hide believers' conflicts; it records conflicts that arose out of sinful attitudes, as when the disciples argued over who was the greatest (Luke 9:46). There were conflicts that arose over doctrinal issues, such as were dealt with in the Jerusalem council (Acts 15); over administrative issues, such as the aid given to widows (Acts 6); over broken relationships through disagreements (Acts 15:36–41); and over personal weakness (Luke 22:24–62).

After surveying the collectivist, shame-oriented culture of the New Testament era, this chapter looks at the major text which seems to advocate a direct approach to conflict that shame-oriented people tend to avoid (Matt

18:15–17). Following that, direct commands on how one is to deal with other believers (especially leaders) in conflict situations (1 and 2 Tim, Titus 1, Phlm) are surveyed. Then attention is given to some descriptive passages on how conflict was dealt with in the early church (Acts 6, John 21), and values that are espoused when handling conflict in the church (Gal 6:1, Jas 5:20).

Honor and Shame in New Testament Culture

Biblical scholars, especially those from the Context Group, have highlighted the importance of honor and shame in the culture of the New Testament. New Testament scholar David A. deSilva claims that honor and dishonor were "foundational social values" in the first-century world.[1] Greco-Roman historians supply ample evidence that their world was characterized by love of honor, in the same way as modern cultures might strive for wealth and possessions. Xenophon described the Athenians as "passionate for praise."[2] Augustine comments on how, for the sake of praise and honor, men overcame all kinds of vices like the love of money and cowardice. Love of honor spurred men to ambition and excellence and extravagant acts of public duty.[3] DeSilva cites the writings of first-century philosophers and statesmen such as Seneca who encourage their fellows to make decisions and choices based on what is honorable. Seneca writes, "that which is honorable is held dear for no other reason than that it is honorable."[4] Aristotle points out to a young protégé that people may choose a particular course of action for one of two reasons: honor or pleasure. Of these, honor was infinitely more to be desired and pleasure without honor was to be deeply despised.[5] Isocrates, giving moral advice, labelled activities "noble" or "disgraceful" rather than "right" or "wrong."[6] The New Testament's ethical teaching is given in that context.[7]

---

1. deSilva, *Honor, Patronage, Kinship*, 23.
2. Malina, *New Testament World*, 111.
3. Malina, 109–111.
4. deSilva, *Honor, Patronage, Kinship*, 23.
5. deSilva, 24.
6. deSilva, 24.
7. For a survey of shame in the Old Testament see Noble, *Naked and Not Ashamed*, Wiher, *Shame and Guilt*, and Lienhard, *Restoring Relationships*. For the importance of the narrative of Genesis 1–3 see George, "Shame, Guilt and the Rites."

New Testament society was collectivistic. Malina describes the first-century Mediterranean personality as "group-embedded, group-oriented, collectivist," to which he applies the term "dyadic."[8] The most important group was the family or kin group. People would also participate in various close associations. An influential voluntary association was formed with friends and patrons. These "dyadic contracts" were based on an informal principle of reciprocity, a kind of non-legal contract unenforceable by anyone and only by a person's sense of honor. By this principle a person selected or was selected by another person for a series of ongoing unspecified acts of mutual support. People could be of equal status (colleague, friend) or of different status (nobleman and peasant). In the latter case, the person of higher status would be "patron" to the person of lower status, who became the "client." In Mediterranean society, those from among the higher status groups, would form partnerships called "friendship" to try and minimize the idea of dependence derived from patron-client relationships. Friendship was not an emotional attachment but a social or political contract based on reciprocity.[9] These relationships were vital for the health of the community. Since movement within society was limited by birth and by the limited supply of goods and services, a person who might be in need of financial help or aspired to a position higher than held, would need help from someone outside the family, a patron. Simply by association, a client would share in their patron's honor.[10]

David deSilva writes positively about the concept of reciprocity within the system of patronage, stressing its relational nature. "The term 'patronage' refers to a system in which access to goods, positions, or services are enjoyed by means of personal relationships and the exchanging of 'favors' rather than by impersonal and impartial systems of distribution."[11] As deSilva points out, such a system would be seen as unfair and even undesirable in a Western individualistic culture, which assumes that the best interests of people are served by a fair and equal process for accessing goods and services. The preferred system in the West would be the concept of barter: buying and selling and

---

8. Malina, *New Testament World*, 62–75. "Dyadism" From the Greek word for "pair" or "two-some," as opposed to "individualism."

9. Meeks, *Origins of Christian Morality*, 40. See also Moxnes, "Patron-Client Relations"; Malina, *New Testament World*.

10. Meeks, *Origins of Christian Morality*, 40.

11. deSilva, "Patronage and Reciprocity," 32.

receiving a fair price.¹² This was not so in the ancient Mediterranean where access to goods and wealth and power lay in the hands of a few. In such a situation of limited goods, other than in the market where basic necessities may be purchased, people relied on favors from benefactors, or patrons. Such a patron might be approached for a variety of needs from food to protection, appointment to a coveted position, or funds to start a business. If such a request was treated favorably, a relationship was formed in which the patron provided what had been requested and continued to be available for similar requests in future, while the client reciprocated by publicizing his patron's generosity and by being loyal and available to serve his patron when possible.¹³ Peristiany observed that reciprocity was valued among the poor. People tried to be good neighbors because their willingness to help another both enhanced their reputation in the community as well as ensured that others would help them in their hour of need.¹⁴ The wider community also relied on public benefactors who used their resources to help the community with building projects and other improvements. While every individual did not become a client of such a benefactor, the community would acknowledge and honor such people publicly as examples with statues and inscriptions in their honor.¹⁵ In the case of the emperor or king, public beneficence was sometimes rewarded with worship since it was considered that the emperor had acted with the aid of and in the place of the deities.¹⁶

Direct Approach to Conflict among Church Members

Usually enshrined in official procedures for, and figuring widely in discussions about, "church discipline," Matthew 18:15–20 is a well-known, if little applied, passage.¹⁷ The actual practice of church discipline is fraught with

---

12. deSilva, 33.
13. deSilva, 33.
14. Peristiany, *Honour and Shame*, cited in deSilva, "Patronage and Reciprocity," 35.
15. deSilva, "Patronage and Reciprocity," 36.
16. deSilva, 37.
17. Turner, *Matthew*, 431. It is hard to read a commentary on Matthew 18:15–20 without the words "church discipline" appearing, but as Turner writes, restricting it to church discipline is "superficial and simplistic."

difficulty, not just in Sri Lanka, but everywhere it seems. In some parts of the world, pastors fear being embroiled in disciplinary issues because it might result in law suits being brought against the church. In shame-oriented cultures, since what people think is so important, church leaders do not generally want to discipline their members, because it will make them unpopular, and cause more trouble than seems worth.[18] The Belgic Confession (1561), which emerged out of the Reformation, enshrined church discipline as one of the marks of the true church, along with the preaching of the gospel and the administration of the sacraments.[19] In fact, Matthew 18 does not address the congregation as a whole, or church leaders in particular. It seems to address individual believers, asking them to take the initiative to bring about reconciliation and restoration with their brothers and sisters. It is one of the clearest explanations of the process to be undertaken by ordinary believers facing the sin of a brother or sister in the church.

Matthew 18:15–20 is largely unique to Matthew with the closest parallel being Luke 17:1–5. It is found within a chapter referred to as the "ecclesiastical discourse" in which the term ἐκκλησία, also unique to Matthew, appears three times. Barclay calls this one of the most difficult passages to interpret in the gospel. "It does not sound like Jesus; it sounds much more like the regulations of an ecclesiastical committee."[20] Some scholars suggest that Matthew 18 is incoherent and that Matthew is caught in an unsolvable tension which he leaves as it is.[21] Luz suggests four different ways in which the passage may be interpreted to deal with the tensions.[22] He favors the idea that Matthew is

---

18. Yang, *Discipline or Shame?*, 32.

19. Laney, "Biblical Practice of Church," 353.

20. Barclay, *Gospel of Matthew*, vol. 2, 188. First, there are variant readings of verse 15. Second, there is the awkward juxtaposition of a seemingly judgmental and condemnatory attitude, especially in verse 17 compared to Jesus's teaching elsewhere in the gospel. Even within the chapter, verses 15–18 do not fit easily in between the exhortation to seek the lost sheep and the command to forgive (Luz, *Matthew 8–20*, 450; Illian, "Church Discipline and Forgiveness," 444). There is also some tension between the apparent strictness of the church's action on the unrepentant believer with the warning against judging (7:12). Third, there also seems to be some tension between Jesus's teaching in Matthew about the church being allowed to be a mixture of wheat and tares until the final judgment (Matt 13:24–43; 22:11–14) and Matt 18:18 where there is a suggestion that an eschatological verdict can be anticipated by the church (Luz, *Matthew 8–20*, 450; Bruner, *Church Book*, 226).

21. Bruner, *Church Book*, 648.

22. Luz, *Matthew 8–20*, 450–451. The grace model: verses 15–18 speak not of excommunication but winning back the lost. In this case the verb ἐλέγχω means not to accuse

recording this teaching within the context of covenant, confirmed by Jesus's presence with the church (Matt 18:20). The covenant confers both privileges and responsibilities. Jesus reminds the church that the seriousness of sin demands prompt action, while forgiveness is always available for the repentant.[23] Bruner suggests that while Matthew 13:24–30 forbids the violent removal of those who are not true believers, it not incompatible with order and discipline within the church.[24] Finally, for some, there is the added problem that it addresses a "church" which did not yet exist, a dilemma that leads them to attribute these words, not to Jesus, but to later editors.[25]

One of the problems with interpreting this passage is the temptation to study and apply it apart from its context within the whole chapter. Before we get to verse 15, Matthew sets the scene by laying down several strands of Jesus's teaching that will impact our understanding of these five verses. The chapter begins with Jesus answering the disciples' question, "who is the greatest in the kingdom of heaven?" by showing them a little child. Considering the social standing of children at the time, the answer would have caused some surprise. Children were loved but seen as needy, dependent, and uninformed.[26] Greatness in the kingdom, according to Jesus (v. 4) is based on becoming like a child. Carson suggests that it is childlike humility and disregard for status that Jesus means.[27] France adds a necessary refinement to this explanation. He argues that it is not the virtue of humility Jesus is referring to, since this

---

or reprove but to reason. Treating the person as a tax collector does not mean expulsion. It might even be that the treatment is meted out by the offended individual not the church. Luz is not convinced by this argument, calling it "absurd." Borderline case model: this passage is referring to an extreme case not the norm. The normal model is the forgiveness which is enjoined in 10–14, 21–22. Luz rejects this since verse 18 suggests a special heavenly sanction for what will be a rare occurrence. The covenant model: Taking verse 20 to be the key to interpreting this passage, Jesus's presence in the church reminds them of the responsibilities and privileges of being the people of God. Jesus's presence and his forgiveness are to be seen in this context as is the seriousness of sin, since they call into question the covenant relationship. The inconsistency model: In this view, there is no recognizable coherence in the passage. Matthew has chosen to place his own church's disciplinary procedure in the most congenial spot he can find.

23. Luz, *Matthew 8–20*, 450.

24. Bruner, *Church Book*, 226.

25. Barclay, *Gospel of Matthew*, 187. Barclay concludes that these are not the words of Jesus but built upon actual sayings.

26. France, *Gospel According to Matthew*, 270. Gibbs and Kloha, "'Following' Matthew 18." Gibbs and Kloha discuss the Mediterranean view of children in their article "'Following' Matthew 18," 6–25.

27. Carson, *God with Us*, 112.

is a virtue that children do not necessarily possess. He suggests that it is their lack of status to which Jesus refers.

Children are not usually humble but perhaps we might say that they are unselfconscious about needing others, and do not possess, nor are interested in, apportioning status in the same way and on the same basis as adults. To "humble himself" is not "an arbitrary asceticism, or a phony false modesty; it does not describe a character trait . . . but the acceptance of an inferior position," and is used of Jesus in Philippians 2:8.[28] "Not 'humbles himself as this little child humbles himself,' but rather 'humbles himself until he becomes like this little child.'"[29] In his continuing discourse, Jesus tells his disciples that God places great value and showers protective care on those "little ones" who place their trust in Jesus (18:5–6, 10–14). This is illustrated by the story of the shepherd who leaves behind the flock that is safe, to go in search of the one sheep who is lost. Bruner calls 18:10–14, 15–20 and 23–35 three "other seeking stories" which sets it in a different light to a procedure for "church discipline."[30]

In having a procedure laid out to deal with a recalcitrant member of a community, the emerging church community was not unique. Voluntary associations, both religious and otherwise, had formal procedures for dealing with discipline.[31] Groups such as the Essenes and the Pharisees had detailed instructions for dealing with offenders within the community. Discipline was, after all, crucial in corporate identity formation.[32] However, in comparison to known practices, the notion of gaining a brother back is distinctively Matthean (16:26, 25:20, 22).[33] The concern for the erring brother or sister

---

28. France, *Gospel According to Matthew*, 271.

29. Morris, *Gospel According to Matthew*, 460.

30. Bruner, *Church Book*, 645.

31. Carter, *Matthew and the Margins*, 367; Duling, "Matthean Brotherhood," 167. Many scholars compare the passage to the by-laws for the *Iobakchoi*, a Dionysian cult in Athens which laid out regulations with penalties for fighting and unruly behavior.

32. Overman, *Church and Community in Crisis*, 268; Duling, "Matthean Brotherhood," 167–169. Nelson, "Exegeting Forgiveness," 44. The writers of the Dead Sea Scrolls had a similar three-step procedure for addressing personal grievances: "They shall rebuke one another in truth, humility, and charity. Let no man address his companion with anger, or ill-temper, or obduracy, or with envy prompted by the spirit of wickedness. Let him not hate him [because of his uncircumcised] heart, but let him rebuke him on the very same day lest he incur guilt because of him. And furthermore, let not man accuse his companion before the Congregation without having admonished him in the presence of witnesses."

33. Overman, *Church and Community in Crisis*, 268.

is consistent with the wider teaching in Matthew regarding love for one's neighbor found in 5:43; 19:19; 22:39.[34]

If Your Brother Sins (Against You)

The two earliest manuscripts as well as patristic commentators omit the phrase "against you" (εἰς σέ) and so some scholars omit the clause finding the flow of the argument more persuasive without it.[35] However, there are compelling reasons for accepting the longer reading. Gundry offers two reasons. First, the next verse has the clause "between you and him alone," which suggests that the person going has been affected by the sin, and second, this section is followed by an expanded teaching on forgiving a brother who has sinned "against you."[36] Blomberg points out that several words found in verses 15–20 are repeated in Peter's question to Jesus. In its most intelligible form, his question is literally "Lord, how often shall against me my brother sin and I shall forgive him? Up to seven times?" The same term for "brother," ἀδελφούς, and ἁμαρτίανω are also used.[37] Blomberg also argues that it is inconceivable that Christians could "monitor all the sins of all their believing acquaintances."[38] Keeping in mind that the New Testament in several places urges believers to intervene when seeing a brother or sister sin, whether or not the sin is against them, (Gal 6:1; Jas 5:19–20), we shall favor the longer reading in this discussion.[39]

We shall concur with Gundry, Blomberg and Luz et al. that the situation being addressed here is the sin (ἁμαρτίανω) of a brother against another. In the context of Matthew 18, the brother or sister who sins is a "little one" who

---

34. Albright and Mann, *Matthew*, 220.
35. Nolland, *Gospel of Matthew*, 745; Bruner, *Church Book*, 225.
36. Gundry, *Matthew*, 367.
37. Blomberg, "On Building and Breaking Barriers," 142; *Matthew*, 278. According to Blomberg, scholars would normally go for the harder reading assuming a later addition of the two words to aid interpretation. However, the word for sin (ἁμαρτήσῃ) ends with two syllables pronounced identically as the words for "against you" (εἰς σέ), which makes it quite likely that they might have been omitted in error by a scribe reading the words aloud, suggesting homophony.
38. Blomberg, "On Building and Breaking Barriers," 138.
39. For a detailed analysis of the arguments for and against both forms of the verse see Gibbs and Kloha, "'Following' Matthew 18."

has gone astray (v6) or might even have been led astray (10–14).⁴⁰ Bruner says that in the parable of the lost sheep this person was "at the beginning of the end" and now they are at "the end of the beginning."⁴¹

This is the first time Matthew uses "sin" (ἁμαρτήσῃ) as a verb.⁴² Since the sin is not specified, we could speculate as to what manner of offences fall into this category. Illian suggests, that in the context of Matthew 18 as a whole, sin is that which causes a little one to stumble.⁴³ Bruner, thinking along the same lines, widens the definition by describing this "sin" as the sin of deliberately and willfully hurting another's faith by "teaching or living unrepentantly and shamelessly, contrary to God's clear Word and commands."⁴⁴ Thompson more expansively states that the sin could be "public or private, serious or slight, accidental or intentional, against God or against one's neighbor."⁴⁵ However, since the sin is serious enough to be the basis for excommunication or exclusion it seems unlikely that it could be something slight.⁴⁶ Since there seems to be a desire to keep the matter private, it is probably not known to many,⁴⁷ which could also be expected to be the case if the matter is being dealt with as soon as it happens.

In applying the command, we need to be clear that what has happened is "sin" as defined by the whole teaching of Scripture rather than what has upset our sensibilities, offended our pride, or gone against our preferences or cultural norms. It is also worth remembering that the Bible does encourage believers where possible to overlook, or cover over the sins of a brother or sister (Prov 10:12; 17:9; 19:11). In the New Testament Paul describes the love between believers as one that keeps no record of wrongs (1 Cor 13:5), while Peter states that such love "covers over a multitude of sins" (1 Pet 4:8). At

---

40. Thompson, *Matthew's Advice*, 176–177. ἀδελφούς is used of a fellow disciple in Matthew 5:47, 18:15, 21 and 23:8 and for "neighbour" in 5:22–24, 7:3–5. Also, of Jesus's own family and the transference of those family ties to the disciples 13:55–56, 12:46–50. Of disciples 25:40, 28:10.

41. Bruner, *Church Book*, 222.

42. Nolland, *Gospel of Matthew*, 745. Nolland remarks that the next time Matthew uses the word as a verb will be when referring to Judas's sin in 27:4. It is an interesting link to Paul's injunction to the church to hand the unrepentant brother over to Satan.

43. Illian, "Church Discipline and Forgiveness," 445–450.

44. Bruner, *Church Book*, 223.

45. Thompson, *Matthew's Advice*, 177.

46. Bruner, *Church Book*, 648; Hagner, *Matthew 14–28*, 551.

47. Davies and Allison, *Gospel According to St Matthew*, 782.

other times believers are warned against being eager to meddle, or engage in useless controversies (2 Thess 3:11; 1 Tim 5:13; 2 Tim 2:23; 1 Pet 4:15). This suggests that the sins being addressed here must be of a serious nature. Ken Sande lays out several conditions for deciding whether a sin can be overlooked or not. He suggests that a person's sin cannot be overlooked if it is "visible enough to obviously and significantly affect a Christian witness," affecting us such that we can no longer maintain the same relationship with them, if it is hurting others, or if it has become a habitual sin that is damaging the person themselves.[48] Keeping these considerations in mind will be helpful in a shame-oriented culture where people refuse to admit openly that they have been offended and who might attempt one of the following: avoid this injunction to go, by saying that they have no problem with anyone; say that they have decided to overlook the offence or "forgive and forget"; or alternatively engage in gossip, or become quarrelsome. Sin is serious, and the church that ignores it does so at its peril (1 Cor 5–6). "If the church refuses to face the stern reality of sin, it will gain no credence when it talks of forgiveness."[49]

Elaine Ramshaw, warning against taking this passage out of context, catalogues a list of offences against women and children that have often been ignored by the church and not counted as "sin." This is particularly pertinent in shame-oriented cultures like Sri Lanka. Women and children generally are treated as of lesser status, and crimes against them ignored or unreported because of the shame attached. Adding insult to injury, the church has then advised relatively powerless victims to forgive (preferring to go straight to Matt 18:21–35), to be silent, or to leave, rather than address issues of abuse.[50]

To be able to discern that there is sin involves an element of "judging," against which Jesus has already spoken in Matthew 7:1–3. In fact, this argument is often used in the church to avoid getting involved in speaking into the life of a brother or sister. However, other New Testament passages make it clear that Christians are expected to be able to discern what is sinful (Matt 7:6; 1 Cor 6:3) and what Matthew sets out is a series of steps in which judgment is suspended until there is discussion and the chance for the alleged

---

48. Sande, *Peacemaker*, 150–153.
49. Bonhoeffer, *Cost of Discipleship*, 288
50. Ramshaw "Power and Forgiveness," 398.

offender to speak for himself or herself.[51] Even the speck from a brother's eye can be a legitimate concern, as long as one has made note of the beam in one's own eye (Matt 7:3). Bonhoeffer says that when people judge, they are detached from the other, observing them from a distance. Love does away with such detachment, for the brother or sister is one who always has a claim on our love and service.[52] "Judging others makes us blind, whereas love is illuminating."[53] If one's motive is sincerely to eliminate evil, we will first look for it in our own hearts where it will certainly be found.[54]

Those who wish to avoid resolving conflict will often not admit, even to themselves, that a brother or sister has offended. Richard Walton has suggested three reasons for this. First, many Christians feel ashamed to admit to feelings of anger or hostility. Second, they balk at expending so much emotional energy in a protracted conflict, and third, they fear the risks involved. The outcome cannot be predicted – there could well be old wounds reopened, unexpected reactions, retaliation and so on.[55] Occasionally, as mentioned, there is uneasiness at "judging" another, and of course, some will assume that this action is incompatible with love. Instead, what is quite likely to happen in Sri Lankan churches is that not wishing to cause any unnecessary unpleasantness, believers will decide to withdraw from the offender. "Real lovelessness, wrong judging, is to drop another person altogether, without any attempt at seeking conversion, repentance or reconciliation."[56]

Go and Point Out Their Fault, Just between the Two of You

Matthew 18:15 delivers a command, not a suggestion, "go and point out." The person who has been affected by the sin must take the initiative.[57] Laney calls church discipline the corollary of evangelism. Just as evangelism seeks out the lost outside the church, church discipline seeks out the lost within the

---

51. Bruner, *Church Book*, 649.
52. Bonhoeffer, *Cost of Discipleship*, 184.
53. Bonhoeffer, 185.
54. Bonhoeffer, 185.
55. Walton cited in Lewis, *Resolving Church Conflicts*, 22–23.
56. Bruner, *Church Book*, 646.
57. Bruner, 226; Gundry, *Matthew*, 367; Luz, *Matthew 8–20*, 451. See Matthew 5. Conversely, the onus is on the offender to go. In either case Jesus commands us to take the initiative to seek reconciliation.

church.⁵⁸ The decision to go communicates the concern and commitment of the shepherd in Matthew 18 who goes after the one sheep who has strayed. It is interesting that the officials of the church are not addressed. It appears that it is the ordinary member of the community who must bear this responsibility.⁵⁹ The command "go" carries with it the idea of a conscious decision. This can be taken prayerfully, at a chosen time and location, with time for reflection, self-preparation, and time to cool down, rather than an unprepared outburst at an inopportune time.

The verb ἔλεγξον occurs only here in Matthew (Luke uses ἐπιτίμησον, "reprove" in 17:3).⁶⁰ The primary meaning of ἐλέγχω is "to take to task," "to call to account."⁶¹ It can indicate any part of a judicial process from initial inquiry to passing judgment, but the fundamental meaning is "to lay open, expose, uncover, reveal, demonstrate the mistake or guilt of another."⁶² It need not include strong rebuke or imply condemnation.⁶³ Bruner translates this as "confront," a word that implies discipline but not necessarily severity⁶⁴ and calls this passage "the magna carta of confrontation."⁶⁵ Pfitzner points out that ἔλεγξον and its Hebrew equivalent יָכַח are used to describe God's actions towards people (Gen 31:42; Ps 6:1; 1 Chr 12:17).⁶⁶ The allusion to witnesses does have the impact of including the meaning "convict" to the semantic range of ἐλέγχω.⁶⁷ The person going is to lay open the incident and invite the person to accept the truth of the matter, but not to take upon themselves the role of judge and executioner.

---

58. Laney, "Biblical Practice of Church," 353.

59. Luz, *Matthew 8–20*, 451; Bruner, *Church Book*, 227. If "against you" is omitted, the grounds for going are that the private sin committed against a fellow believer is never purely private. Sin always affects the whole community (Luz, *Matthew 8–20*, 451).

60. It is worth noting that Jesus was not averse to rebuking his disciples as part of his training (Luke 9:54).

61. Luz, *Matthew 8–20*, 451. The same verb occurs in 1 Tim 5:20; 2 Tim 4:2; Titus 2:15; cf. 1 Thess 5:14; 2 Tim 2:25; Gal 6:1.

62. Thompson, *Matthew's Advice*, 178.

63. Thompson, 178.

64. Bruner, *Church Book*, 647.

65. Bruner, 224.

66. Pfitzner, "Purified Community," 35.

67. Luz, *Matthew 8–20*, 451.

The background to this command to go and speak openly to the offending brother or sister is found in the Old Testament, specifically Leviticus 19:17.[68] "Do not hate a fellow Israelite in your heart. Rebuke your neighbor frankly so you will not share in their guilt. Do not seek revenge or bear a grudge against anyone among your people, but love your neighbor as yourself. I am the Lord" (Lev 19:17–18).

Rabbinic interpretations of this text recognized the public admonishing of a fellow Israelite as a sign of neighborly love and of solidarity within the community of God.[69] The Pharisees and the Essenes both used this verse as the basis for their own code of conduct.[70] The connection made in Leviticus 19 to revenge might suggest that the face to face conversation is meant to stop a person allowing anger to fester in their heart, and allowing hatred to develop because of a supposed offence against them. The theme of speaking openly with a brother is a wisdom theme (Prov 26:24–25; 10:18; 25:9–10). It is a sin to keep these negative or hostile feelings hidden. They must be brought into the open.[71]

"Christian discipleship requires confrontation because the peace that Jesus has established is not simply the absence of violence. The peace of Christ is nonviolent precisely because it is based on truth and truth telling."[72] Although the truth is hard to hear and sometimes hard to deliver, leaving it unuttered is not love but abandonment of the brother. Truth telling in Mediterranean society was not owed to those who were outside one's kin group, but it was obligatory within the family.[73]

The conflictual issue is to be discussed "just between the two of you," μεταξύ σοῦ καὶ αὐτο μόνου. By bringing up the matter quickly and privately there is a chance to do away with gossip and innuendo that is common to every community to a lesser or greater extent. The honor of the offender is preserved, and it might be that in the private talk, the confronter is proved to be mistaken.[74] The person is forced to face up to what they are alleged to

---

68. Luz, 451; Bruner, *Church Book*, 225; Gundry, *Matthew*, 367.
69. Luz, *Matthew 8–20*, 451.
70. Illian, "Church Discipline and Forgiveness," 446.
71. Thompson, *Matthew's Advice*, 179.
72. Hauerwas, *Matthew*, 166.
73. Barchy, "Divine Power," 94.
74. Bruner, *Church Book*, 647.

have done wrong, but the possibility of being exposed or shamed is kept to the minimum while repentance is made as easy as possible.[75] We are tempted to believe that time will heal conflicts but this is not the case. If the sin is serious enough that we cannot overlook it, then time will not heal it. The grievance festers, the sin becomes habitual. Time merely makes one offence into a "spiral of unmanaged conflict." Robertson suggests that an unresolved issue (X), far from being healed by time, gains momentum and reappears with increased intensity under different guises as time progresses (X2, X3, etc.).[76]

X1: Presenting issue / problem arises.

X2: Sides form along the lines of the issue (that is, I am for issue X; you are against issue X).

X3: Positions harden (I see myself as pro-X; I see you as anti-X).

X4: Communication between parties breaks down. Any meaningful dialogue between us ceases.

X5: Resources are committed to the cause (I invest time, energy, and money in X).

X6: Conflict spills outside the parties (I talk to others about you, instead of to you).

X7: Perceptions of reality become distorted (I see you only as the Enemy, not as a person with whom I happen to disagree on issue X).

X8: A sense of crisis emerges, and the result can be litigation, dissolution, or war.

The text does not decree that there should be only one meeting between the parties. It is possible that this first step, as with all the others, takes time. In a shame-oriented culture, time and space and the willingness to listen, heals and offers grace to the one who has been shamed by having their fault exposed, even if only to themselves and one other. Lynd explains that exposure to oneself is as painful as being exposed to the gaze of others, so there is a need to be mindful both in speaking and listening to prevent adding shame.[77]

---

75. Yang, *Discipline or Shame?*, 43.

76. Robertson, *Conflict in Corinth*, 594–595, cites Susan Carpenter and William Kennedy's research.

77. Lynd, *On Shame*.

If He Listens You Have Won Back Your Brother

Whereas Luke in the parallel passage about forgiving an offending brother seems to make a condition "if they repent" (Luke 17:3), Matthew talks of winning back a brother if he listens (Matt 18:15). In Matthew, there is an emphasis on the importance of hearing the word, and listening (e.g. Matt 13:9; 17:5), for discipleship.[78] "Listen" is more than merely giving someone a hearing. It means "to respond properly."[79] What constitutes "responding properly"? Is it acknowledging one's fault and repenting?[80] Although the term "repent" is not made explicit, it is hard to see how the erring brother or sister can be "won back," or reconciled, without their agreeing with what is said to them, accepting their fault, and being willing to change. It is important then, that repentance, however it is expressed, is genuine. Repentance is not the same as remorse, which is being regretful that one has failed one's expectations, neither is it the same as shame that one has been discovered, nor is it merely external manifestations, such as tears. Roberts argues that not even reformation of character is proof of true repentance (1 Kgs 21:19–24). Fear of consequences, or an attack of conscience might trigger a short-term change of behavior, but that is not true repentance.[81] Godly sorrow at falling short of God's expectations leads to repentance. Paul writes,

> For even if I made you sorry with my letter, I do not regret it (though I did regret it, for I see that I grieved you with that letter, though only briefly). Now I rejoice, not because you were grieved, but because your grief led to repentance; for you felt a godly grief, so that you were not harmed in any way by us. For godly grief produces a repentance that leads to salvation and brings no regret, but worldly grief produces death. For see what earnestness this godly grief has produced in you, what eagerness to clear yourselves, what indignation, what alarm, what longing, what zeal, what punishment! At every point you have proved yourselves guiltless in the matter. (2 Cor 7:8–11 NRSV)

---

78. Bruner, *Church Book*, 227.
79. Blomberg, *Matthew*, 278.
80. Carter, *Matthew and the Margins*, 367.
81. Roberts, *Repentance*, 94. See Roberts 85–103 for seven myths of repentance.

Repentance will be seen in a willingness to do whatever it takes to change. True repentance will be shown in the willingness to deal with deep rooted causes of certain behavior and it will not be selective in its abhorrence of sin.[82] Someone who is truly repentant will be willing to face potential disgrace, for example, being set aside from ministry, being willing to submit to processes and procedures set out by the fellowship and will be willing to accept that there might be consequences to their actions that repentance cannot erase (Luke15:17–19). Roberts casts doubts on the genuineness of repentance that is accompanied by defensiveness and bargaining.[83]

The aim of going is to "win back." Bruner makes the point that while Paul seeks to win non-Christians to Christ, Matthew concentrates on winning Christians.[84] The term "win back" suggests humility and winsomeness. Wherever the term κερδαίνω is used to mean "winning over," it has overtones of humility.[85] The person who wins back the brother or sister must have observed the injunction to humble themselves like a child (Matt 18:4).[86] Matthew does not say "shamed back" or "proved yourself right" as we might sometimes want to say.[87] "Win back" or "have gained" is in contrast to "be lost" in Matthew 18:14. Grace is an antidote to shame, offering the warmth of acceptance to the one who has been exposed. Yet grace cannot be the "cheap grace" that Bonhoeffer so scathingly attacks.

> Cheap grace is the preaching of forgiveness without requiring repentance, baptism without church discipline, Communion without confession, absolution without personal confession. Cheap grace is grace without discipleship, grace without the cross, grace without Jesus Christ, living and incarnate.[88]

There is another reminder in this verse that this person is a brother (or sister). Matthew takes pains to emphasize the brotherhood of the disciples (v.

---

82. Roberts, 2001, 99.
83. Roberts, *Repentance*, 96.
84. Bruner, *Church Book*, 649.
85. Thompson, *Matthew's Advice*, 180.
86. Thompson, 180.
87. Bruner, *Church Book*, 649.
88. Bonhoeffer, *Cost of Discipleship*, 44.

15),[89] using the term "brother" thirty-nine times (as opposed to Mark's twenty times and Luke's twenty-four times).[90] Just as the conflict between brothers is a matter of concern for the whole church, the winning back of the brother is also more than personal reconciliation. It is winning back to the church a disciple who might have been lost because of their sinning.[91] Neyrey interprets this passage as upholding the general code of honor found in Mediterranean society.[92] Mediterranean society was an agonistic society in which an affront to honor must be addressed. A challenge had to be answered by a riposte to maintain one's honor. According to Neyrey this passage reinforces cultural norms by telling an offended brother or sister to "seek some redress" by telling the one offering a challenge, their fault or "accusing him before some assembly" or even "expelling the offender from the group."[93] According to Neyrey, though, Jesus undermines the general code of honor both in verses 21–22 and in Matthew 5:6 by "declaring praiseworthy the acceptance of insults and injury without a riposte." His argument that Jesus "replaces" verses 15–17 with verses 21–22 is not convincing.[94]

So, does Jesus maintain or challenge the status quo? It seems that he issues a challenge to both offended and offender. The offended must risk further shame by going alone to meet the offender. In a shame-oriented culture, for a person who has offended, to acknowledge or confess to the offence is to add to their shame. So, the alleged offender could well react with accusations of meddling or denials, and retaliate by engaging in gossip, bringing up the faults of their "accuser" and plan some kind of revenge, perhaps blocking the progress of the one who has come by passive-aggressive behavior. Honor that seems to have been lost in this exchange can be regained by gaining support within the church or getting revenge, but Jesus expects that the offender

---

89. Gundry, *Matthew*, 367; Duling, "Matthean Brotherhood," 165

90 Duling, "Matthean Brotherhood," 165. Duling, 165–172, points out that the term is used to allude to fictive kinship in seven Matthean passages (5:21–26, 7:1–5, 12:46–50, 18:15–22, 35, 23:8–10, 25:40, 28:10). Aasgaard, *"My Beloved Brothers and Sisters!,"* 3. Aasgaard finds that the family is Paul's most frequent mode of speaking of Christians, occurring 122 times in the seven letters Aasgard attributes to Paul: Romans, 1 and 2 Corinthians, Galatians, Philippians, 1 Thessalonians, and Philemon.

91. Gundry, *Matthew*, 368.

92. Neyrey, *Honour and Shame*, 183.

93. Neyrey, 183.

94. Neyrey, 193.

must be willing to listen and presumably to show repentance in some way. Jesus also assumes a high level of trust between the two, for each has to be vulnerable before the other.

These are some of the negatives of a shame-oriented culture, but there are values, positive aspects of the culture that can be harnessed to bring about the objectives of Jesus's teaching. In shame-oriented cultures today, as in the Mediterranean of New Testament times, the family is the most significant kin group.[95] Belonging is the most significant aspect of personal identity. A vital consideration when seeking out the erring brother or sister, is how the church sees itself. Robertson, remarking on Paul's advice to the Corinthian church on an incestuous relationship in the church, notes that the church has the choice between identifying with the world or seeing itself as set apart from the world as one family. "The Corinthians' choice of self-definition would, in turn, determine how they would deal with internal disputes."[96] The family is a powerful metaphor for the church in the New Testament, both for Jesus and Paul. New Testament scholarship has identified the disciples as a "fictive kin group," one of many voluntary associations which were formed on common interests or some other criteria (age, sex, work) rather than natural kinship.[97] In the church, the borders of family are extended to include all believers, regardless of ethnicity, gender, or status.

In times of conflict, it was understood that brothers and sisters would not go outside the household network, but rather would find a way to coordinate with the *paterfamilias* and with one another to find a way forward together. That way forward was known as the *concilium*, an intentional gathering of the adult members of a household network for the purpose of addressing problematic issues and allowing warring siblings to attain compromise and conciliation.[98]

In Scripture, discipline is a family matter (Deut 8:5–6; 21:18–21).[99] God is revealed as the father who disciplines as part of his love (Heb 12:7–9. See

---

95. Bartchy, "Undermining Ancient Patriarchy"; Robertson, *Conflict in Corinth*.

96. Robertson, *Conflict in Corinth*, 597.

97. Duling, "Matthew," 215; see also Burke, *Family Matters*, deSilva, *Honor, Patronage, Kinship*, Meeks, *First Urban Christians*.

98. Robertson, "Courtroom Dramas," 602.

99. See Burke, *Family Matters*, for a discussion of the role of fathers in authority and discipline from both Jewish and non-Jewish sources.

also Prov 3:12 and 25:9).[100] Burke states that the *paterfamilias* had the role of socializing his children into the family. Imitation of the father was part of that socializing.[101] Meeks says, of the terms and the affectionate language of Paul's epistles, "especially striking is the language that speaks of the members of the Pauline groups as if they were family."[102] The terms "brother" and "sister," though used in all early Christian literature, occur most frequently in Paul's writings.[103] Paul refers to believers as his children, occasionally naming individuals as "son," like Timothy, Titus, Philemon, and others.[104] Bartchy writes that this is in the context of a time when sibling relationships were generally expected to offer "the deepest experience of emotional bonding, psychological intimacy and loyalty."[105] Burke highlights Paul's use of terms of affection for the church, including the endearment "beloved" (1 Thess 1:4; 2:8, 17) and the establishment of a kinship activity, the kiss of greeting, as part of the church's ritual.[106] Bartchy lists some of the "obligations of kinship."[107] Whereas among strangers, honor was considered a limited good and constantly competed for, within the family, honor was freely shared among siblings who were not to compete, challenge, or respond to a challenge to honor from within the family. Honor was to be extended to brothers and sisters in Christ who might not have been deserving of such honor according to cultural criteria (Phil 2:3, Rom 12:10, 1 Cor 12:23–26). "The tightest unity of loyalty and affection in the ancient Mediterranean world was experienced in the sibling group of brothers and sisters."[108] This "general reciprocity" was to be extended to surrogate kinship groups like the church. Other characteristics included: loyalty and trust, truth telling, an obligation to meet one another's material needs, and opening the home. Members of these groups had a sense of a shared destiny.

---

100. Evans, *Matthew*, 334.
101. Burke, *Family Matters*, 160–161.
102. Meeks, *First Urban Christians*, 86.
103. Meeks, 87.
104. Meeks, 87. This practice of using household terms to refer to members of a group was found in Judaism but also in pagan clubs and cults.
105. Bartchy, "Undermining Ancient Patriarchy," 69. See Bartchy, 70 for a breakdown of the number of times Paul refers to his readers using "brothers", "sisters" or "brothers and sisters".
106. Burke, *Family Matters*, 4.
107. Barthcy, "Undermining Ancient Patriarchy," 72.
108. Bartchy, "Divine Power," 93. Bartchy contrasts this with the modern western view of marriage as the closest bond. See also deSilva, *Honor, Patronage, Kinship*, 76.

Barnabas (Acts 4:36–37) is an example of one who embodied these values.[109] Loewen therefore calls Matthew 18:15–17 "face to face soul nurture."[110] Lynd in her treatise on the search for identity says:

> Enlarging the possibilities of mutual love depend upon risking exposure. This risk of exposure can come about only with respect for oneself, respect for the other person and recognition of non-personal values and loyalties that both persons share. Through such love one comes to know the meaning of exposure without shame, and of shame transformed by being understood and shared. Aristotle distinguishes between feeling ashamed of things shameful "according to common opinion" and things shameful "in very truth." In love there can be the exploring together of things shameful "in very truth."[111]

Bonhoeffer in his reflection on the beatitudes describes the characteristic of being merciful thus:

> They go out and seek all who are enmeshed in the toils of sin and guilt. No distress is too great. No sin too appalling for their pity. If any man falls into disgrace, the merciful will sacrifice own honor to shield him, and take his shame upon themselves. They will be found consorting with publicans and sinners, careless of the shame they incur thereby. In order that they may be merciful they cast away the most priceless treasure of human life, their personal dignity and honor. For the only honor and dignity they know is their Lord's own mercy, to which alone they owe their very lives.[112]

Bartchy makes the point that scholarship has engaged in debates over the issue of the structure of the church as either patriarchal or egalitarian, assuming the two to be at opposite ends of the same power spectrum. He argues out that the two terms operate in two different, and the two most important, social structures of society – kinship and politics. He suggests that while the church

---

109. Bartchy, "Divine Power," 94–95.
110. Loewen, "Four Kinds of Forgiveness," 159.
111. Lynd, *On Shame*, 239.
112. Bonhoeffer, *Cost of Discipleship*, 111.

was non-patriarchal, that did not mean it was egalitarian.[113] Paul's goal was "not the creation of an egalitarian community in the political sense, but a well-functioning family in the kinship sense."[114] This leaves room for different roles, strengths, and resources being brought by different members of the family for the good of the whole. While the responsibility towards our brothers and sisters should be stressed, churches should work to bring believers to grow in wisdom and spiritual maturity. In Galatians 6:1 Paul urges the church to look out for and restore those who have been "overtaken" or "ensnared" in sin. There is a necessity for those who undertake this task be spiritually mature, and be careful they do not get similarly ensnared. Laney suggests that not everyone is qualified to deal with sin in another's life. "Those who are weak, easily tempted, or unable to forgive should allow others to take the lead in the task of restoration."[115] Could it be that if the brother or sister does not listen, it is because we have failed in our communication? If so, taking others along could well be a form of protection for the offender rather than for us.

But If He Does Not Listen Take Witnesses

If the brother does not listen, the offended believer is to take along "one or two witnesses." Who are these witnesses and what are they supposed to contribute to the process of reconciliation? At this point, the offended party has to examine their motives and attitude closely. The offender has not listened. What feelings and motivations are most likely to occur if unchecked? Self-righteousness, anger, a desire to make sure the offender pays, exaggeration of the offence? In those circumstances, choosing two or three witnesses could well become a pretext for shaming someone who has offended us. To be shamed is to be exposed to the rejection of others, to be found wanting. Therefore, to have one's wrongdoing exposed to more and more people can be seen as a deliberate attempt to shame.

Some scholars suggest that the two witnesses are eyewitnesses to the offence.[116] This certainly seems to be the case in the Old Testament reference in the text. Deuteronomy 19:15 states: "One witness is not enough to convict

---

113. Bartchy, "Divine Power," 97–98.
114. Bartchy, 98. Petersen, (*Rediscovering Paul*, 157) disagrees, saying that Paul levels the playing field, so that the church consists of brothers and sisters with no fathers and mothers.
115. Laney, "Biblical Practice of Church," 357.
116. Laney, 353–354.

anyone accused of any crime or offence they may have committed. A matter must be established by the testimony of two or three witnesses." This concern for ensuring fair play is repeated in the New Testament when Paul writes to Timothy, "do not entertain an accusation against an elder unless it is brought by two or three witnesses" (1 Tim 5:19). In 2 Corinthians 13:1, Paul uses the same text in the context of repeating a warning to the church, "This will be my third visit to you. 'Every matter must be established by the testimony of two or three witnesses.' I already gave you a warning when I was with you the second time. I now repeat it while absent: On my return I will not spare those who sinned earlier or any of the others," (2 Cor 13:1–2). Some scholars suggest that the witnesses here are not individuals but Paul's three visits.[117]

While the allusion to Deuteronomy and the plain reading of the text seems to indicate that the two or three are eyewitnesses to the offence, many scholars conclude that they are eyewitnesses not of the initial offence, but of the conversation between the offender and their aggrieved brother/sister.[118] France points out that the context in Matthew is different to that in Deuteronomy, since the brother/sister is not on trial.[119] Pfitzner says the witnesses are there for the sinner rather than against them. They witness to the fact that the sinner was given every chance to repent. Every word will be attested to so that the sinner cannot claim that they were accosted in anger, that their accuser is biased or pursing a hidden agenda.[120] Adams's argument that there is no point trying to keep the matter private if there have been witnesses to the incident must be tempered since there are bound to be occasions when a person's offence against another is witnessed or known about.[121] Horning argues that assuming they are eyewitnesses is in tension with the pastoral and redeeming purpose of the passage as a whole. Their role is not primarily that of witnesses for the prosecution in case the matter goes before the church. In Deuteronomy, the witnesses are to help establish the guilt of a person before the judges. In Matthew, in contrast, the role of the witnesses is to discreetly

---

117. Davies and Allison, *Gospel According to St Matthew*, 785.

118. Luz, *Matthew 8–20*, 452; Gundry, *Matthew*, 368; Albright and Mann, *Matthew*, 220; Blomberg, *Matthew*, 138; Thompson, *Moral Formation*, 183; France, *Gospel According to Matthew*, 274.

119. France, *Gospel According to Matthew*, 274.

120. Pfitzner, "Purified Community," 39.

121. Adams, *Handbook of Church Discipline*, 59–60.

help convince the fellow disciple of the need for repentance.[122] Gibbs and Kloha strongly disagree and argue that the witnesses are eye witnesses to the incident since that is the sense in Deuteronomy.[123]

Taking into account the broad brushstrokes with which this vignette is painted, where the sin is not specified, it seems likely that these instructions can be applied in situations where there are no eyewitnesses to an offence. It seems reasonable to suppose that while the two witnesses might best be chosen from those who have witnessed an offence, thereby keeping the matter as private as possible, where there are no witnesses, the one who is going might take with him people who will serve as witnesses to the attempt to reconcile. The allusion to the Old Testament text then is not to be followed literally but serves to reinforce the principle that "multiple testimony is more convincing."[124] Bonhoeffer also deals with the situation where the member of the congregation denies the charge and it cannot be proven to the satisfaction of the witnesses. In those cases, the matter should be left in God's hands for "they are witness not inquisitors!"[125]

If they are not eyewitnesses, they cannot give their account of the incident to the church. The witnesses add their persuasion to that of the one who goes. The witnesses are there to persuade, as is seen from the fact that the offender is supposed to listen to them (Matt 18:17). The words they speak are first to the offender rather than to the church as a whole. They are counsellors who become witnesses only if the offender does not listen to them, says Adams who suggests that they are witnesses to "every word" in this conversation.[126] They represent the community's authority and its desire for reconciliation.[127] If they have this important function, presumably some care must be taken in choosing them. Important aspects to consider will be their character, integrity,[128] their relationship to one or other or both parties, perhaps even their spiritual authority in the church, which is not the same as their positional authority. Osborne suggests that they should be leaders in the

---

122. Horning, "Rule of Christ," 74.
123. Gibbs and Kloha, "'Following' Matthew 18," 20–25.
124. France, *Gospel According to Matthew*, 274.
125. Bonhoeffer, *Cost of Discipleship*, 291.
126. Adams, *Handbook of Church Discipline*, 60.
127. Carter, *Matthew and the Margins*, 368.
128. Blomberg, *Matthew*, 278.

community.[129] In a culture rife with gossip, the ability to keep a confidence is vital. Counselling skills and training might be useful. The one going must avoid the temptation to choose only those who will show unswerving and uncritical loyalty to them. It is to the church's shame that there is in many congregations, a dearth of people who might fit these criteria.[130]

The text does not say that the church leaders need to be involved here, but Adams suggests that the qualities required of such people would quite likely make church leaders suitable candidates. He stresses that they go initially in their private capacity though he admits this would be hard to do.[131] A practical suggestion for maintaining confidentiality is that the name of the offender should not be disclosed to a potential "witness" until they have agreed to take on that role.[132] Barclay offers the insight that a person may find it harder to listen to the one they have offended. "A man often hates those he has injured most of all,"[133] so that the presence of others who will also listen to the other side could well be beneficial and make it easier to "hear." Blomberg suggests that a person who is repeatedly offended might be too "co-dependent" to effectively deal with the sins of people close to them.[134] Here too, taking others who can be more objective will be helpful.

In rabbinic texts the witnesses' duty is to warn the offender about their deed. The use of witnesses also makes it harder to condemn an offender for a first offence. They have to be warned more than once before being condemned in a legal sense.[135] Taking this meaning, the purpose of the witnesses would be either to provide the warning or to strengthen the reproof.[136] Great damage can be done to a believer, especially a leader, if false accusations are believed or slander is spread. Jesus's instructions here avoid the danger of false accusations, slander, and gossip, all prohibited by Scripture and damaging to the individual and community. This extra work of going again shows patience,

---

129. Osborne, *Matthew*, 686.

130. 1 Cor 6:1–11. Paul comments on the Corinthian church's inability to mediate and deal with conflict in the church especially in vv. 2–5.

131. Adams, *Handbook of Church Discipline*, 61.

132. Adams, 61.

133. Barclay, *Gospel of Matthew*, 188.

134. Blomberg, *Matthew*, 279.

135. Luz, *Matthew 8–20*, 452.

136. Gundry, *Matthew*, 368.

it acts to protect the sinner from "arbitrary and precipitous" action, prevents coercion, and means going the extra mile to bring back this brother or sister into fellowship.[137] It also allows fresh perspective and objectivity.

It might be good at this point to stop and consider the alternatives to the church's involvement in the disputes between members. In 1 Corinthians 6:1–11, Paul admonishes the church for allowing members to go outside the church to the courts to settle a dispute. In Sri Lankan culture, litigation is not as easily resorted to as in some parts of the world-wide church. However, it is the underlying principles that are helpful in reinforcing Jesus's teaching in Matthew 18. Robertson sees the link between Leviticus 19 and Matthew 18 as reflecting the familial nature of the bond between believers.[138] It seems like there is a long tradition of assuming that the people of God will be able to find within its ranks wise people who will be able to adjudicate between siblings when necessary. Robertson points to the similarity between Deuteronomy 1:12–18 and 1 Corinthians 6 which he links to Leviticus 19.[139]

If They Still Refuse to Listen, Tell It to the Church

The attitude of the erring believer seems to harden as they move from "not listening" to "refusing to listen."[140] The focus narrows to the one who originally went – they must now undertake the difficult task of taking the matter to the church.[141] Ideally, no matter should come to the attention of the church that has not already been carefully and caringly worked on by one or a few brothers and sisters in the church. There is nothing in the text to tell us how many meetings and how many days should elapse before it is assumed that the offending brother or sister will not listen. Scripture does give instances, though, of matters reaching this stage without going through the previous two stages. In 1 Corinthians 5, the church seems to have been unconcerned at

---

137. Bruner, *Church Book*, 649.

138. Robertson, "Courtroom Dramas," 593–594, 598. Robertson points out that in this context, any victory gained outside the church is still a defeat for the entire church as relationships change and factions develop. When brother takes brother to court in the sight of outsiders, their familial bond is broken.

139. Robertson, "Courtroom Dramas," 600.

140. Nolland, *Gospel of Matthew*, 747.

141. Nolland, 747.

the sinful behavior of the man who was committing incest and Paul decrees on behalf of the church that stage three has been reached.[142]

Matthew is the only gospel writer who uses ἐκκλησία, and this is his second of three uses of the word (16:18; 18:17a, 17b).[143] The passage does not specify to whom the original party should report. It does not state that they should be the leaders of the church or a particular body charged with handling conflicts within the community. Thompson argues that the use of the term ἐκκλησία suggests some kind of organizational structure and formal procedure, but there is insufficient evidence to specify what that might be.[144] Blomberg suggests that flexibility and sensitivity should feature in the procedures adopted, especially since rigid guidelines are not laid down.[145] For instance, considerable damage could be done if a sin that few know about is now publicized to the whole church. This leads Blomberg to suggest that the text leaves it vague enough to allow the church to exercise its discretion. He suggests that the matter is kept "as private or public as the original offence."[146] However, if there is a need for excommunication, then the whole church needs to be told.[147] The church's role is "not to rebuke or condemn, but rather to support the individual disciple in his final attempt to convince and reconcile his brother."[148]

If They Refuse to Listen, Treat Them as You Would a Pagan or a Tax Collector

If the person still refuses to listen, drastic measures are taken to treat them no longer as a brother or sister but as a tax collector or pagan. This verse raises two questions. First, who is supposed to treat the offender as a tax collector/pagan? Is it the church or the individual? Second, what does it mean to treat a believer in that way? Is it some kind of limited exclusion such as denial of participation in the Lord's Supper or is it excommunication? (Of course, the

---

142. Horning, "Rule of Christ." In Gal 6:1, Paul calls for a community rather than individual response (the "you" is plural).
143. Gundry, *Matthew*, 368; W. G. Thompson, *Matthew's Advice*, 183.
144. Thompson, *Matthew's Advice*, 184.
145. Blomberg, *Matthew*, 279.
146. Blomberg, 139.
147. Blomberg, 139.
148. Thompson, *Matthew's Advice*, 184.

answer to the second question will be linked to the answer to the first, since only the church, not the individual, can excommunicate.)

The phrase "he shall be to you (σοι)" is addressed to the individual,[149] which leads some scholars to suggest that it is the individual who is to shun the unrepentant offender, so that it is a "quarantine *within* the church, not . . . expulsion *from* her."[150] However, the verse which follows speaks of binding and losing in the plural, which does not make it so easy to settle. Brunner therefore favors the view that it is the whole church that performs this action.[151] Gundry takes a similar view and explains that the singular is used because of the parallel with the preceding instruction.[152] Similarly, Luz, who says that although this is addressed to the offended party, for all practical purposes this means expulsion from the church, rather than that the individual offended has nothing to do with the offender.[153] No mention is made of the formalities of how this is to be done and no mention either of the role of officials of the church in this process.[154] Other texts suggest that leaders should play a central role here (cf. 2 Thess 3:14–15; 1 Tim 5:20; Titus 3:10–11). However, if it is not the individual, neither is it the leaders alone who undertake this responsibility – it belongs to the whole church. "When the whole assembly participates in this decision, and not just the leaders, the whole assembly experiences the fear of the Lord and the gravity of sin."[155] Pfitzner states that this is not a high-handed authoritarian act but recognition of what the sinner has done, cut themselves off from forgiveness and fellowship.[156] In 1 Corinthians 5:1–12, we read of an example of such action recommended to the church by Paul. Carter argues that this is not excommunication based on the emphasis on mediation and conciliation, and since there are no procedures laid out.

---

149. Bruner, *Church Book*, 650.

150. Bruner, 650; France, *Gospel According to Matthew*, 275. Thompson also sees this as a "threefold attempt at reconciliation than a juridical process of excommunication" (*Matthew's Advice*, 185).

151. Bruner, *Church Book*, 651–652.

152. Gundry, *Matthew*, 368.

153. Luz, *Matthew 8–20*, 452.

154. Luz, 452.

155. Bruner, *Church Book*, 650.

156. Pfitzner, "Purified Community," 39.

In his opinion, it is more a recognition that the offender has placed himself or herself outside the community.[157]

Blomberg observes that Matthew 18:15–17 "resembles the Old Testament practice of 'cutting' someone 'off' from the assembly of Israel (e.g., Gen 17:14; Exod 12:15, 19; 30:33, 38)."[158] Bruner comments that many commentators find it hard to reconcile this teaching with Jesus's own gentleness and generosity with such people from whom Matthew himself was called.[159] It gives us a clue as to the church's agenda for the expelled believer – they are to be treated as a lost sheep to be brought back to the fold. To be treated thus does not mean condemnation, but does suggest ceasing to have Christian fellowship with them. They can no longer be treated as fellow believers. Although most commentators take this positive view of the church's concern for the excommunicated brother or sister, Illian points out that in Matthew, few Gentiles and tax collectors are portrayed positively. More often they are shown to be hostile to God and negative examples (5:47; 6:7; 6:32; 20:25). The disciples are told not to waste time on them (10:5). They are outsiders.[160] This must be clear in the church's mind. Fellowship activities such as the Lord's Supper or privileges of membership of the church such as leadership or voting rights would be withheld.[161] Blomberg goes so far as to suggest that this person should not be allowed to participate in public corporate fellowship, but that individual Christians should reach out to them.[162] They are "objects of mission."[163] Excommunication, says Hauerwas, is a "call to come home by undergoing the appropriate penance."[164] This suggests that believers still need to be involved in the life of the offending brother or sister, exhorting and wooing them back.

Church discipline that leads to exclusion causes a person to lose their social standing. Not only the person but their family is shamed. It might be that within the Christian community, the church is shamed. Yang states from his

---

157. Carter, *Matthew and the Margins*, 368.
158. Blomberg, *Matthew*, 279.
159. Bruner, *Church Book*, 651.
160. Illian, "Church Discipline," 449.
161. Blomberg, "On Building and Breaking Barriers," 140.
162. Blomber, *Matthew*, 279.
163. Carter, *Matthew and the Margins*, 368.
164. Hauerwas, *Matthew*, 165.

survey of Malaysian churches that church discipline is rarely practiced, and if practiced in the form of excommunication, does not result in restoration. Furthermore, reconciliation is never achieved.[165] In a shame-oriented culture, a person who is publicly disciplined by excommunication, for example, will not normally return to the church because they have lost face. This inhibits Asian pastors from such practices for fear of the repercussions. Yang also mentions that his survey showed that there was little pastoral care offered to those who had been excommunicated. Pastors were simply not equipped to deal with the complications of church discipline in a shame-oriented culture honor.[166]

Disciplining a church member in this way in a shame-based culture will make the pastor unpopular, raise strong emotions that might well be difficult to control, alienate other members, especially the offender's family and close friends, and possibly lose the offender altogether.[167] In his survey Yang received varied responses to the question of excommunication. Several pastors felt that in shame-oriented cultures, such a treatment was inappropriate. Others felt that shame could not be avoided if church purity was to be safeguarded. One Nagaland pastor replied that public shaming ought to be carried out. His reason was that when a person sinned, they had already done something that society considers shameful. The church cannot be seen to have a lower standard than society. Public announcement of the sin causes shame but this losing face is an important step towards repentance. In local idiom, "the skin of his face must be removed" so that all can see the true self.[168] Yang extended his research from Malaysia to six Asian countries to include six pastors and two seminarians. The reality was that excessive shaming resulted in the member being lost to the church, partly because of the experience of being shamed and partly because the church rarely provided a way back for the offender. However, face saving alone would result in all manner of sinful behavior being left unaddressed.[169]

---

165. Yang, *Discipline or Shame?*, 4.
166. Yang, 7.
167. Yang, 32–34.
168. Yang, 37.
169. Yang, 38.

Since the New Testament was written to people in a shame-oriented culture, it seems that both Jesus and Paul (1 Cor 5) taught that there was a point at which shame could no longer be hidden. Yang concludes that there is a difference between shaming someone intentionally and with a desire for vengeance, and allowing them to "sense" their own shame. Feeling shame can lead to positive results. Perceptions of "being shamed" can have disastrous results. Paul allows the offender to feel the shame of their position and be forced to make a decision about their allegiance.[170]

Shame is "a good tool in the hands of a loving community," says Yang. The person who is disciplined longs to return to the community. Shame in this positive sense motivates healing and reconciliation. If the community is uncaring, the person feels alienated. The negative side of shame will overcome the positive.[171] Of course, there is no guarantee that this process will work. Ramshaw points out that in Matthew 18:12–14, the shepherd who goes out to find the one who has strayed rejoices if they find it, but there is the possibility that they might not.[172]

Excommunication in this day and age would not have the same effect as it did in New Testament times. The person who has offended merely needs to go down the road to another church, whereas in New Testament times they would have been bereft of Christian fellowship.[173] Auli, in his research into the effect of church discipline on Chagga men in Africa, discovered that they were more ashamed of what was socially unacceptable, namely childlessness, than they were of being excommunicated.[174] Overman points out that unlike Paul in 1 Corinthians 5:5, Matthew does not mention the expected benefit of the excommunication to the offender in the long term.[175]

In the history of interpretation, these texts have been understood differently over time and within different Christian communities. In the early church, there is evidence that there was the kind of excommunication of which Matthew speaks. Then after Constantine, expulsion was both with the authority of the church and also with secular penalties like banishment, loss

---

170. Yang, 46.
171. Yang, 59.
172. Ramshaw "Power and Forgiveness," 399.
173. Blomberg, "On Building and Breaking Barriers," 140.
174. Auli, "Shame, Guilt and Church," 67.
175. Overman, *Church and Community*, 270.

of property, and so on. In the Middle Ages, there were varying degrees of excommunication, major and minor. Minor became part of church discipline and penance, major consisted of a public rupture between the offender and the church, with severe penalties like banishment, loss of citizenship rights, and so on.[176] The reformers wanted a separation of church and state. However, in practice, they tended to treat public sins the same way the Catholic church did. Sins such as murder, adultery, heresy, and the like were matters that affected public order and so it was assumed that in those cases, the offender would be charged publicly with the offence with no need for private admonition. The text is probably most well applied in small communities like the monastic communities. Both Basil and Benedict ensured that discipline according to Matthew 18 was part of community life.[177]

In the radical Reformed churches like the Anabaptists, exclusion was based on who was and was not a believer and this had to do with having received baptism as a believer. They too wanted separation of church and state but were more consistent in their treatment of offenders than the reformed churches.[178] In modern times, excommunication is rarely applied or even interpreted as a communal exercise. To many believers it might seem superfluous as Luz suggests. They will either identify with the church or leave it voluntarily. Some scholars argue that excommunication is no longer desirable since these practices will not have the desired effect on modern Christians. Others warn of lawsuits against the church.[179]

Carter points out that many voluntary associations and groups in New Testament times had procedures for dealing with inter-community conflict. Matthew differs in its process by its emphasis on restoration over punitive measures, its lack of specified regulations and roles for leaders, and the lack of specified fines and penalties and formal procedures for reinstatement.[180] Illian cites Josephus's description of the Essene community and compares the church's attitude favorably with that of the Essenes whose expelled brethren were often at a loss in society and being bound by strict food laws were

---

176. Luz, *Matthew 8–20*, 455.
177. Luz, 456.
178. Luz, 456–457.
179. Luz, 229.
180. Carter, *Matthew and the Margins*, 367.

often on the verge of death before they were taken back in.[181] The rabbinic community likewise had occasion for expelling members, though it is not clear from records what those occasions might be (apparently becoming a tax collector was one). However, those who were expelled were expected to dress distinctively, like a mourner or leper, and thus be kept literally at a distance. The banned person was still allowed to enter the temple, listen, and even teach![182] The goal of this treatment was repentance on the part of the offender and their eventual reintegration into the group.[183]

Ramshaw suggests, however, that the church has often taken this passage out of context. Whereas Matthew's emphasis is primarily on how to win a believer back, the church often uses this as a means of getting rid of people on whom it has given up. This passage is usually labelled "church discipline" and discipline is usually the concern of leaders, and of organizations for the purposes of order and conformity.[184]

Hand This Man Over to Satan (1 Cor 5:1–5, 6–13)

In 1 Corinthians 5:1–5 Paul seems to describe the excommunication process using different terms. Here the opportunity for steps one and two of the process have passed, unutilized. Paul's rebuke is then first aimed at the church, not the man who has committed this act of sexual immorality that even the Gentiles would have found difficult to accept. Witherington remarks that only one verse in Paul's treatment of the issue addresses the individual while twelve deal with the congregation's responsibility in the matter.[185] Robertson argues that what Paul was addressing in the Corinthian church was an underlying confusion about group identity. This resulted in conflict where there should not have been conflict (taking one another to court), and acceptance where there should have been a confrontation (the incestuous brother).[186]

---

181. Illian, "Church Discipline," 448.
182. Illian, 448.
183. Illian, 449.
184. Ramshaw "Power and Forgiveness," 397–398.
185. Witherington, *Conflict and Community*, 151. Witherington avoids attributing a grid-group analysis on this community, preferring to see Paul as attempting to bring structure without quenching the Spirit.
186. Robertson, *Conflict in Corinth*, 2.

The man in question is in a sexual relationship with his father's wife. The word *porneia* was used to describe a variety of sexual aberrations including incest.[187] Although the situation in this family is not entirely clear (e.g. was the father dead or alive? Was his alliance legal?), both the Old Testament and the surrounding culture held certain strictures against a son marrying the wife of his father (Lev 18:8).[188]

Paul declares that the church ought to be in mourning.[189] He does not enter into a discussion of how he knows what had happened. By not disclosing his sources, he prevents the church from being distracted from the issue at hand by trying to identify those who had reported to Paul.[190] Instead he points to the deep gravity of sin that ought to have made the church mourn as if for the dead. Sin ought not to be trivialized, excused, or relativized. It is unclear if the church was boastful in spite of or because of the man's behavior. They might have been boasting in their wisdom and giftedness while ignoring the blatant sin in their midst,[191] alternatively, the reason for boasting might have been in the spiritual freedom being practiced by the man.[192] Others suggest that the man was a patron of the church and thus in a privileged, high status position.[193] Honor was closely bound to power and authority in the culture[194] and therefore the best response to the indiscretions of a patron would be to ignore them. Furthermore, the honor due to a patron would include loyalty and support. Robertson, who supports this latter view, says that by refusing to judge him, the church was implicitly stating that the network of relationships outside the church, including the status it achieved, was more important

---

187. Witherington, *Conflict and Community*, 156; Bailey, *Paul through Middle Eastern Eyes*, 162.

188. Interestingly, the sin in Leviticus 18 is said to "dishonor your father."

189. Baird, *Corinthian Church*, 62–63. The precise nature of the man's situation is not clear. The woman in question is probably his stepmother, either the widow of the man's father or is divorced from him. Baird suggests the former since no mention is made of further relationship with the father. The bottom line is that the relationship is known to be prohibited (Lev 18:8). Since the woman is not addressed, she is probably a non-believer.

190. Bailey, *Paul through Middle Eastern Eyes*, 162.

191. Hays, *First Corinthians*, 85.

192. Morris, *1 Corinthians*, 83.

193. Chow, *Patronage and Power*, 137; Robertson, *Conflict in Corinth*, 194.

194. Witherington, *Conflict and Community*, 154.

than the relationships shared inside the church.[195] The text does not make it explicit.

Paul's command is to expel the brother.[196] Later on he will go on to say, "expel the wicked person from among you" (1 Cor 5:13). The Old Testament background for this command is found in several places in the book of Deuteronomy (13:5; 17:7; 19:19; 21:21; 22:21, 24; 24:7) where the community of God was meant to rid itself of evil influences within them. Paul's dismay at the church's lenient attitude to this situation is clear. He stresses the power of sin and its ability to spread and infect the whole community. Paul is clear that what the man has done is sinful and not to be tolerated. However, he expects the church to join him and take responsibility for taking the next step.

Some scholars suggest that the "handing over" is to be a formal pronouncement, perhaps in the form of a curse, effecting a ban. The "flesh" to be destroyed then is not the sinful nature but, taken literally, the physical body. If this is so, Paul intends sickness, or even death, so that the man's soul may be saved on the day of judgment (11:29–31).[197] The shocking incident of Ananias and Sapphira would be an example of such a result.[198] There are several problems with this view. It tends towards a dualistic view of the person, which Paul has not previously endorsed and in fact is challenging in this letter in chapter 15.[199] Furthermore, the instruction not to eat with the man suggests that death is not imminent. Finally, it is out of character for Paul to suggest that this man's sins have put him beyond the reach of restoration and redemption and the love of the community. In 2 Corinthians 2:5–11 he urges the church to take back a man who has been excluded (some suggest it is the same man).

Most likely, Paul hopes the fleshly nature will be destroyed and the man (oriented to the Spirit) will be saved, not only on the last day but the day (eschatological reality in the present).[200] The man is being excluded from

---

195. Robertson, *Conflict in Corinth*, 195.

196. Verses 3 and 4 both present problems for interpretation. How is Paul present with the church? And what happens "in Jesus's name"?

197. Meeks, *First Urban Christians*, 130; Morris, *1 Corinthians*, 86; Smith, *"Hand this Man over to Satan"*; Conzelmann, *1 Corinthians*, 97. Smith, *"Hand this Man over to Satan"*, provides a comprehensive survey of the literature giving both options.

198. Morris, *1 Corinthians*, 86.

199. Baird, *Corinthian Church*, 66; Robertson, *Conflict in Corinth*, 192.

200. Fee, *First Epistle to the Corinthians*, 212.

the communion of the church where Christ reigns. He is forced out into the realm where Satan is considered to hold sway. The flesh, σάρξ, to be destroyed, is the power of sin under which the man now lives bound. Lee A. Johnson suggests that Satan is a tool for the man's salvation and for re-aligning the church under Paul's authority.[201] Kistemaker arguing that Satan never works to bring a person closer to God, only further away thus prefers to interpret this as meaning that the man is physically weakened by Satan but over a period of time, giving him the opportunity to recognize his mistake.[202] He gives the example of the prodigal son who when far away from the protection of his father's house came to, his senses and made his way back.[203] That Satan may be used by God in this way is evidenced in Job's experience as well as in Paul's own life (2 Cor 12:7). However, even in this view Satan's role is to be God's instrument whereby the excluded brother comes to his senses and is brought back to the fold.[204]

Paul has a unique position as the "father" of the squabbling family of brothers and sisters in the church at Corinth. Paul uses familial terms for the church more than any other writer of early Christian literature.[205] This position gives him the authority to make a judgment. But he makes it clear that the church ought to have made this decision and now empowers them to continue the process as a *concilium*.[206] Robertson's thesis is that the church is a "family-like" system for which the family systems approach is suitable. A church like a family is:

- *Particularistic rather than universal*: treating its own members differently to outsiders.
- *Diffuse rather than specific*: members interrelate on a wide variety of issues not merely a few.
- *Achieved rather than ascribed*: membership is based on who people are rather than through some form of achievement.

---

201. Johnson, "Satan Talk in Corinth," 149.
202. Kistemaker, "Deliver This Man to Satan," 43.
203. Kistemaker, 42.
204. Johnson, "Satan Talk in Corinth," 149; Baird, *Corinthian Church*, 66; Fee, *First Epistle to the Corinthians*, 209.
205. Meeks, *First Urban Christians*, 87.
206. Robertson, *Conflict in Corinth*, 195.

- *Affective rather than neutral*: members relate in emotionally affective rather than emotionally neutral ways.[207]

Robertson argues that one of the complications of conflict in Corinth is that believers belonged to a number of small groups, or "overlapping networks." Their allegiances to various people, like patrons, clashed with their relationship within the church as family.[208] Members of the church were unclear as to what relationship should take priority. This Robertson calls an "identity crisis."[209] Church members saw their relationship with other members of the church as one set of relationships among many and Paul as one leader among many.[210] "*Who* we are is grounded in the reality of *whose* we are . . ."[211] Paul wants the church to see its relationships as familial.[212] "Ἀδελφός runs like a thread throughout the entire letter."[213] Although in Paul's context the terms were used to refer to one's countrymen and women, Paul chooses to use it liberally of relationships in the church.[214]

Paul makes a pronouncement as to the man's guilt but he does not act unilaterally to pronounce judgment. He expects the church to act with him (1 Cor 5:5). Sin in one believer affects the whole church both in the sense of "infecting" others as well as being the responsibility of all.[215] This, together with the similarity found in Matthew 18 suggests that the phrase "in the name of the Lord" (v. 4a) applies to the gathering of the church.[216] To take such an action would cause the person involved to be shamed. If he was, as some think, a wealthy and influential man, this would be a "daring move."[217]

---

207. Robertson, 43.
208. Robertson, 53–98.
209. Robertson, *Conflict in Corinth*, 117–164.
210. Robertson, 116.
211. Robertson, 119.
212. Robertson, 143. Robertson distinguishes between calling the church a family and saying it has familial characteristics.
213. Robertson, 143.
214. Robertson, 144.
215. Baird, *Corinthian Church*, 68.
216. Witherington, *Conflict and Community*, 158.
217. Witherington, 159.

Not only is this the only way remaining for the man to be brought to repentance, but the church will be made healthier (5:7–8).[218] Fee points out that there is a distinction between the anticipated result of the action and the objective or purpose. The destruction of the flesh is the anticipated result but the purpose is the man's redemption.[219]

The problems that many churches face today is that, first, most people do not care if they are excluded from the church. This is a demonstration of "how far many of us are removed from a view of the church in which the dynamic of the Spirit was so real that exclusion could be a genuinely redemptive action."[220] Second, the action Paul takes is in the face of a serious sin. Such extreme measures were clearly not taken for every sin, but he shows that there will be some circumstances under which an unrepentant person should be excluded from fellowship. Some might even suggest that no further association is allowed, even on a personal basis, though the text is not explicit.[221] The church is bound over to this action because it has failed to act at the point when the man entered into this relationship. The failure of those who had leadership in the church has resulted in them being publicly shamed when they are castigated by Paul in this letter.

Baird tackles the seeming inconsistency of Paul's teaching. On the one hand, the church has to associate with evil people in the world, and even within the church, all are sinners. Yet on the other hand, certain evil people must be put out of the church (see also 1 Tim 1:20 where Hymenaues and Alexander are handed over to Satan) and others might remain in the church but believers should not associate with them (1 Tim 5:9–10, 11). "The advice seems to be varied depending on the magnitude of the sin and the character of the association."[222]

> I wrote to you in my letter not to associate with sexually immoral persons – not at all meaning the immoral of this world, or the greedy and robbers, or idolaters, since you would then need to

---

218. Baird, *Corinthian Church*, 68. Baird says sin is contagious especially because the relationship between believers is likened to being one loaf, where sin spreads like yeast.
219. Fee, *First Epistle to the Corinthians*, 209.
220. Fee, 214.
221. Witherington, *Conflict and Community*, 160.
222. Baird, *Corinthian Church*, 69.

go out of the world. But now I am writing to you not to associate with anyone who bears the name of brother or sister, who is sexually immoral or greedy, or is an idolater, reviler, drunkard, or robber. Do not even eat with such a one. (1 Cor 5:9–11 NRSV)

The association within the church was of such an intimate nature that certain sins precluded fellowship. The word translated "associate" literally means "to be mixed up together with." Believers will have to be discerning to avoid such intimate association with those who persist in serious sins, while calling themselves brothers and sisters.[223] Harris explains that the vice lists Paul refers to in his letters make it plain that the situation in the church is not dissimilar to that in the surrounding culture (6:9–11; 5:10–11).[224] Fee states that sexual immorality, idolatry, and greed were all prevalent in Corinth at the time of this letter.[225]

Hays shows how Paul's list in 1 Corinthians 5:11 is in fact taken from six passages in Deuteronomy which require the death penalty. See table 4.1 below.

Table 4.1. Comparison of 1 Corinthians with Deuteronomy by Hays[226]

1 Cor 5:11	Deuteronomy
Sexually immoral	Promiscuity, adultery (22:21–22:30)
Greedy	No parallel, but in 1 Cor 5:9 is paired with "robbers"
Idolater	Idolatry (13:1–5; 17:2–7)
Reviler	Malicious false testimony (19:16–19)
Drunkard	Rebellious drunken son (21:18–21)
Robber	Kidnapping, slave trading, "thief" in LXX (24:7)

The point of the comparison is to show that Paul is addressing the church as God's elect, transferring to them the ethical and disciplinary principles of Israel.[227] In this passage, says Hays, we encounter Paul's vision for the church, not one voluntary association among many, but the unique covenant

---

223. Baird, 69; Morris, *1 Corinthians*, 89.
224. Harris, "Beginnings of Church Discipline," 135.
225. Fee, *First Epistle to the Corinthians*, 224.
226. Hays, *First Corinthians*, 88.
227. Hays, 88.

community of God. To be within the community was light and life and to be excluded was to be "in the realm of death."[228] The holiness of the church was paramount. The important thing is the distinctiveness between the church and the world. Not that "the church go out of the world but that the world go out of the church."[229] As we saw with Matthew 18:17, excommunication is the final step to be taken with someone who has shunned every other attempt to cover his or shame with privacy. Yang says that Paul probably saw something positive about the experience of shame that Asian pastors have missed.[230] The shame of public exposure will cause feelings of anger directed both at self and the church. The anger at self, arises out of the feeling of missing the mark as set by the ego ideal. The rage towards the church and especially those who caused this exposure is because of the feeling of humiliation.[231]

Direct Approach to Conflict among Leaders

Paul provides guidance for church leaders in dealing with conflict among other leaders. This subsection examines how he instructs Titus to protect the church in Crete from false and divisive teachers; how he confronts the erring apostle Peter; and how he instructs Timothy to rebuke erring church elders.

Rebuke False and Divisive Teachers

Paul's vilification in Titus 1:10–16 is a rhetorical devise not aimed at ordinary members of the congregation but to discredit illegitimate leaders, whom the elders must reprove. He uses a technique which Genade calls "emphatic clustering," to do so.[232] Vilification was a well-known and widespread technique in the Mediterranean world, aimed at persuading the audience to disassociate themselves from those being thus characterized, and side with the speaker.[233] Paul uses kinship language both to establish the οἴκος (household) of the church as well as to demonstrate that the false teachers are a threat to the stability of that household. In Titus 1:4, God is referred to as Father while

---

228. Hays, 88.
229. Baird, *Corinthian Church*, 70.
230. Yang, *Discipline or Shame?*, 47.
231. Yang, 54.
232. Genade, *Persuading the Cretans*, 38.
233. Genade, 29.

Titus is called Paul's "loyal son," affirming the family closeness but also Titus's responsibility to act as a faithful son.²³⁴ In Titus 1:6, one of the responsibilities of the elder is to maintain his own family order. The false teachers are by their teaching, "upsetting whole families" (Titus 1:11). Sri Lankan culture holds respect for church leaders in accordance with cultural values. They too should take note of Paul's injunctions.

At the beginning of his letter Paul chooses to describe God as the one "who does not lie," using a term ψεύστης, which is not used of God in either Jewish or Christian writings but was applied to pagan prophets in Greek writings.²³⁵ Towner cites evidence of the fact that lying was considered acceptable among the Cretans to the extent that the term Κρητες arising from the name of the island meant "to lie" or "to play the Cretan."²³⁶ The best known lie was the Cretan claim that their island contained the grave of Zeus, who being a god, could not die!²³⁷ Alternatively, Towner suggests that Paul might be hinting at the well-known Cretan mythology of Zeus who deceived a human woman by pretending to be her husband in order to have sex with her.²³⁸

Having established God's character as truth teller, Paul "also raises the specter of the ancient critique of the flawed Cretan religion and morality."²³⁹ In verses 12–13 Paul quotes an unnamed Cretan teacher/prophet whose description of the Cretan culture is far from flattering.²⁴⁰ His aim is twofold, both as polemic and as the basis for the presentation of the gospel. "Paul, the missionary, enters the Cretan religious arena; he submits a challenge to the Cretan religious mind, using the words of a Cretan prophet about religious lies and ungodly behavior, on which he will build with alternative and remedial truth claims."²⁴¹ Mounce wonders at the offensive tone of the quote

---

234. Towner, *Letters to Timothy and Titus*, 675.
235. Towner, 670.
236. Towner, 670.
237. Witherington, *Conflict and Community*, 123.
238. Towner, *Letters to Timothy and Titus*, 670.
239. Towner, 671.
240. See Towner, 700, and Mounce, *Pastoral Epistles*, 398 for a discussion of the possible source of the quote including Epinmenides and Callimachus. The most obvious reason for the appellation of being liars was attached to the fact that the Cretans claimed that Zeus's grave was on their island. Mounce suggests that the Cretans being addressed were the false teachers only, not to all Cretans or else this would apply to the church.
241. Towner, *Letters to Timothy and Titus*, 703.

and suggests that either the letter was meant to be private or else that the congregation would have interpreted the condemnation to be aimed at the Cretan teachers or the unbelieving outsiders.[242] Witherington states that it was the Cretan teachers who were living up to the stereotype.[243] The one who is to rebuke them is Titus, in his role as pastor of the church. The necessity to "rebuke" (ἐλέγχω) is laid out in verse 9 as part of the pastor's responsibilities. Group-oriented people desire to gain honor through conformity to group values, as described in chapter 2. What Titus has to do is to "prevent the members 'primary socialization' from overriding or short-circuiting their full secondary socialization into the Christian worldview and ethos."[244]

The word "severely" (ἀποτόμως) and related words occur in the context of warning and discipline.[245] Paul's only other use of it is in 2 Corinthians 13:10.[246] The reason for the severity of the action is the seriousness of the threat to the church. Paul's hope is that those who are rebuked may be restored to a healthy ("sound," a medical term),[247] life-giving faith as opposed to the diseased and destructive faith they had espoused. Sri Lankan church leaders often suffer from isolation and loneliness brought about by various circumstances, including jealousy, lack of close friends, and poor pastoral support. This often precludes the possibility of hearing these severe warnings within a supportive environment.

In 3:10, these instructions are reinforced. However, this section ends with the note of finality: "have nothing to do with them." The Cretan teachers are not to be engaged on their terms. The reason is that such debates would be vain and fruitless. The divisive person who is part of the band of Cretan teachers must receive a verbal warning. Once again, the word used is of the same semantic range as in 1:9 with the specific meaning of "admonition."[248]

---

242. Mounce, *Pastoral Epistles*, 399.

243. Witherington, *Conflict and Community*, 124.

244. deSilva, *Honor, Patronage, Kinship*, 74. deSilva, (74–75) describes how the New Testament consistently combats the tendency to understand honor from one's culture. Jesus challenges the cultural norms of power (Mark 9:34–35; Luke 9:48), James and Paul challenge partiality towards the rich (Jas 1:9–10; 1 Cor 11:20–22), ethnocentrism (Rom 1–3), and views of spirituality (1 Cor 4:7).

245. Towner, *Letters to Timothy and Titus*, 704.

246. Lea and Griffin, *1, 2 Timothy, Titus*, 291.

247. Witherington, *Conflict and Community*, 124.

248. Towner, *Letters to Timothy and Titus*, 797.

The divisive person receives warning, instruction, and correction with a view to restoring him (see 2 Tim 2:25–26).[249] If the three efforts to persuade are ineffective, the person was to be excluded from the congregation ("reject," "refuse"). Towner sees this to be in keeping with both Jesus's teaching in Matthew 18 and Paul's teaching elsewhere.[250]

Paul gives justification for this step in the following verse. First, it is known that such a person is "perverted," that is, already corrupted as shown in their refusal to listen. Towner calls this a "hardened state of mind."[251] Second, they are "sinful" or more accurately, as the present tense verb suggests, keep on sinning, following a distorted message and disrupting and confusing the minds of believers, and finally they have condemned themselves.

Challenge an Erring Leader

It says something about the honesty of the biblical reports that it reports an incident in which no less a leader than Peter faces public rebuke. In Galatians 2:11–14 a situation is described where Paul says he opposed Peter "to his face" (v. 11), and told him his fault "in the presence of all" (v. 14). Whether Paul first aired his concerns with Peter privately we do not know. We do know that Paul seems not to have taken his own advice, given to the Galatians, that if someone is caught in a transgression, they are to be restored "in a spirit of gentleness."[252] Paul's reason seems to be that what Peter has been caught in is not a mere transgression, but the "effective preaching of an anti-gospel" in the church.[253] In "playing the hypocrite" Peter has acted and led others to act against what they have professed to believe. The power of this play-acting to confuse and mislead is demonstrated in the fact that even Barnabas follows (Gal 2:13). Martyn suggests that the reason Paul does not record Peter's reply or the way in which the matter was settled is because Paul lost.[254]

The incident does disclose the obligation Paul felt to deal with divisive issues within the one community instead of splitting the church by withdrawing with his supporters. In this incident Paul seems to demonstrate

---

249. Towner, 797.
250. Towner, 798.
251. Towner, 798.
252. Martyn, *Galatians*, 235.
253. Martyn, 235.
254. Martyn, 236.

a guilt-oriented type of approach, valuing straight talking and public confrontation over his relationship with a fellow apostle. Perhaps the conviction that Peter's action already was condemned (v. 11 "clearly in the wrong") had something to do with this. As with Matthew 18:1, we need to be sure what we are ready to condemn is sin and not something else.

The emphasis on truth here is on the truth of the gospel, which Peter, by denying it through his action, was jeopardizing his position as a leader is also important. As we have seen in the passages discussed above, all the incidents of public rebuke in the epistles are aimed at leaders in the church. We could add to this the instances where Jesus rebuked the religious leaders (e.g. Luke 11:37–54). It is also noteworthy that the result of Jesus's rebuke was they "began to oppose him fiercely." Perhaps if Sri Lankan leaders were reminded of the influence in transforming the lives of those under them, they may be challenged to a greater sense of responsibility. And by the power of the Holy Spirit they might be willing to face rebuke for the sake of the church.

Rebuke an Elder Publicly

In 1 Timothy 5:19–20 the question of ascertaining the validity of a charge against an elder is addressed. It is Timothy as the leader who is addressed by Paul, rather than any member of the congregation. The verses imply a more or less formal hearing or a legal accusation brought against a leader.[255] The concern is on the process of evaluating the charges and gathering evidence. Timothy must take care not to accept an accusation without proper procedures, which is the evidence of two or three witnesses. The present tense imperative ("stop accepting accusations") might imply that there were others, or perhaps even Timothy, who had done so. What Paul is enjoining is an attitude of assuming "innocent until proven guilty."[256]

What Paul says is the combination of two texts from LXX Deuteronomy, "on the basis of two or three witnesses." Deuteronomy 17:6 states "On the testimony of two or three witnesses a person is to be put to death, but no one is to be put to death on the testimony of only one witness" and Deuteronomy 19:15 "One witness is not enough to convict anyone accused of any crime or offence they have committed. A matter must be established by the testimony of

---

255. Johnson, *First and Second Letters to Timothy*, 279.
256. Towner, *Letters to Timothy and Titus*, 331.

two or three witnesses."²⁵⁷ Since the death penalty is not in view, Deuteronomy 19:15 is the more likely source. Paul was not teaching something new. Jesus refers to it in Matthew 18, (also Matt 27:38; Mark 6:7; Luke 9:30, 32, 10:1; John 20:12; Acts 1:10; Heb 6:18; Rev 11:3–4).²⁵⁸

While Timothy is to take care not to entertain accusations lightly, neither is he to shrink from his duty. "Those who are sinning" in verse 20, based on the present continuous, are those who persist in sin.²⁵⁹ They must be rebuked in the presence of all. Fernando, writing in a Sri Lankan context, says that this verse was "the most jolting and troubling statement in the whole epistle" to him, highlighting the passion the leader should have to maintain holiness and deal drastically with things that dishonor God.²⁶⁰ The word used for "rebuke" is ἐλέγχω, which has overtones of confrontation. The semantic range of the verb has a range of possibilities: exposure, refutation, correction, reprimand, censure, or discipline. Within Timothy and Titus, the term takes its place within the vocabulary of community discipline (2 Tim 4:2; Titus 1:9, 13; 2:15). Johnson suggests that the public rebuke is what is being talked about in Deuteronomy 19:17–18.²⁶¹ The extent of the rebuke cannot be determined but it could have included the threat of removal from leadership (Titus 1:9), or excommunication (2 Cor 5:4–5; 1 Tim 1:20; Titus 3:20).²⁶²

This seems to be a rather harsh treatment of a leader, if the approach laid out in Matthew 18:15–17 is recalled. Marshall suggests that the first few stages of the traditional approach (speak privately, Matt 18:15–17, Titus 3:10) have been tried and failed. Towner adds that if that is not the case, the behavior of the leader is so serious that it poses a threat to the well-being of the church and must be exposed. This could also account for Paul's treatment of Peter in Galatians 2:14.²⁶³

This is borne out by the purpose clause הִנֵּה *hina* (which discloses the results of the actions taken). Deuteronomy 19:20 is in the background here

---

257. Towner, 368.

258. Towner, 369. Josephus and Qumran show this principle was well known in Jewish life.

259. There is some question over who this group is, the elders or those who accuse (Johnson, *First and Second Letters to Timothy*, 279).

260. Fernando, *Leadership Lifestyle*, 135.

261. Johnson, *First and Second Letters to Timothy*, 279.

262. Towner, *Letters to Timothy and Titus*, 371.

263. Towner, 371.

– after laying out the process to be followed in terms of ensuring reliable witnesses, the purpose of the process is set out "so that the rest of the people shall hear and fear."[264] "Fear" is the realization of the gravity of sin. The purpose of this fear is to prevent further sin. "Fear of punishment seems a very lowly motive for holiness, but, considering human nature, we sometimes need such jolting truths to keep us from yielding to temptation."[265] The motive for the public rebuke is that others will be warned against following in this leader's footsteps.

The solemnity of Paul's instructions is communicated first by the use of the verb "to charge." Second, the charge is made in the sight not of the congregation but of the angels and of God and Jesus. The reference to the angels might have been prompted by the mention of three witnesses.[266]

Lessons from Community Conflicts

Scripture is clear about dealing with conflict in its teaching, commands, and exhortations. Lessons can also be learned from narratives of community conflict.

Acts 6 – Inter-ethnic Conflict

Most commentaries on the book of Acts pay scant attention to the conflict between the two groups of widows in Acts 6.[267] Leaving aside the identification of the two groups and the reasons for the neglect, which are not important for our study, we see a conflict between two groups who are distinguished by language if not ethnicity. The problem gives rise to a "murmuring."[268] The perception is that there has been an injustice – discrimination on the basis of language.[269] The church is both new and growing, the ideal breeding ground for conflict. In Sri Lanka, growing churches, especially those with a thriving

---

264. Johnson, *First and Second Letters to Timothy*, 279.
265. Fernando, *Leadership Lifestyle*, 280.
266. Towner, *Letters to Timothy and Titus*, 372.
267. Gooding, *True to the Faith*, 44.
268. There are similarities between the description of the early church and the Old Testament people of God who murmured in the wilderness over the lack of food and challenged the leadership (Exod 16; Num 11).
269. Peterson, *Acts of the Apostles*, 230.

congregation from one ethnic group, will face similar problems as language and ethnicity become more pronounced.

We do not know how the murmuring reached the ears of the apostles, but busy as they were, at this early stage in the formation of the church, they do not dismiss the problem as unimportant, nor do they hope it will resolve itself if ignored. The group that was disadvantaged was a vulnerable group, the kind of people who should have found that they were no longer in need. The problem was an embarrassing, but also a potentially divisive, one. Where divisions exist within the church, based on ethnicity, age, gender, or financial status, even an unintentional slight appears deliberate. Unfortunately, the church sometimes is blind to the divisions and prejudices within its members. This is certainly true in Sri Lanka, where many Christians assume that no communal/ethnic feeling exists in the church.

The apostles do not assume that increased teaching on how to give and receive charity will solve the issue. They do not take affront at the implicit criticism of their leadership, since they had been undertaking the distribution of food. They also do not attempt to solve the problem on their own, but bring it to the community. The apostles recognize that if they attempt to continue to administer the concerns of the growing community, they will be unable to satisfy the community or properly steward their own calling to preach. The apostles then trust the community to propose the names of those they feel are suitable for the task. They show a willingness to be flexible, to change the existing structures to fulfill an unanticipated need and to delegate to others.[270] Perhaps this is due to the clear vision of the church's calling. It is worth noting that even though the choice of leaders is left to the community, there are some criteria for leadership, which includes "Spirit inspired wisdom."[271] The people chosen for the task are people of good repute. Similarly, we find in the letters to Timothy and Titus, the qualifications for pastoral ministry are primarily to do with character (1 Tim 3:7; Titus 1:5–9).

The researcher's interviews revealed that many church conflicts arise among leaders. Often in the church the qualifications for leadership are academic qualifications, efficiency, skills, gifts, charisma, and status. Could this be one of the reasons why so many conflicts involve church leaders? We also

---

270. Peterson, 233.
271. Witherington, *Acts of the Apostles*, 250.

see that the task of "waiting on tables" is seen as an important service to the community. Both preaching and serving the widows are a "public religious service"[272] and the position of deacon is treated with honor in that the men are prayed for and commissioned.

The men chosen all have Greek names. Witherington suggests that this was no accident and that the men chosen are deliberately chosen to avoid even the hint of favoritism.[273] This decision is unusual in antiquity and the "first example of affirmative action."[274] Munck warns us not to read too much into the Greek names saying that there was archeological evidence that some Jews had Greek names.[275] However, one wonders if his reasoning is colored by the fact that he views the choice of men from one of the "feuding parties" would be inefficient and cause more problems as the Hebrews would complain.[276]

Acts 6:7 records the result of the swift resolution – the church grew. "The satisfactory resolution of the conflict in the Jerusalem church made it possible for this ministry of the gospel to flourish and for church growth to take place even more rapidly."[277] The method of conflict resolution depicted here could be compared to the collaborative model, where discussion and representation form part of the solution.

Acts 15 – Doctrinal Conflict

Acts 15 records the process of resolving the potential conflict between the Jewish and Gentile Christian communities. The pressure was on the Jewish leadership to impose strict controls on the Gentiles entering the church. Once again, we see a collaborative style of conflict resolution. Witherington says that in antiquity, the way to resolve conflicts of this kind was to call a meeting of the assembly and allow people to speak and debate. Listening to speeches crafted according to the rules of rhetoric, and considering them, the

---

272. Witherington, 250.
273. Witherington, 250.
274. Witherington, 248.
275. Munck, *Acts of the Apostles*, 57.
276. Munck, 57.
277. Peterson, *Acts of the Apostles*, 236.

community would reach concord.²⁷⁸ He cites Johnson's analysis of the steps to resolution as follows:²⁷⁹

- A process of discernment and recognition of God's activity
- The interpretation of Scripture to make sense of what had happened
- Assuming that debate and discussion are a necessary part of discerning
- Consent or agreement by the church leader (James)

Witherington adds that the procedure followed is not unlike the secular assembly in the Greco-Roman world. Witnesses would be called, authoritative documents analyzed, a formal agreement drafted, and the document sent to the bodies who had asked for a ruling. "Theophilus is being presented here with a picture of the church as a self-governing entity, a subculture in the Roman Empire, a people living in orderly fashion by their own rules, but nonetheless following procedures not unlike those recognized in the larger culture to be proper."²⁸⁰ It is not often that the Sri Lankan church sees this kind of close collaboration. It is noteworthy that at times of persecution, the church is more united and willing to collaborate. Cooperation and a kingdom perspective, rather than the desire to build one's own empire, can and should be fostered during the leaders' seminary training.

Lessons from Interpersonal Conflicts

Broad community-based conflicts between sub-groups require wise, collaborative leadership. Records of more focused, interpersonal conflicts also offer valuable lessons.

Euodia and Synteche

In Paul's letter to the Philippians, unity is an important theme. Paul mentions two women who are in conflict and asks that another believer addressed as "loyal yokefellow" act as mediator (Phil 4:3). He does not shy away from

---

278. Witherington, *Acts of the Apostles*, 450.
279. Witherington, 450.
280. Witherington, 451.

mentioning these two ladies by name. Presumably their conflict is known by the church and Paul clearly demonstrates that a conflict between two people is sufficient cause for concern that the church must actively seek to resolve it, rather than ignoring or avoiding it. Paul's tone is not condemnatory. He affirms the women's sincere ministries. Success in ministry, however, cannot replace reconciled relationships. As we have seen, conflicting parties in the Sri Lankan church often seek a mediator but cannot find one.

Peter and Jesus

In John 21, there is the interesting pericope of the restoration of Peter. Peter denied Jesus when confronted by a servant girl as he stood by a charcoal fire (John 18:18). To be disloyal to a friend and leader is surely a shameful act which dishonors Jesus. After the act, Peter weeps bitterly which could be understood as a sign of repentance. However, there is no recorded conversation between Jesus and Peter before this incident on the beach. John 21:9 records that Jesus had lit a charcoal fire on which fish for breakfast was being cooked. Jesus addresses Peter by his full name, "Simon, son of John." Bruner ponders the possibility that this form of address is a semi-rebuke.[281] Michaels suggests Peter is being treated as if he was no longer, or not yet, a disciple, since it was thus Jesus addressed him when they first met in John 1:42.[282] At the very least there is an air of solemnity.[283]

Jesus's question to Peter is ambiguous: "Do you love me more than these?" Scholars debate the three possible ways of interpreting this question.[284] Bruner's suggestion that Jesus is asking Peter if he loves Jesus more than the other disciples do is based on Peter's previous boasts about his devotion to Jesus. Even if the others desert Jesus, he would not, he claimed (John 13:37; Matt 26:33–34).[285] "In all the Gospels, Peter had quite inappropriately elevated

---

281. Bruner, *Gospel of John*, 1227.
282. Michaels, *John*, 359.
283. Morris, *Gospel According to John*, 767.
284. This could mean "do you love me more than these others do?," "do you love me more than you love these others?" or "do you love these things more than you love me?"
285. Much has been made of the different words used for "love" but most modern commentators agree that the words can be used interchangeably (Morris, *Gospel According to John*; Carson, *Gospel According to John*; Bruner, *Gospel of John*).

himself above his fellow disciples when he claimed his exceptional loyalty to Jesus."[286]

Peter's replies to Jesus indicate his acknowledgment that he can only trust in Jesus's perfect knowledge of Peter's heart. Peter will no longer claim what he cannot be sure of. Neither will he compare himself with the other disciples any longer.[287] Malina concludes that Peter was shamed by Jesus's questions. That was the "satisfaction" Jesus was entitled to after Peter's disloyalty, but Jesus's final assertion of the way Peter would glorify him was an intimation of reconciliation with his Lord.[288]

Peter was restored to friendship, service, leadership, and ministry. He was given a position of trust, based on one qualification, love for Jesus.[289] It is noteworthy that this reinstatement happens publicly. This is not a private conversation between Jesus and Peter but one that is carried out with the other disciples looking on. Carson suggests that there might have been a private transaction of repentance and forgiveness when Jesus appeared to Peter alone (Luke 24:34; 1 Cor 15:5). However, just as Peter's boasts of loyalty had been in the disciples' hearing (John 13:38; 37–38), so this restoration must also be carried out in their presence.[290]

If Jesus wanted to provide us with a formal model of repentance and forgiveness in interpersonal conflict, this would surely have been a good opportunity to do so. Instead what we see here is an emphasis on what is most important: "Do you love me?" If there is true love for Jesus, surely one would accept being shamed momentarily in order to become more like him. If one truly loves Jesus, one would accept rebuke, and willingly change so as to honor Christ's name.

Bruner lists several church commentators (e.g. John Chrysostom, Gary Burgess) who speak of this incident as signifying Jesus's forgiveness of Peter. Peter's confession of love for the Lord was the truest repentance.[291] Jesus entrusts a weak, failed man with the supreme task of caring for his people. Restoration, for Peter was not restoration to a lower position, with a time of

---

286. Bruner, *Gospel of John*, 1227.
287. Bruner, 1227.
288. Malina and Rohrbaugh, *Social Science Commentary*, 290.
289. Morris, *Gospel According to John*, 772.
290. Carson, *Gospel According to John*, 675.
291. Matthew Henry, cited in Bruner, *Gospel of John*, 1225–1226.

probation, but an immediate "ordination" as Bruner calls it, to mission.[292] Of course, Jesus was able to see into Peter's heart in a way we cannot do with one another. Yet it does show that for Jesus, past failure could be overcome with one qualification, true repentant love for Jesus. Could it be that the question, "do you love Jesus?" will help ease the pain and shame of words that come next as a brother or sister comes to us to show us our fault?

Paul and Barnabas

In Acts 15:36–41 Luke records a disagreement between Paul and Barnabas over the suitability of Mark as a missionary partner. They had such a "sharp disagreement" (παροξυσμός) that they parted company (Acts 15:39–40). Barnabas's desire to take Mark along could have been to do with the relationships between them, but could also have been due to Barnabas's personality which was more inclined to give a person the benefit of the doubt, and a second chance.[293] No details of the disagreement are given. There was a difference of opinion on Mark's suitability and each missionary felt it sufficiently important not to acquiesce to the other's demands. There is no accommodating or compromising or collaborating.

What we can tell is that no animosity lingered between the parties concerned, since Barnabas is mentioned as a colleague of Paul's again in 1 Corinthians 9:6, and Paul commends Mark as a valued colleague in later years (Col 4:10; Phlm 24; 2 Tim 4:11). Sri Lankan Christians would find it hard to speak well of someone who had once caused them pain. Equally, a Sri Lankan Mark might find it hard to serve a leader who had once found him wanting. There is insufficient information for us to know if Paul regretted his decision, and what conversations he had with John Mark when they met later on. However, unlike with many of the case studies in the Sri Lankan field research, true fellowship was restored.

Philemon and Onesimus

New Testament scholar Max Turner suggests that Philemon is "probably the most detailed discussion in the New Testament" on Paul's view on

---

292. Bruner, *Gospel of John*, 1233.
293. Peterson, *Acts of the Apostles*, 447.

reconciliation although the term καταλησσω does not occur.²⁹⁴ The conflict is between the runaway slave Onesimus, and his owner Philemon, the respected leader and patron of the church that meets in his house. Not only has Onesimus run (or stayed away) but he may have stolen something from his master.²⁹⁵ Philemon possesses both ascribed and acquired honor and is greeted by Paul as a fellow worker, brother, and exemplifier of brotherly love. Onesimus is a slave and as such possesses no rights and no status. In social terms Paul is Philemon's inferior. Paul is not wealthy, works with his hands, and has only his Roman citizenship to commend him.²⁹⁶ In the letter however, Paul portrays himself not just as Philemon's equal, but as his benefactor or patron based on the fact that Paul led Philemon to Christ. Paul also identifies with Onesimus, making him an equal. This is implied in the interchangeable relationships: "welcome him as you would welcome me" (v. 17), "that he might be of service to me in your place" (v. 13).

Family reconciliation

Paul's injunctions to Philemon and to the church can only be made sense of when we recognize the importance of the church as a believer's closest kin group. Paul identifies himself as both the father figure as well as the brother of both the respected church leader and the runaway slave. For Paul, Onesimus is not defined by his slave class, as the honor-shame culture dictates, but by his being in Christ. Neither is Onesimus's future determined by social status. He is not stereotyped as the "typical slave type."²⁹⁷

Paul does not fear to address a situation that has the potential to shame one of the most influential people in the church. Not only that, but by writing a letter that would be read by the church, he has made the matter known in the whole church. In the Sri Lankan culture church leaders and/or affluent donors would be deeply offended that such a matter that involved them was made public knowledge, or that anyone should advise them to do what they "ought to do" (v. 8). If the matter did become public knowledge, most

---

294. Turner, "Human Reconciliation," 37.

295. Barclay, "Paul, Philemon and the Dilemma," 163–165. Barclay lists various wrongdoings Onesimus might have committed (163–165). Onesimus might have been sent to Paul and then absconded.

296. deSilva, *Introduction to the New Testament*, 671.

297. de Vos, "Once a Slave," 95.

people would probably want to support the cause of the wealthy patron who provided the church somewhere to meet. It is quite likely that a lot of gossip would arise about what Onesimus had done and how undeserving he was of the privilege of being owned by a Christian master.

Why does Paul not write privately to Philemon? Would that not be more in accordance with Jesus's teaching in Matthew 18:15–17 and serve to save face for Philemon? The situation is one in which Philemon is not yet the offender. The letter is written to give him an opportunity to respond wisely to a situation that must be known to many in the church already, and to act in a way that will prove his honor. Philemon's decision about Onesimus's future cannot be private because Onesimus is now part of the larger household of God and not merely Philemon's household.[298] However, Paul chooses not to command, but to entreat as brother and co-worker as well as apostle. Since he occupies a position of authority, in saying what he does, he does not shame Philemon. It is not a humiliation to obey the words of someone who is recognized as having the authority to command.[299]

What Paul calls for is a changed attitude from both Onesimus and Philemon. Onesimus has to face the consequences of his actions. Facing the consequences of our actions is difficult in the Sri Lankan culture. To own up to a fault is to shame oneself. Paul defers to cultural values of honor and shame, patronage and clientele, but molds them to the needs of the church.

Paul the family mediator

Paul takes the initiative to be a mediator. In Sri Lankan culture, weaker persons might require a mediator to speak on their behalf. For example, a person in domestic employment who has fallen out with their employer, or needs to ask for some special favor may seek out someone of the same social standing as the employer to speak on their behalf. deSilva points out that this kind of mediation was common in the Greco-Roman world. Citing Pliny's letters to the emperor Trajan on behalf of Voconius, he shows that a client may approach a patron to ask a favor on behalf of another. When considering the request that Voconius be given a senatorial office, Pliny stands as guarantor of Voconius's character. Trajan's assessment of Pliny, not Voconius will be the

---

298. deSilva, *Introduction to the New Testament*, 669.
299. Pitt-Rivers, "Honor and Social Status," 58.

basis of his decision.[300] In a similar way, Paul asks that Onesimus be judged and treated, not on the basis of his past behavior but on the basis of Paul's reputation (v. 17).

In verse 8, Paul declares that instead of commanding he will appeal. Barth suggests that the whole of Philemon, especially verses 8–9 "can be considered a discussion of the proper and improper use and recognition of authority."[301] Paul's authority comes through in his request but it is a spiritual authority that he has earned so that even though he does not invoke his apostolic identity, we are still aware of it. Paul clearly relies heavily on his relationship to Philemon. Paul shows the fruit that is borne when he can appeal to someone whom he genuinely appreciates in the Lord rather than command. Barth remarks that Paul lays on Philemon's shoulder a hand that is both warm and heavy. The warmth is experienced through the genuine appreciation and commendation he receives, and the pressure is felt in the exhortation to continue to be the leader Paul can be proud of.[302]

"In the service of Christ, the free man Paul asks for a free man's response."[303] Paul has faith that the Spirit's work in Philemon will produce the required fruit. Authoritarian leadership in the church makes the assumption that the ordinary believer cannot be trusted to follow the Spirit's leading, but true spiritual maturity cannot come through coercion or pressure. A free choice means that there can be reconciliation. A forced taking back will result in bitterness and resentment. Also, Philemon's honor is maintained. By responding positively, Philemon gains greater honor as someone who is trusted to do the right thing (v. 8 "what you ought to do"). Paul shows that he has complete confidence that Philemon will do the right thing – he expects the best from him and gets it. If we expect very little from one another, we will probably get what we expect.[304]

Philemon is given the benefit of time and the discretion to decide "what you ought to do" (v. 8). The word implies a code of conduct that befits someone of Philemon's status.[305] The church benefits from being encouraged to

---

300. deSilva, *Introduction to the New Testament*, 674.
301. Barth and Blanke, *Letter to Philemon*, 309.
302. Barth and Blanke, 253.
303. Barth and Blanke, 316.
304. Barclay, *Letter to the Philippians*, 283.
305. Barth, *Letter to Philemon*, 313.

think that there is a correlation between holiness and high social status. Throughout history, the concept of *nobless oblige* suggested that privilege entails responsibility. In Sri Lankan culture, however, the higher the social status, power or privilege, the lower the responsibility one is expected to show others. This attitude can infiltrate the church if not challenged.

The letter, says Lucas, "in the deepest sense . . . is a family letter, from brother to brother, concerning a third brother."[306] The church is a "fictive kinship group." It is the household of God.[307] Mutual love, demonstrated in sharing resources, covering up rather than broadcasting a family member's shame, commitment to another's spiritual welfare, mutual honoring (Rom 12:10, Phil 2:3) commitment to unity, and the replacement of competition with cooperation were some of the important characteristics of this family.[308]

Paul's role as *paterfamilias* includes a continuing educational role with three components: teaching, being a role model, and correction.[309] This relational model shapes the church's mode of response to him – not as duty to an outsider but in the context of a family relationship.

God the arbiter of honor

God was "the supreme member" of this new court of reputation. He would bestow honor on the believer on the final day, but even before that, his approval could be experienced through the believer's own conscience (Rom 8:16–17; 1 John 3:21–22), through the Scripture's affirmation and through the recognition of virtue by the church, the new family of God.[310] The leadership of the church played a vital role in bringing believers before this "court of reputation," by describing their behavior as being either commendable, praiseworthy in God's eyes or not (Rom 1:8; 1 Cor 1:4–9; Col 1:3–8; 1 Thess 1:2–10; 2:13–16).[311] Paul therefore is one channel of God's approval when, as a church leader, he affirms what is honorable in a given situation.

Philemon like Paul and Jesus (Heb 12:2; 1 Pet 2:4–8) must "despise shame" that society conferred on him in favor of the honor that would be conferred

---

306. Lucas, *Message of Colossians and Philemon*, 186.
307. deSilva, *Honor, Patronage, Kinship*, 200–239.
308. deSilva, 220.
309. Holmberg, *Paul and Power*, 78.
310. deSilva, *Honor, Patronage, Kinship*, 55.
311. deSilva, 59.

on him by God and the church, who together make up his court of reputation.[312] Paul constantly reminds Christians that it is God who decides what is honorable. Sri Lankan Christian leader Fernando points out that in the New Testament, categories of shame and honor are used to promote holiness (Eph 5:3–4; 1 Cor 15:34; see also 2 Thess 3:14).[313] Fernando, a Methodist, draws a parallel between this New Testament emphasis on accountability (with the community encouragement of holiness), and the early Methodist "class" and "band" system in which believers sought holiness through close fellowship and accountability.[314]

Response to grace

Paul asks Philemon to return grace for grace. In terms of patron-client reciprocity, God is the supreme patron who has showered favor or "grace" on his church. Although Paul does not remind Philemon of the grace he has received from Christ, there is sufficient mention of the relationship he has with Christ to form a basis for the appeal to grace (vv. 4, 9, 16). What Paul encourages Philemon to do is to make a response of grace in the face of the grace he has received, not just from Paul but from God himself. The fundamental ethos governing relationships of patrons and clients, benefactors and beneficiaries, and friends is that grace must answer grace. The receiving of favor must lead to the return of gratitude, or else the beauty and nobility of the relationship is defaced (disgraced).[315]

In the world of the New Testament, "grace" was not purely a religious term. It was used to refer to the reciprocity between patrons and clients, between friends, and between humans and their God or gods.[316] Grace referred both to a particular act or gift of generosity from patron to client, as well as the attitude of a favorable disposition which gave rise to the act. The same term is also used to describe the response of gratitude at receiving the gifts from a benefactor or patron. The use of the same word for both the action and the response imply that one gives rise to the other, grace must be met with

---

312. deSilva, 54.
313. Fernando, "Wesley Groups and Holiness."
314. Fernando.
315. deSilva, *Honor, Patronage, Kinship*, 155.
316. deSilva, "Patronage and Reciprocity," 38.

grace.[317] Thus, Philemon is being asked to forgive rather than take revenge. Jesus recounted the parable of the unforgiving servant that illustrates this principle. The first servant having received grace in the form of forgiveness of his debt and release from a prison sentence must show such grace to his brother. If he does not, he suffers the retributive justice of the king.[318]

"Paul, by his actions, refused to allow his audience the comfort of two worlds (religious and social) independent from one other."[319] Peterson states that Paul's demand "transforms Philemon's previously comfortable double life in the two domains by rendering the institution of slavery in the domain of the world as a rock and the institutional domain of the church, whose support Paul has cultivated in this letter, as a hard place."[320] This case represents for Paul a case not just of personal relationships but more deeply, of conflicting identities. Will Philemon view his primary identity as being "in Christ" or as "master"? Paul, writing in a time when the church was a minority, like it is in Sri Lanka, sought the "establishment of little oases where an alternative way of life was being practiced and could be observed."[321] In Sri Lanka, some churches and Christian organizations are seeking to do that – to intentionally create counter-cultural, alternative societies where reconciliation is a greater virtue than revenge, where truth is more honorable than lying, and where mutual submission takes the place of unassailable autocratic leadership. The question is why this endeavor should be limited to some. Perhaps the rest of the church is guilty not so much of being blind to gospel claims but of assuming that those values will spring up without being planted, nurtured, and guarded.

Overall Attitude Toward Those Who Need Correcting

In his letter to the Galatians, Paul advises the church on helping a person who has been overcome by sin. The church is addressed as "brothers and sisters."

---

317. deSilva, 39. deSilva points to the well-known artistic depiction of the "three Graces" which in which the three young women represent the benefactor, the one who receives a gift, and the one who returns it. The unbroken circle in which they dance suggests the continual giving and receiving giving beauty and continuity to the relationships.

318. Little, "Different Kind of Justice," 70–72.

319. Lyons, "Paul's Confrontation with Class," 334.

320. Petersen, *Rediscovering Paul*, 289.

321. Lucas, *Message of Colossians and Philemon*, 188.

Paul does not define what the sin might be that needs intervention. Martyn remarks that having written extensively on how the church is free from the law, Paul still expects them to be able to identify sinful behavior. He has given listed characteristics of the flesh, he has warned against community-destroying behavior, and finally he has confidence that the Spirit himself will identify those things which mar the church's witness and community life.[322]

When Paul refers to "you who are spiritual," he is not speaking to an elite group in the church. He is talking to the whole church.[323] Once again, as in Matthew 18:15–17, the purpose is restoration. The word translated as "restore" means "to make perfect" or "to equip" and can refer to restoring something to its original condition, like fishing nets (Mark 1:19; Matt 4:21) or a dislocated bone.[324] Believers are led by the Spirit who binds them together as family, to deal gently with those who err, remembering that they too are as liable to fall. James writes to the church "My brothers and sisters, if any one among you wonders from the truth and is brought back by another, you should know that whoever brings back a sinner from wandering will save the sinner's soul from death and will cover a multitude of sins" (Jas 5:19–20).

All the members of the church are addressed here. The person who has wandered (cf. Matt 18:15–17) has wandered from the truth. For James "truth" is both what a person knows and how they live.[325] The one who guides the lost one back, protects both the individual and the community. Both James and Peter (1 Pet 4:8) draw on Proverbs 10:12 which says, "Hatred stirs up strife, but love covers all offenses" (ESV). McKnight states that Peter knows that love shared creates community and conciliation.[326] James adds to that the fact that the experience of forgiveness promotes personal and communal holiness.[327] "There is no surer test of the spiritual person than his treatment of another's sin. Note how he takes care to deliver the sinner rather than triumph over him, to help him rather than punish him, so far as lies in his capacity, to support him."[328]

---

322. Martyn, *Galatians*, 546.
323. Martyn, 546.
324. Fung, *Epistle to the Galatians*, 286.
325. McKnight, *Letter of James*, 454.
326. McKnight, 460.
327. McKnight, 460.
328. Augustine, cited in Edwards, *Ancient Christian Commentary*, 93.

In 1 Timothy 5:1–2, Timothy is exhorted to be respectful towards the members of his church and is given instructions regarding his interactions with those members. "Do not rebuke an older man harshly, but exhort him as if he were your father. Treat younger men as brothers, older women as mothers, and younger women as sisters, with absolute purity" (1 Tim 5:1–2). In this way, Paul directs Timothy regarding the proper demeanor towards different age groups. Paul deals with the relationship primarily with those who are older, and also those of the opposite sex, for two reasons: one being Timothy's comparative youth, and the other, because this is the subject of Greek moral teaching.[329] These two verses fall within a general subsection devoted to the different relationships within the church, this fictive kinship group. The church is expected to relate with "respect and intimacy," the structure and behavior of the typical family in the ancient Mediterranean. As such, age and gender would play an important part.[330] This attitude was enjoined by secular philosophy and so was part of general moral conduct.[331]

There are two main difficulties with understanding to whom Paul was referring in this verse. First, the term Paul uses for the "older man" is the term Πεσβύτερος. The cognate πεσβυτέριον has been used by Paul in 4:14 (and later in 5:17 and 19) to refer to a committee of elders who hold an official status of leadership in the church. Second, in the later texts Paul refers to a process of disciplining elders.[332] It is therefore unclear whether Paul is referring to an older man purely in the sense of age, or if he is referring to an elder in the church. However, what Paul is prohibiting here is some kind of harsh rebuke. The term ἐπιπλήξῃς refers to a sharp rebuke, even striking another.[333] What is encouraged instead is a term which encompasses the meaning of "exhorting, urging, encouraging, consoling and comforting." Correcting must be done but it ought to be done in a "conciliatory and positive way" designed to restore fellowship.[334]

In the Greco-Roman world, the father was owed complete respect. For those in the same age groups, the young leader is advised to exhort and

---

329. Towner, *Letters to Timothy and Titus*, 329.
330. Towner, 329.
331. Diebelius and Conzelmann, *Pastoral Epistles*, 72.
332. Towner, *Letters to Timothy and Titus*, 331.
333. Johnson, *First and Second Letters to Timothy*, 260.
334. Towner, *Letters to Timothy and Titus*, 331.

correct as would be expected between peers. This does not reduce Timothy's authority but it does shape how he will use it. The word translated "exhort" is παρακαλέω, which is literally "call aside" and can mean encourage, or comfort, as well as admonish. When the young leader has to admonish an older man, he must do so, but as a son, rather than as "a superior."[335] When dealing with young widows, Timothy must take pains to guard himself from sexual impurity and even the appearance of it, "from getting into a situation in which his propriety could be called into question."[336]

Values and Virtues for Honor

In the cultures of the Mediterranean, virtues that were valued were, on the one hand, those that facilitated the competition for honor (φιλοτίμως); but on the other hand, virtues that cultivated peace and harmony were also valued although they might undermine one's competition for honor. Inscriptions on tombstones show that "good," "harmless," and "friend of all, troubling no-one" are extolled.[337]

The early church as a small, marginal group developed an "alternative culture" in which a new status was given to many who were the least in society.[338] These people were assigned power through their association with Jesus, the sovereign king. They received the appellation "children of God," and were trusted with behavioral ideals which were typically the ideals of the aristocracy or king, values like mercy, generosity, and peace making.[339] Property was shared and even the poorest were encouraged to give and share. Wisdom, which was seen as the province of the nobility who had the leisure and education to pursue it, was offered to all who were weak and heavy-laden (Matt 11:28–30). In this way, says Theissen, power, possessions, and education were status symbols conferred on the mainly poor community of the church.[340] Meeks compares the church with other small groups in society, primarily the household, the voluntary association, synagogue, and philosophical or rhetorical school. He points to similarities and differences

---

335. Fernando, *Leadership Lifestyle*, 122.
336. Towner, *Letters to Timothy and Titus*, 331.
337. Meeks, *Origins of Christian Morality*, 41.
338. Theissen, *Social Reality*, 279.
339. Theissen, 280.
340. Theissen, 280–281.

with all.³⁴¹ His conclusion is that the household remains the basic context in which the church established itself, though it drew from aspects of all the other groups as well.³⁴²

As we have seen, what is honorable is decided by the community or subgroups. The powerful and the masses, the philosophers and the Jews, the pagans and the Christians all regarded honor and dishonor as their primary axis of value. Yet each group would fill out the picture of what constituted honorable behavior or character in terms of its own distinctive set of beliefs and values. They then would evaluate people both inside and outside their group accordingly.³⁴³

At its best, the pursuit of honor brought great feats of valor and noble virtues, but at its worst, this love of honor caused disruption and fighting.³⁴⁴ What were the values that the New Testament church held and how did that shape their attitude towards conflict? Rather than use the term ethics, or values, Meeks prefers to use the term "early Christian morality." Morality "names a dimension of life, a pervasive and, often, only partly conscious set of value laden dispositions, inclinations, attitudes, and habits."³⁴⁵

In the New Testament, love and unity were to be hallmarks of the community of faith (John 13:35, 17:23; 1 Cor 1:10; Eph 4:3, 11–13; Col 3:13–14; 1 Pet 3:8; 1 John 4:12). Believers were to honor one another, consider another's needs before their own (Rom 12:3, 10; Phil 2:3–4). Competition was to be replaced by cooperation. Humility and service were to distinguish the

---

341. Meeks, *First Urban Christians*, 76–77. For example, the household model does not address issues like rituals and structures for leadership; churches were similar to voluntary associations in that they were joined freely and had a place for rituals but dissimilar in that they were exclusivistic in a unique way (78). In spite of many similarities with the synagogue, the New Testament refuses to allow believers to simply continue with a Jewish identity and forces us to look elsewhere for a suitable comparison (81).

342. Meeks, *First Urban Christians*, 84.

343. deSilva, *Honor, Patronage, Kinship*, 25.

344. Neyrey, *Honour and Shame*, 17.

345. Meeks, *Origins of Christian Morality*, 4. Meeks gives the illustration of a child who asks why he cannot do something. The parent by appeal to a higher authority (I said so), or moral sense (it's wrong), or family standards (we don't do that), or appealing to a sense of empathy (how would you feel) helps the child to internalize moral values or rules. Meeks distinguishes between ethics and morality in this way. Ethics, in his view, is the self-conscious reflection on morals, which seeks reasons, validity for a course of action. "It is morality rendered self-conscious . . ."

greatest among them (Matt 18:3–4; Mark 9:35; Rom 12:16; Eph 4:2; Jas 4:6). Of course, the reality was that conflict was still inevitable.

Summary

From this survey of New Testament texts, a few common themes can be can summarized. First, the importance of reconciliation between believers is both explicitly and implicitly stated. Commands guide believers to live in unity and peace, to forgive liberally. Values and virtues are stressed, which make for peace, honoring one another, humility, dealing with anger promptly, not taking revenge, and speaking the truth in love.

Second, while the New Testament nowhere advocates retreating from the world, it does make a sharp distinction between those who are in the light and those who still walk in darkness. One of the primary social functions of conflict is to establish social boundaries, between the "them" outside the group and the "us" inside the group. Robertson remarks that the absence of conflict between the church in Corinth and wider society shows that there was a "deficiency of the church's identity markers and boundaries."[346] In order to lessen the conflict within the church, Paul needed to make the church aware of the gulf between the church and the world. "For divisions within the ἐκκλησία to abate and boundaries to be drawn tighter and made clearer, a *larger shared division* from the rest of the world had to be perceived..."[347] The morals and values of the world must not be allowed to permeate into the fellowship of believers.

The following table summarizes the New Testament literature using the seven-element conceptual framework.

---

346. Robertson, *Conflict in Corinth*, 28.
347. Robertson, 28.

Table 5.1. Conflict and Shame in the New Testament

Shame-oriented culture characteristic	New Testament
Goal of conflict resolution	To restore fellowship with God and fellow believers. Substantive issues are less important, though both truth and mercy are required. Reparation is sign of repentance.
Identity of self and other	Primary identity is as child of God. Church family is new kin group. As brothers and sisters, they have responsibilities towards one another. Exhortation to trust, confess, repent, forgive and seek Christlikeness together rather than seek to save face.
Style of communication	*Elegkein* – reveal and lay open for discussion in a context of respect and intimacy. Appeals to conform to Christian character. Obstinate refusal to listen requires open and even public confrontation.
Conflict resolution style	Take initiative to restore relationships that may involve confrontation (in case of persistently offending leaders) and/or collaboration (Jerusalem Council). Avoidance is challenged. Competition is re-formulated to be "win back" not "win-lose."
Power distance	Status entails responsibility, not special privilege. Leaders must mediate, confront, and set an example. Leaders must accept correction. Humility a prized virtue while pride is serious sin.
Relative morality	Virtue is honorable. Direct challenge to cultural sins of envy, lying, boasting, gossip, and revenge. Non-exhaustive lists of vices show absolutes do exist.
Extreme reactions	Being a fighter is condemned. Extreme reactions of Judas (suicide) and the Jewish leaders (murder) are noted. Possibility that violent quarrels existed (James), which are strongly condemned.

CHAPTER 6

Recommendations and Conclusions

This study has shown that urban Sri Lankan church culture displays the characteristics of shame-oriented cultures. Believers have learned a conflict script from their culture which has not been critiqued by a reconstituted worldview.

Major Discoveries Emerging from the Study

The research shows that although shame-oriented cultures are collectivistic, relationships tend to be superficial and even avaricious beyond the person's kinship group. Ascribed and achieved honor is largely based on cultural norms rather than on virtue. Conflict becomes intractable because at the heart of most conflicts is the issue of identity. Face saving techniques preclude ready repentance and forgiveness. The goal of conflict resolution is usually the appearance of harmony rather than true reconciliation.

A positive finding is that extreme reactions of violence or suicide are not found in the selected sample. Another positive finding is that intentional investment of time to listen without judgmentalism, but with demonstrations of grace can help foster communities that are fictive kinship groups in which a different conflict script is learned.

New Testament studies show that there is no one prescribed approach to conflict resolution, though avoidance challenged. Instead, values and virtues of leading to peacemaking are extolled. Primary among them is the value of the church as a fictive kinship group where restoration of the sinner and brotherly love characterize the community. Leaders play the important role as parents who teach and exemplify values and virtues, rather than claim the privilege of honor without virtue.

Recommendations for the Church

A person's approach to conflict is molded within their social groups amidst the surrounding culture. Sri Lanka culture clearly exhibits characteristics of a collectivist, shame-oriented culture. There are seven aspects of shame-oriented cultures that have a major impact on how conflicts are experienced and managed. Field research revealed that except for extreme reactions to shame, conflict between church members exhibited all aspects of the characteristics of the larger culture that mold conflict responses.

However, a social group, for example a church, can regulate its own community and mold the values and behavior of its members. The New Testament records and recommendations for dealing with conflict showed that the church as kin group played a vital role in challenging cultural norms of its day and reinforcing honorable values which made for peace.

In collectivistic communities, people are socialized into the community through observation, imitation, and absorption.[1] Taylor describes four aspects of conversion that combine to form the model of conversion as re-socialization.[2] The first is what he calls "autobiographical reconstruction," which is the reinterpretation of one's past in the light of conversion, leading to an alienation from past relationships and lifestyle. Second, there is "comprehensive attribution," which refers to the way the convert will now interpret their symbolic universe through the lens of their new religious beliefs. Third, there is "suspension of analogical reasoning," which is to say converts will accept the new system of beliefs as unique and incapable of comparison with other belief systems. Finally, there is the assumption of a master role. The convert now identifies completely with the new community of faith, assuming its moral code and living according to its prescribed way of life.[3]

The church community plays a vital role in modelling this new identity and nurturing new believers, helping them to go through these phases to find their new identity within the worldview of the grand narrative of Scripture. It is not an easy process. The New Testament documents show that the church struggled with this re-socialization. It was not complete in some converts (1

---

1. Luzbetak, *Church and Cultures*, 188–189.
2. Taylor, "Social Nature of Conversion," 134. Taylor builds on the work of previous sociologists whose work he discusses in this chapter.
3. Taylor, 134–135.

Cor 5:1; 6:1; 14:16; 1 Tim 3:7). Today, New Testament teaching (understood with a lens focused on how honor and shame are related to conflicts) combined with insights specific to Sri Lankan culture, can aid the church there to further the conversion process of re-socialization in its members.

To do that, the church needs to intentionally address the seven aspects of shame-oriented culture that have major impact on how conflicts are experienced and managed.

Goal of Conflict Resolution

The literature review on shame-oriented cultures revealed that the conflict goal was relational rather than substantive. The New Testament research showed that the goal of conflict resolution is restoration of the erring party's fellowship with God and the church. While substantive issues are important, the relational aspect is more important with believers being willing to suffer loss (1 Cor 6:7) and cultivate a lifestyle of forgiveness (Eph 4:32). The reason for addressing the parties involved is not to remove them from the church so that the church might attempt to form a sin-free society. The goal is that through facing up to the wrong they have done, and through repentance and a changed life in the power of the Spirit, the erring brother or sister is brought back into the fellowship of the church. Those who fall are to be met with grace, though not cheap grace.

However, the field research showed that shame-oriented people seek harmony, which is not the same as shalom. It is the appearance of peace rather than restored relationships that people in our case studies sought. Thus, the shame-oriented person's desire for harmony can be used to advantage if the church teaches believers the true meaning of harmony, not as the absence of conflict or the avoidance of conflict but shalom. Shalom requires truth and mercy, justice and forgiveness. An important aspect of the church's education program should be conflict resolution. At present, there is rarely any teaching in the church about conflict and conflict resolution. Ken Sande's book *The Peacemaker* sets out a readily accessible discussion on conflict as an opportunity to glorify God. A similar educational curriculum for a Sri Lankan context could be part of the church's regular teaching program. This should begin in Sunday school and be continued in age appropriate ways for the whole congregation. This would gradually change the church's understanding of peace and the elements of reconciliation.

Another way the church can help believers learn a new conflict script that challenges the cultural norm would be to put in structures for pastoral care and church discipline. In Sri Lankan churches, the process for dealing with those who stray is vague and varied. In some churches, authoritarian pastors administer discipline with no participation by ordinary members of the congregation and very little consistency. A person may be asked to leave the church because they asked awkward questions about finances or chose to marry the "wrong" person, while in other churches grave misdeeds by leaders or clergy are ignored because of the status of the offender. A worship leader may be ordered, in front of the congregation, to leave the podium and take himself home because he has not shaved, while in another church the pastor who has sexually assaulted a member of his congregation is given a rap over the knuckles or transferred to another church so that he is not shamed by visible disciplinary action.

Many believers do not have close relationships within the church and have no one to go to in a conflict situation. Pastoral care is often equated with visiting the sick or elderly. A system of care that ensures every believer is "spurred on to love and good works" (Heb 10:24–25) is vital to foster a culture of peace.

Identity of Self and Others

The field research revealed that believers tend towards superficial relationships outside of their extended family. In Sri Lanka, if the church wishes to model a reconciled community, it must foster deeper relationships within the family of believers. As mentioned before, Sri Lankans value strong family ties but are weak in showing family-like regard for those outside their biological family. Caste, ethnicity, age, marital status, and financial well-being are some of the barriers that arise within a single congregation.

Having seen the importance of one's in-group for collectivistic, shame-oriented cultures and having also surveyed the New Testament teaching on life in the new community, one vital element for dealing with shame is the fostering of healthy church life. In terms of the collectivistic identity of the shame-oriented person, the New Testament emphasizes identity of the church as family, a fictive kinship group. deSilva shows how Paul, by writing to the whole church, allows the Christian community that meets in Philemon's house to be the "court of reputation." The court of reputation is the "sole body of significant others whose approval or disapproval should be important to the individual."[4]

Paul writes as *paterfamilias* to his children. He uses familial language to remind believers that they are brothers and sisters first and members of other associations and kin-groups second. There is to be a clear distinction between the church and the world.

The New Testament challenges the cultural desire to save face by insisting that matters that cause disunity, or are contrary to the morals and values of the kingdom are brought into the open, even if it causes embarrassment to the people concerned. Leaders are not exempt from rebuke as seen from the fact that the letter to Philemon is read to the church and Peter is confronted with his weaknesses to the face, in front of others, both by Jesus and by Paul. To rebuke, even if it is a last resort, is still a valid and necessary option, especially for the pastor who must be concerned for the spiritual maturity of his flock.

Unnecessary shame is avoided as much as possible because the first approach is to go personally and show someone their fault; to be gentle, show respect, and not judge without evidence. Confession is part of church life (Jas 5:16) and thus not shameful. Humility is a virtue, both before God and others (Col 3:12; 1 Pet 5:7). Interestingly, no specific type of apology is described in any of the conflict situations.[5]

This familial view of the church is something that would help the Sri Lankan church with three provisos. If the church is family, there is the temptation to expect the pastor to be *paterfamilias*, with children who will not grow up and take responsibility. Family dysfunctions can be carried over into church life.[6] Sometimes churches fall victim to their own publicized ideals. The congregation expects the church to fulfill their need for acceptance, comfort, emotional support, exercise of power, use of gifts, and so on, all under the rubric of being family.[7] It is not unknown for Christian leaders in Sri Lanka, especially in some types of church government, to assume a paternal role towards their followers. However, this role has not been redeemed by being brought under the lordship of Christ. That means that the role they assume is

---

4. deSilva, *Introduction to the New Testament*, 674.
5. The most elaborate apology is made by the Prodigal Son in Luke 15:21.
6. Fleckenstein, "Congregation as Family," 189–191.
7. Greenwood, "Beyond Shame," 3.

more similar to the role of the Roman *paterfamilias* who had absolute authority over his children, even the right of life and death. Christian leaders who abuse their workers verbally and even physically, who make decisions about who should marry and whom they may marry, who demand unquestioning obedience and exert draconian methods of discipline exist and seem to thrive. To those new to the faith, these models are not questioned because they are culturally acceptable (as seen in some political leaders). What is required are church leaders who will assume the role of the father described by Jesus – the one who sets aside dignity and offended pride and runs to welcome the prodigal home (Luke 15:11–32).

Second, this fatherly care must be devoid of favoritism. Paul modelled Jesus's own way of gentleness with the weak while being ready to sharply admonish those who continued to sin. Unfortunately, the church can often be swayed to discriminate against the weak in favor of the strong: the male, the rich, the powerful, the confident have a voice and find privileges denied to the woman, the poor, the weak, and the timid.

Third, Sri Lankan Christians need to see that while the gospel upholds family life, it also enlarges the borders of family so that family includes all those who love the Lord. The downside of a society in which family is important is that Christians assume their responsibility to others ends at their own front door. "We have a tremendous opportunity before us to honor Christ by saying his blood is more important than our own in determining who shall be our family."[8] In Sri Lanka, close, honest, accountable relationships are hard to come by for Christian workers in general and church leaders in particular. An inability to keep confidences, competitiveness, and judgmentalism on one side, and insecurity, pride, and defensiveness on the other are some of the reasons for this.

In the Sri Lankan church, it would take considerable resolve and courage to break the barriers that divide – between ethnic groups, genders, between those of the "middle class" and those of the "lower class" or "servant class" (even though the term "servant" is rarely used now). Would a white-collar, middle-class CEO find it "normal" to have a "brother" from another class/caste socialize with them, question them, or teach them? Some might find it difficult to share the communion cup with someone from a lower status.

---

8. deSilva, *Honor, Patronage, Kinship*, 55, 238.

When honor is conferred on leaders in the church, new barriers are sometimes formed, not only through a sense of status but also through suspicion and insecurity. Paul who had in every aspect "reason to be proud" (Phil 3:4–6) was able to truly love and appreciate a fellow believer from a completely different background and what is more, to place his own reputation on the line to speak on his behalf. Paul's intervention on Onesimus's behalf not only changed Onesimus's life but also the life of the church. Paul chooses in his letter not to identify himself as "apostle" but "servant of Christ" (Phlm 1). He is comfortable identifying himself as brother to both slave-owner and slave.

The Spirit's gift of community might be the most under-utilized of all gifts, says Albers.[9] In the early church, identity, strength, nurture, purpose, and direction were derived from the believing community. It was a healing, *therapeuo*, community and the healing of shame is an important aspect of the church's mission.[10] As seen from the New Testament texts surveyed, the church was constituted as a new community with a striking resemblance to the Mediterranean family, the most significant "in-group" in their culture. One way the early church preserved its values in spite of being a minority group in a hostile environment, was to ensure that it functioned as a "fictive kinship group," incorporating, or often replacing, the natural kin group.[11]

While ancient biblical and non-biblical texts record similar injunctions to unity, safeguarding family honor, respect for parents and brotherly love, Paul, in his letters to the Thessalonians emphasizes that brotherhood was the most intimate of family relationships.[12] Paul differs from other non-biblical writers by including within the brotherhood those from different geographical locations and also insisting the church show concern for outsiders (1 Thess 3:12). Writers such as Plutarch show little consideration for the honor of outsiders and even advise brothers to vent their hostility on outsiders rather than on each other.[13] Paul upholds the tradition of maintaining the family honor by

---

9. Albers, *Shame*, 131.
10. Albers, 131.
11. deSilva, *Honor, Patronage, Kinship*, 76.
12. Burke, *Family Matters*, 254.
13. Burke, 254–255.

instructing the church to demonstrate honor towards brothers, as well as by holding older brothers as worthy of greater respect.[14]

Not only did the church then become the "public court of reputation," recognizing honor and using shame as a sanction, but "God becomes the most important judge of one's honor or lack of honor since only his knowledge is complete and only his sanction matters beyond this life."[15] The early church thus rejoiced in being counted worthy to be dishonored for the name (Acts 5:41). Paul uses this motivator repeatedly (Rom 2:29; 2 Cor 5:9–10; Gal 1:10; 1 Thess 2:4). The author of the epistle to the Hebrews likewise exalts Jesus as the one who, having been shamed in his public crucifixion (Heb 12:2), has been exalted as Son of God and King (Heb 1:1–3; 1:13; 2:6–9).[16] The honor of the Father means acquired honor for the children. Children, in turn, will desire to uphold the honor of the Father and of the family name. Wu, constructing a Chinese ecclesiology, suggests that believers should be taught that confession magnifies God, even as it humbles the confessor, while hiding sin dishonors God. Paradoxically, as the Father receives honor, his children are also honored.[17]

Within the family of believers, people can find acceptance but also the challenge to change. Fernando writes of the time when he preached from 2 Timothy 2:21 (on fleeing youthful passions), in his seminary class. After his sermon, his professor remarked that he had omitted to address Paul's injunction that this was to be done "along with those who call on the Lord from a pure heart." Fernando urges the church to recover this body identity in which we pursue holiness with one another.[18]

Grace and mercy

The story goes that C. S. Lewis once walked into a room where a group of people were discussing the question of what distinguished Christianity from

---

14. Burke, 255. Burke's thesis is that the early church was not entirely non-hierarchical. Paul shows that some brothers in the church were worthy of more respect because of their hard work (1 Thess 5:12-15) and because they are called to "rule over" the brothers. (Burke, 256).

15. deSilva, *Honor, Patronage, Kinship*, 171. This technique was used by other minority groups and individuals like Plato, Socrates, Epictetus etc as well as Jewish groups as evidenced in 2 Maccabees (deSilva, 172).

16. deSilva, "Despising Shame."

17. Wu, "Biblical Theology," 20.

18. Fernando, *Jesus Driven Ministry*, 135.

the other major religions. The answer, he said, was easy – it was grace. Smedes writes of how grace deals with both guilt and shame. We experience grace as pardon for guilt, and as acceptance for shame. "We are reunited with God and our true selves, accepted, cradled, held, affirmed, and loved. 'Accepting' grace is the answer to shame."[19] The church is the place where we are meant to experience that accepting grace, and yet the church is often a place where people are hyper-critical of one another. The case studies revealed that conflicts frequently arose when one person was criticized by another. Those who are most active in the church know only too well the pain of friendly fire. It is probably true that those who are most active in the church are most likely to become involved in conflict in the church because they have invested so much of themselves in the church. They are more likely to care passionately about what happens in the church, most likely to have an opinion on how the church should respond to challenges and in which direction it should move. However, when there is conflict, these leaders are often either allowed to get away with all manner of un-Christian behavior because of their status or because the church cannot afford to lose them. Alternatively, the church deals harshly with them. In either case, they do not receive grace, as pardon or as acceptance. Few churches have a satisfactory program of pastoral care. While clergy might visit the sick or bereaved, many sincere believers who are struggling with painful relationships suffer alone.

The New Testament texts constantly urge the church seek out and restore those who have fallen into sin, including the sin of unresolved conflict with its attendant unforgiveness, lack of repentance, anger, bitterness, and, in shame cultures, hypocrisy. Covering a multitude of sins does not mean covering up unresolved conflict. Bonhoeffer interprets Matthew 5:7 ("blessed are the merciful") thus:

> If any man falls into disgrace, the merciful will sacrifice their own honor to shield him, and take his shame upon themselves . . . (I)n order that they might be merciful, they cast away the most priceless treasure of human life, their personal dignity and honor. For the only honor and dignity they know is their Lord's own mercy to which alone they owe their very lives.[20]

---

19. Smedes, *Shame and Grace*, 108.
20. Bonhoeffer, *Cost of Discipleship*, 125.

Jewett, addressing American culture, writes that internalizing the message of grace – the knowledge that we are loved and accepted by God even though we are not perfect, and not loved and admired by the world as we would like – is what will set us free from the fear that suppresses the truth.[21] What he writes is equally applicable to those in shame-oriented cultures.

While shame often hides a deep-seated arrogance, grace releases us from pride into grace-filled acceptance of ourselves. Smedes describes the distinction between "graceless arrogance" and "grace-based pride": graceless "arrogance is pride without gratitude, while grace given pride is nothing but gratitude."[22] Smedes goes on to describe this grace-based pride as "a kind of elation" which leads us to want to share with someone what we have done. Yu writes of the Korean concept of *unhae*, meaning "gracious favor" exemplified by the care given to children by their parents. The receiver is morally obliged to reciprocate. When one does not pay back the grace one has received, it gives rise to shame.[23] The Christian concept of grace is wider. One "repays" not the human giver but the divine giver when one extends grace to those who are undeserving.

Within a grace-filled community, holding one another accountable becomes family business. It is only when community is strong that being shunned becomes the ultimate shame and punishment (Matt 18:17; 1 Cor 5:1–13). If relationships are weak, all that is necessary is for the person to leave the church and find another more suitable to their needs. Yang states that in the Old Testament community of God as well as the New Testament community of God, the community's moral code was taken seriously. Not to do so was a great shame to the community. The community's reputation was more important than the honor or face of any one individual.[24] Writing on Paul's injunction to expel the incestuous man in 1 Corinthians 5, Yang says "Thus saving the spirit of the sinning individual, protecting the community from contamination and safeguarding the community's reputation are more important than saving the face of the recalcitrant sinner."[25]

---

21. Jewett, *St Paul at the Movies*, 39–40.
22. Smedes, *Shame and Grace*, 150.
23. You, "Shame and Guilt Mechanisms," 63.
24. Yang, *Discipline or Shame?*, 51.
25. Yang, 51.

As seen in the field research, the typical reactions to conflict among shame-oriented cultures is found at the two extremes of the peacemaking spectrum (attack to save honor and escape to hide shame). Christians are able to offer a different response; one that seeks the good of the other rather than one's own security (honor). Toorman, who has worked as a missionary in shame-oriented cultures, warns that such cultures can be devoid of selfless love in their relentless search for honor at all costs. A right understanding of the God of love, the story of salvation taking us from shame to honor, and a people who are willing to offer selfless love must prevail to prevent a culture of lovelessness.[26]

Baptism as identity formation

In many churches which practice what is called "believer's baptism" the ritual of baptism is primarily an act of public confession of the believer's new allegiance. It is often portrayed as an individual's decision to follow Christ, to die to sin, and be raised with Christ. Although the church community witnesses the event, not much is made of the believer's new identity "in Christ." Paul uses the believer's baptism as an identity marker. The believer who is "in Christ" has a new identity that supersedes all others. It relativizes all other relationships and confers a status: adopted child of God, co-heir with Christ, and member of one family of God. This is more important than other identities, position, and status from birth or accomplishments. It is a sign of acceptance into a new family.[27] Baptism and the cross were supposed to mark Christians off from those who were outside, those who were perishing. Real status is belonging to God, being in Christ.[28]

Whatever else is involved, the image of the initiate being adopted as God's child and thus receiving a new family of human brothers and sisters is a vivid

---

26. Toorman, "Selfless Love," 166. Toorman gives as an example the case of Tsunami relief which first poured in from Western countries and only much later and slower from Islamic groups. Toorman, 162.

27. Baptism which should have been a key identity marker, identifying those who were members of one family, was even being used as a cause for division in Corinth (Robertson, *Conflict in Corinth*, 123). The closeness within the group was meant to promote a sense of separation from "outsiders" (1 Cor 5:12, 13; 1 Thess 4:12; Col 4:5). These outsiders are also characterized in evaluative terms such as "unrighteous," "those who do not know God" (1 Cor 6:1, 9; 1 Thess 4:5; Gal 4:8; etc.) (Meeks, *First Urban Christians*, 94).

28. Witherington, *Conflict and Community*, 155.

way of portraying what sociologists call the re-socialization of conversion. The natural kinship structure into which the person has been born and which previously defined their place and connections with the society are here supplanted by a new set of relationships.[29]

Binau suggests that baptism should be explained as the promise of relationship with the one whose covenant can be trusted and who will not allow us to be put to shame.[30] It is the unconditional promise of acceptance by a heavenly father and adoption into a family in which we are co-heirs with Christ (Rom 8:15–17; 1 Cor 12:13; Gal 3:27–29). Churches should treat baptism as important so that new believers will recognize "a warm welcome in their new family."[31] In a country like Sri Lanka, where for a significant number, baptism is saying farewell to existing family relationships, this welcome has a special significance.

Baptism is also a ritual that should be remembered as a symbol of a new life. Paul asks the Roman Christians to remember their baptism and to become what they already were through conversion. Perhaps there can be deliberate reminders of one's baptism within the liturgical life of the church, to encourage believers to remember the vows they took and the new allegiances it marked. In many churches, the congregation also makes promises at the baptism, to uphold and encourage the new believer in their faith. Perhaps it is time to take those promises more seriously. In a shame culture, when a child errs, blame falls not just on the child but the parents, teachers, and community who are meant to nurture the child and guide them in their choices and behavior.[32] It is only from within a community in which there is a caring and interdependence can there be church intervention or discipline.

Rituals

Closely connected to the previous point is the whole concept of rituals. Hiebert includes in his conclusions regarding methods of transforming worldviews,

---

29. Meeks, *First Urban Christians*, 88. Resocialization is the process by which a person, in this case the convert, replaces the primary socialization process which occurred though the normal process of being reared in one social world, with a new social reality.
30. Binau, "Shame and the Human Predicament," 142.
31. Fernando, *Sharing the Truth in Love*, 193.
32. Wu, "Biblical Theology," 5.

the importance of creating "living rituals."[33] During the performance of living rituals, a change occurs in those participating. Although Buddhism and Hinduism are replete with rituals, Protestant Christianity in Sri Lanka has been devoid of them. Living rituals, as Hiebert defines them, speak of what lies deep within us, point to the transcendent, and to our deepest allegiances.

Rituals of transformation like baptism, mark the change of allegiance and the paradigm shift that has occurred and witness to the community of one who has become a member of the church family. "Rituals of intensification," like the Sunday service, are periodic, and function to recall and reaffirm worldviews.[34] "Without living rituals, we have no appropriate ways to affirm our deepest beliefs, feelings and morals, which lead to new lives in a new community and in the world."[35]

> Rituals such as eating or worshipping together, whether formal or informal often have the effect of binding individuals and groups together. In creating a sense of group solidarity and well-being they help people to de-objectify themselves and to forget their sense of shame.[36]

In traditional societies, says Pattison, rituals help turn shame to beauty. He testifies to the "shame-reducing effects" of participating in corporate worship, especially singing. Some rituals, he warns, can have the opposite effect, making a person stand out, feel isolated or alienated.[37] In some churches, the sharing of the peace is meant to be a ritual that encourages people to remember the gift of unity given by the Spirit to the church, because of Christ's death. In other churches, the ritual of the Lord's Supper is used to remind believers of the importance of reconciled relationships. Despite the tremendous rupture in the fabric of Sri Lankan society from thirty years of conflict, few rituals of reconciliation have become part of the church's pattern of worship.

---

33. Hiebert, *Transforming Worldviews*, 322.
34. Hiebert, 324.
35. Hiebert, 324.
36. Pattison, *Shame*, 160.
37. Pattison, 160.

Style of Communication

In terms of styles of communication, the onus is on any party in a conflictual situation to take the initiative to reconcile. Whether one has been offended (Matt 18:15) or is aware that they might have offended another (Matt 5:23), the command is to go to the other party with the view to reconcile. This suggests that in a shame-oriented culture, a way has to be found to challenge the indirect method of communication.

The role of teaching and care

The field research showed indirect communication was one of the main causes for the prolonging of conflict. In the New Testament, "going to" is a priority regardless of whether one has been offended or has offended. However, the going ought to be with the right attitude and motivation. The church needs to speak and teach more openly about the issues involved in conflict resolution. We can value the shame-oriented culture's sensitivity to another's honor, by consistently practicing humility, gentleness, and discretion. In addition, believers need to be taught the principle of going to the one who has offended, rather than to partisan factions. In this way, a transformed conflict script can emerge.

Instead of pastoral care being restricted to visits to the sick and elderly, it should take seriously the care of those involved in conflict. Church disciplinary processes should be well formulated and consistently applied. The goal should be the emergence of a church where conflict is prayed about and practical help offered; where apology and forgiveness are "natural" ways of relating; and broken relationships are considered to be shameful.

The role of mediation

We have seen that people from shame-oriented cultures prefer to have a mediator bridge the gap between them and the conflicting party. In a close family situation between siblings, a mediator should not be necessary. However, our New Testament analysis revealed Paul taking the role of father and mediator, for example with Philemon and Onesimus. Taking into account the reality of the depth, or lack of depth, of relationships within the church, the size of an average congregation, and the reticence of shame-oriented people to take the initiative in seeking reconciliation, a ministry of mediation would be a helpful tool. Field research revealed that church members who know that there is a conflict between two parties in the church will talk about it to others, or at best advise one or the other, but will stop short of bringing people together.

Who can be a mediator? Elmer, writing for cross-cultural missionaries, advices them that people might approach them as mediators. If the missionary, in accordance with their own cultural values, merely tells the local person to go and speak directly to the person concerned, the local person is hurt and confused.[38] Initially, believers may need to be helped with approaching someone who is in conflict with them. A mature believer should be equipped and ready to be such a mediator. Mediation is a risky venture and can be costly, since one or both of the parties might accuse the mediator of interference or bias, and even feel the need to shame the mediator in order to save face for themselves. However, as the cross demonstrates, peace-making is costly.

Even when using a mediator, speech ought not to be too direct. To accuse someone directly is to shame them before the mediator.[39] The role of the mediator is not to find the solution but to bring people together, strengthening the bonds between people and affirming their identity and affirming community.[40] Saving face involves intricate finesse, in which care must be taken to preserve the honor of both sides. A mediator can diffuse anger, help clarify perceptions and negotiate demands, especially relating to substantive issues.[41]

The mediator must be trusted by both sides, respected, neutral, objective, someone who will seek to protect both parties from shame. Other qualifications would include the ability to listen impartially, suspend judgment, accurately gather information, and assess it. In a shame context, people will seek out a mediator who is perceived as powerful, in terms of money, status or position.[42] The advantage to this is that if one of the two refuses to listen to the mediator, they will face the shame of losing face before the mediator and the community. If that possibility does not exist, then the mediator is ineffective.[43] Elmer suggests that if the mediator lacks power, another way to gain trust and credibility would be to use the "one down" position. A mediator may choose to make themselves vulnerable to the person to indicate that without their

---

38. Elmer, *Cross Cultural Conflict*, 72.
39. Elmer, 71.
40. Elmer, 75.
41. Augsburger, *Pastoral Counselling*, 133–134.
42. Elmer, *Cross Cultural Conflict*, 76.
43. Elmer, 76.

help the mediator will lose face. A person who has the opportunity to help you save face and does not do it, will themselves lose face.[44]

In a hierarchical society like Sri Lanka, there is a danger that if a mediator is too powerful, and too directive, they might coerce the two parties into a show of reconciliation that is not real. Just as parents may say to a child "say you're sorry" and assume that this resolves the child's conflict with a sibling, so a leader can enforce a pseudo-reconciliation if not careful. The field research showed that pastors and peer group alike can be mediators if they are trusted, sensitive to saving face, and impartial.

Conflict Style

The field research showed that the most common style of conflict management was avoidance, especially among women. The New Testament suggested that of the five main conflict styles, avoidance was the least used and affirmed (see table 6.1). In fact, a new style of confrontation with the "win back" rather than "win-lose" scenario seems most frequent.

In terms of conflict resolution style, there is no prescribed model for seeking and receiving forgiveness. There are no formulaic phrases, no methodology laid out. What is important is that the brothers and sisters in conflict be treated gently, be helped back into fellowship with one another and with God. Discussion and even open confrontation are preferred over avoidance. Table 6.1 shows that it is the compromising and avoiding style that seem to be least affirmed in the New Testament. The so-called "competitive" style predominates but with one important departure from the secular model. The goal is not the "win-lose" scenario, but a "win back" scenario. It is based on the seriousness the gospel places both on relationships, and on holiness, that is, on unity and on purity.

---

44. Elmer, 80.

Table 6.1. Conflict Management Styles in the New Testament

Style	Examples	Goal	Comments
Competitive	Paul with Peter Jesus with Peter Believers with the brother who sins against them (Matt 18) Paul and Barnabas The church leader with false teachers	Reconciliation Holy church Pure doctrine	When the gospel is at stake When sin must be repented of Initial confrontation leads to collaboration through repentance Goal is not "win-lose" as in secular model but "win back"
Collaborative	Distribution to widows (Acts 6) The Jerusalem Council regarding the inclusion of Gentiles (Acts 15) Paul and Philemon (Phlm)	Inclusion breaking of barriers	Where an organizational principle needs changing Where a deeply rooted belief/value must be challenged
Compromising			No positive examples within narrative or epistles.
Accommodating	Where our preferences cause a stumbling block (Rom 14:13–23; 1 Cor 8:13)	Consider others' needs	Where conflict is not due to sin but diversity of opinion. Christian freedom is balanced with responsibility
Avoiding	Judas		No positive examples within the NT narratives

Based on the literature reviews (including NT research) and the field research, a basic conflict resolution model would be:

Table 6.2. Sri Lankan Conflict Resolution Recommendations

Framework	Steps to take	Steps to avoid
Goal	Pray Desire to convict; win back; reconcile	Peace-faking (avoidance, overlooking)
Identity	Recognize that the person and problem are linked; not only the person but the person's family and friends (kin group) are affected	Shaming the person by being too direct. Encouraging people to take sides
Communication	Save face for the other. Protect the person's honor by seeking them out separately to clarify issues Listen carefully and decipher indirect communication including avoidance, silences and assurances that nothing is wrong. Persevere Affirm relationship Do not demand confession Ask if mediator is required	Forcing person to admit guilt Demanding an apology Passive-aggressive revenge methods (e.g. ignoring them, undermining them)
Conflict style	Collaborate to see God's perspective Do not avoid Do not compromise on moral issues. Persevere Pray together Consider the other's needs	Competing "win-lose" and avoiding styles
Status	Be first to apologize, offer reparation	Pride
Relative morality	Guard against gossip, lying, envy, suspicion, self-preservation. Give time to build trust	Giving in to norms of gossip, resentment, lying
Extreme reactions	Be aware of defensiveness and anger, or withdrawal and flight	Self-centeredness. Self-protection

Status Orientation

The field research showed that believers defer to those with status and prestige. They maintain a cultural fear of crossing the boundaries of those that have titles, leadership roles, and age. In the New Testament, leadership is not about status and prestige. Instead there is a fearsome stewardship responsibility for leaders. The harshest treatment of accountability is reserved for leaders. It is they who are to be confronted even publicly if they do not repent of sin. However, they are also to be respected, and treated in accordance with the customs of address for age and gender. Accusations against them should not be entertained without sufficient evidence.

Leaders are called to act as "parents" in the church family. They are to be role models, to teach, and to take on the role of peacemaker and mediator, especially speaking up for the weaker members of the family. It is worth pondering Bartchy's contention that the beginning of the end of the "brother-sister" ethos was when the Roman emperor who had taken the title of *paterfamilias* became patron of the church, bringing with him "a virulent form of hierarchy and patriarchy."[45] The church must beware of those who bring with them a different model of the parent role. Instead of looking to the surrounding culture for guidance, the values and worldview taught by Jesus and Paul should be studied, adopted, and reinforced.

In a culture where status and power are synonymous, leaders in the church should stand out as the epitome of servant-stewards with vulnerability and authenticity. Criteria for selection of leaders, and leadership training in seminaries should also be founded biblical, not merely cultural values. Unfortunately, churches often make the mistake of appointing leaders based on their personality, giftedness, financial wealth, or availability, with lesser regard for character traits.

Relativistic Morality

The field research revealed several cultural sins that are common to shame-oriented cultures. These include envy, falsehood, gossip, and pride. These kinds of vices existed in the New Testament world and believers were explicitly warned that continuing in those ways was unacceptable. Paul's unusual use of a culture's own critique of itself in Crete suggests that there are cultural

---

45. Bartchy, "Undermining Ancient Patriarchy," 77.

sins which every culture must recognize and critique. Culture cannot triumph over church in matters of purity and holiness. In the Sri Lankan church, cultural sins include lying, envy, and abuse of power as well as abdication of responsibility, gossip, and slander.

Approaches to ethics

How are we to deal with the fact that a significant contribution to conflict and lack of reconciliation between believers is sin which is excused as "part of the culture"? There are several views on intercultural ethics. Ethical absolutism is the view that there is a set of universal principles that apply to all cultures. While the obvious benefit of this approach is that all cultures can appeal to the same fixed set of principles, the weakness of this approach is that the ethic of one culture (usually the dominant culture) is assumed to be the universal ethic. For example, many Westerners find the idea of arranged marriages unacceptable. Absolutism assumes that those who apply ethical principles are free from fallibility.

A second approach would be ethical relativism. Ethical relativism states that right and wrong are determined by a particular culture and cannot be evaluated by outside criteria.[46] Although this approach is sensitive to cultural values, it allows certain practices to continue unchallenged within a culture. Mayers calls this an "abandonment of principle" giving rise to irresponsible behavior.[47] Cultures, like the people who inhabit them are by nature both good and fallen.[48] In the past, missionaries have challenged and stopped practices like *sati* (the burning of widows on the funeral pyre of their husbands), because they maintained that ethical relativism cannot be upheld in the light of God's revelation. Mayers suggests what might be called "cultural realism," "cultural relevance," or "cultural integrity." This approach develops and maintains principles, "from the inside out," recognizing cultural relativism but not ethical relativism.[49] Cultural relativism is compatible with a belief in the supreme authority of Scripture (absolute morality) while taking into account human fallibility, which prevents any culture from being infallible

---

46. Ting-Toomey, *Communicating across Cultures*, 273.
47. Mayers, *Christianity Confronts Culture*, 245.
48. See the Lausanne Covenant for a biblical explanation of this view of culture.
49. Mayers, *Christianity Confronts Culture*, 245.

interpreters of Scripture. It attempts to guard against ethnocentrism, by which we may claim that our culture's norms are in fact biblical values. Adeney, discussing bribery, concludes that

> the person who successfully navigates the shoals of corruption is likely to be someone who is living the right kind of story. The kind of person we are and the way we are oriented to God, to our neighbor, and to our own self-interest will most likely decide for us.[50]

Thompson explores the methods Paul employs to "re-socialize" converts, and the coherence of his teaching.[51] The church in Sri Lanka on the whole has given little attention to this re-socializing. Many in the church have never had their worldview and values challenged. Ethical teaching tends to be in the form of commands to be obeyed, often without application to the ordinary believer's life. Respectability and niceness take the place of transformation. New Testament research showed that cultural norms and values were critiqued by the values of the kingdom. On the one hand, New Testament injunctions to the church uphold certain values that were widespread. They were to act in such a way that outsiders would recognize their goodness (Matt 5:16; 1 Pet 2:12). At least some virtues were shared with the wider community.[52]

Although Paul does not formulate an exhaustive ethical guide, he has a method in his approach. First, Paul calls believers to remember Jesus's own life as a model for behavior as well as a challenge to die to themselves.[53] Second, Paul places the narrative of the believer's life and Jesus's life within the story of Israel, providing a "symbolic world and an identity."[54] "The community's knowledge of 'what is' is the basis for its knowledge of the 'ought.'"[55] They are no longer merely citizens of the Roman Empire but part of the elect of God, his holy people. Third, Paul appeals to the Torah, especially drawing from

---

50. Adeney, *Strange Virtues*, 162.
51. Thompson, *Moral Formation*.
52. Meeks, *Origins of Christian Morality*, 49.
53. Thompson, *Moral Formation*, 207; Rom 6:1–11; 1 Cor 11:17–34; 2 Cor 5:14–15; Rom 15:1–3; 1 Cor 11:1; 2 Cor 8:9; Phil 2:1–11; 3:17.
54. Thompson, *Moral Formation*, 208.
55. Thompson, 208.

Leviticus 17–26.⁵⁶ Although he does not always cite specific laws, they give shape to his teaching. He seems to place special emphasis on sexual ethics and love for neighbor.

Centrality of love

The centrality of love is a distinctive feature of Paul's teaching. This love (Lev 19:18) is no longer limited to one's fellow Israelite. It is now to be extended to the mixed community of the church. "For him love is a familial term."⁵⁷ Love is understood through the sacrificial death of Christ and is the lens through which the law is interpreted.⁵⁸ Thompson states that Paul does not use the term φιλάνθρωπα popular with Greek philosophers but instead uses the concept of φιλαδελφία, which in Greek writings was used for the love of siblings. "Paul envisions the church as a family that provides the emotional support, general welfare, protection, and sacrifice that correspond with the larger society's ideals about the family."⁵⁹

It is interesting that Paul reinforces the ideals for family, which New Testament society held but enlarges the concept of family to include fellow believers. In Sri Lanka too, the ideals of family are mutual love, support, shared honor, and protection from shame. Some of Paul's teaching is common to Greek morality that counted as vices theft, drunkenness, quarrelling, and murder.⁶⁰ Thompson suggests, from Paul's numerous lists of vices and virtues that where society's morality was consistent with the Torah, Paul reinforced society's virtues. But he also strongly urges separation from society's vices.⁶¹

> Letters written to churches created a communal consciousness and a shared ethos that separated the converts from their past and from the society in which they lived. Instructions were not written to isolated individuals, but to those who shared a common story. The vices and virtues called for a united stance of the community towards possessions, sexuality, and their neighbors

---

56. We have already seen in this representative study of the New Testament's ethical teaching how Jesus and Paul draw from Leviticus 19 in Matthew 18 and 1 Corinthians 5.
57. Thompson, *Moral Formation*, 209.
58. Thompson, 180.
59. Thompson, 209.
60. Thompson, 208.
61. Thompson, 211.

and a demarcation between insiders and outsiders. Paul discouraged anti-communal behavior involving strife, jealousy, and division; and encouraged a loving behavior toward the new fictive family.[62]

Meeks states that Paul rarely fixes the norms of Christian lifestyle by laying down rules. While there are rules, most of his writing is "rather general in scope, more suggestive than prescriptive."[63] The most striking aspect of Paul's application of the rules are "the remarkable freedom of his interpretation and the flexibility of the decision apparently required of his readers . . . The impression is one of great fluidity, of a complex, multipolar, open-ended process of mutual discipline."[64] Meeks argues that "moral confidence, not moral certainty, is what we require."[65] That confidence does not come from solitary reflection or philosophical soliloquy, though they have their place. Confidence emerges from healthy communities.[66]

For the church in Sri Lanka, there is a challenge for leaders as well as believers to unite to honor those who embody Christian virtues. What difference might it make in a society where dishonesty, corruption, violence, and even murder can be and often are rewarded by other "in-groups," if the church was to unite behind believers, to encourage them to despise shame, and live by principles of truth, honesty, justice, forgiveness, and other biblical values, in the face of insults or persecution by society. Although the church espouses these values, it is still tempted to honor the rich donor over the poor evangelist; to sympathize with, but think unworldly, the person who loses their job because they will not massage the figures; to forget rather than learn from the faithful disciple whose body is now too weak to allow her to serve. What would happen to the church if honor was heaped on those who embody Christian virtues rather than on those who hold social status or office (though one hopes the groups will not be mutually exclusive).

---

62. Thompson, 211.
63. Meeks, *First Urban Christians*, 139.
64. Meeks, 139.
65. Meeks, *Origins of Christian Morality*, 217.
66. Meeks, 217.

Role of conscience

Building on Meeks' argument for moral confidence, and allowing for mature Christian freedom, the role of the conscience is now considered. Priest suggests that missionaries often fail in their attempts to impress upon people of other cultures a proper understanding of sin, because they fail to understand that their own understanding of sin is culturally conditioned. He suggests that the preaching of sin, repentance, and guilt be done with reference to the hearers' own culturally conditioned but God-given conscience.[67] Dye, writing on cross-cultural mission and the mistakes missionaries make in their preaching on sin, suggests that the church does well to preach first on sins that are already regarded as sin by the culture. In that way, the believer's conscience, which has been culturally shaped (Rom 2:15–16), is pricked, and there is conviction.[68] It is the role of the Holy Spirit to illumine a person's fallen, dulled conscience.

Dye gives an example from a small village in which he was involved in Bible translation. He was working on translating Jesus's list of sins in Mark 7, and the local people gave him the correct term. He then records the conversation below:

> "What did your ancestors tell you about these things?" I asked them.
> "Oh, they told us we shouldn't do any of those things."
> "Do you think these were good standards that your ancestors gave you?" They agreed unanimously that they were.
> "Well, do you keep all these rules?"
> "No," they responded sheepishly.
> One leader said, "Definitely not. Who could ever keep them all? We're people of the ground."[69]

Dye is certain that conversion followed rapidly from the fact that the villagers discovered that what God was revealing was in line with their own conscience. Kraft takes a similar line arguing that God, by the Holy Spirit,

---

67. Priest, "Missionary Elenctics."
68. Dye, "Toward a Cross-Cultural Definition of Sin," 31.
69. Dye, 39.

first leads people to live closer to their own ideals and then in a "second step," guides and empowers them to live up to his ideals.[70]

Wiher states that sin and salvation are conceived of in different ways by different conscience orientations. His results are summarized in table 6.3. The middle column denotes the neutral terms, while left and right columns deal with shame, and guilt conscience orientations, respectively. The columns show the movement of the conscience from bottom to top, which is from a bad to a good conscience, from sin to salvation.

Table 6.3. Soteriological Model of Conscience[71]

Harmony	Salvation	Innocence
Honor	Righteousness	Rightness
Prestige	Blessing	Justice
Glory/Power		Law
Virtue/Pride		
Reconciliation (mediator)	Forgiveness Repentance	Reparation Justification
Shame	Sin	Guilt

Wiher suggests that while the shame-oriented conscience must be understood and affirmed as valid, elements of the guilt-oriented conscience's preferences should be added to balance the shame-guilt axis. So, it is good to set moral standards that should be adhered to, and it is good to affirm the need for reparation.[72] Wiher uses the model of covenant, which brings together both shame and guilt axes. The covenant is relational but is codified in identifiable ways of behaving corresponding to justice. "Righteousness is the behavior that corresponds to covenant community and law."[73] Because it brings together both covenant partners as well as laws, it is "relational and legal, person and object oriented, shame and guilt-oriented."[74]

---

70. Kraft, *Christianity in Culture*, 245.
71. Wiher, *Shame and Guilt*, 402.
72. Wiher, 407.
73. Wiher, 371.
74. Wiher, 371.

Both orientations are necessary, Wiher claims. A shame orientation is necessary for our relationships with one another (and with God) and for our identity formation. On the other hand, a guilt orientation is also necessary to maintain fixed moral standards in society. Therefore, both orientations are necessary and desired by God, in "balance" though "balance" does not mean equilibrium but ". . . a combined shame and guilt-oriented conscience with a tendency towards equilibrium."[75]

We could combine this with Mayers' advice to the cross-cultural missionary. He suggests that there are four questions to be asked:[76]

1. What is the norm (culture)?
2. Is the person living according to the norm?
3. Does the norm need to change?
4. Who is responsible for changing the norm?

Starting with question 1 forces us to understand the reasons why something is done in a particular fashion. Question 3 forces us to engage with Scripture and with our own norms if they differ from the other person's norm. Experience, Scripture, the Holy Spirit, and culture are all involved in the transformation of the norm.

Extreme Reactions

Extreme reactions of violence or, at the other end of the spectrum, suicide, are hardly mentioned in the New Testament church. A notable exception is the story of Judas, who unlike Peter chose that route of escape from his guilt and shame. James speaks of fights and quarrels and even murder (Jas 4:2). Most commentators suggest this is a metaphorical use, but some commentators suggest that the phrase "so you kill" (4:2) refers to believers engaging in actual acts of violence.[77] For Paul, even taking another believer to court is extreme (1 Cor 6). Similarly, in Jesus's own teaching, anger is likened to murder (Matt 5:22; also 1 John 3:15).

Extreme reactions, such as physical violence or at the other extreme suicide, are rare in interpersonal conflict between believers in Sri Lanka. This

---

75. Wiher, 178.
76. Mayers, *Christianity Confronts Culture*, 255–260.
77. Adamson (*Epistle of James*, 168) suggests that *phonneute*, translated "you kill," should actually be *phthoneite* "you are envious" which fits in better with the context.

might suggest that the gospel has impacted that aspect of the cultural tendency in conflictual situations. It is possible that believers recognize that such reactions would not be condoned in the church and shame is working as a positive sanction.[78] However, the New Testament teaching, especially that of the Sermon on the Mount (Matt 5–7) elevates attitudes of the heart and the spoken word to equate them with extreme reactions like murder (Matt 5:21–22).[79] Therefore, the church cannot be complacent about the outward appearance of peace as proof of a reconciled community.

Using Positive Aspects of Shame

There are positive aspects of a shame-oriented culture that can be harnessed for peace-making. Proper shame, "discretionary shame" as Albers calls it, is the sign that a person cares what others think, and that they desire to live up to ideals they have internalized. Christians should care what others think about them. Our lives must cause others to glorify God, even though they might be at enmity with us (Prov 22:1; Matt 5:16; 1 Cor 10:31; 1 Tim 3:7; 5:10; 1 Pet 3:16). A good reputation is expected, especially for those in leadership.[80] A person who feels shame at falling short, desires to be better. Yang says, "Only a shameless person would continue to live in blatant sin."[81] It is only because people care what the community thinks that discipling and discipline will work in a church context.

While shame pushes people apart and sends the shamed one running for cover, shame also longs for reconciliation. Shame suggests the desire for belonging and acceptance by the community. If, therefore, the church community is truly precious to believers, knowing that they have been excluded through their actions will lead the sinner to repentance. If, on the other hand, the community is judgmental and cold, church discipline will be the final straw. Yang holds that "Shame is a powerful psychological tool in the

---

78. There is a widespread belief amongst Christians that suicide is an unforgivable sin.
79. See also 1 John 2:3; 3:15.
80. Wu, "Biblical Theology," 18.
81. Yang, *Discipline or Shame?*, 58.

hands of a loving community. It can be a source of motivation for healing and reconciliation."[82]

A desire to maintain God's honor allows the church to follow a quest that is not self-serving or competitive but selflessly oriented around God's reputation, with a secondary focus on his church.[83] Roberts argues that true repentance goes deeper than repentance for deeds that are done, to repentance for the people we are.[84] Referring to Nathan's confrontation of David, he points out that Nathan did not merely chastise David for the acts of adultery and murder but for an underlying attitude towards God. In 2 Samuel 12:9–10, the Lord's word to David is that David has despised the Lord and his word. This is what has been made known in his actions towards Uriah and Bathsheba.[85]

In feeling shame for sin, we are making space for the Holy Spirit to do a deep work in bringing us to repentance not only of actions and words that are seen by others but of the attitudes and values that have shaped, or perhaps more accurately, warped our personalities and crippled our lives. A conscience sensitive to the Holy Spirit will awaken shame at the thought of sin.

Theological Resources

The church in shame-oriented cultures is often heavily influenced by guilt-oriented theological formulations. It is time to redress the balance by offering theological resources that also speak to the shame-oriented person. One such resource is the presentation of the atonement in terms of Christ as shame-bearer rather than the predominant justification model.[86]

Re-envisioning the Cross

Kraus takes shame into account in his *Jesus Our Lord*. He shows how sin can be explained as defilement, falling short of God's glory (Rom 3:23). "We have disappointed and dishonored God in that we have fallen short of the

---

82. Yang, 59. Yang also remarks on the fact that many honor-shame cultures regularly carry out public discipline in the form of floggings, public expulsion, etc. (Yang, 63).

83. Wu, "Biblical Theology," 18.

84. Roberts, *Repentance*, 113–114.

85. Roberts, 113.

86. Kraus, *Jesus Our Lord*; Tennent, *Theology in Context*; Binau, "Shame and the Human Predicament"; Muller, *Honor and Shame*.

covenant goals which would have fulfilled the divine image."[87] Chapter 3 in the Genesis narrative describes how the fall arouses feelings of shame as well as guilt and fear. However, this is often neglected by theologians. Adam and Eve hide from God and attempt to cover their nakedness. In his shameful death on the cross, Jesus identifies with our shame. The cross restores purity (Col 1:22–23). The love of God which results in the anguish of watching his son become an object of scorn is the anguish of one who has been dishonored, betrayed, and disappointed by those he has created.[88]

Kraus argues that the cross exposes "false shame," which is our society's own identification of shamefulness. This, in Sri Lankan culture, would include such things as physical deformity or disability, mental illness, illegitimacy, low caste, barrenness, widowhood, being the victim of sexual abuse, and so on. Jesus's teaching was that what was shameful was what came out of a person (Mark 7:21–23), the acts that might be hidden from many but not from God.[89] "We might note here that Jesus did not shift the categories from defilement and shame to transgression and guilt but gave to shame an authentic moral content and internalized norm, namely exposure to the eyes of the all-seeing, righteous, loving God."[90]

Binau, tracing the theme of shame in the Bible, points out that shame is often portrayed as the experience of being let down by the ones we trust. It is the exposure of our misplaced trust in promises that were not kept. In response to this confusion and distress, people cry out to God to keep them from being shamed (Ps 119:31; Isa 50:7). God promises to deliver them from shame (Isa 54:4). Shame is then reserved for the enemies of God. Salvation from the consequences of the law, which we experience as shame, is through grace, which is the relationship we have with God, through faith which is the trust we put in someone whose promises will not be broken.[91]

---

87. Kraus, *Jesus Our Lord*, 215.
88. Kraus, 216–217.
89. Kraus, 221.
90. Kraus, 221.
91. Binau, "Shame and the Human Predicament," 138.

Redefining "Honorable" and "Shameful"

What is honorable is defined by each society. Yet all people share certain aspects of "face," a desire for respect and protection of their self-image. Field research also showed how important people's self-image (or sense of identity) was. Thus, what is important is not that the church requires believers to abandon their desire for honor and protection of self-image. Rather, the church needs to re-define what is honorable for its own society and teach believers to seek honor from other sources than the wider culture. They should seek honor from the church and from God.

In his writings, David A. deSilva points out that the early church had a method for preparing believers to stand against the values of their culture. This involved a clear identification of insiders and outsiders, declaring that it is the community of faith whose opinion mattered, and that God was the primary giver of honor.[92] Paul re-defined what was to be considered "honorable" and what was "shameful." Fernando remarks:

> Paul said that sexual sin "must not even be named among you, as is proper among saints" (Eph 5:3 ESV); that filthiness, foolish talk and crude joking was "out of place" (Eph 5:4 ESV); and that "it is shameful even to speak of the things they do in secret" (Eph 5:12 ESV). When rebuking the Corinthians for unholy behavior, he said, "I say this to your shame" (1 Cor 15:34 ESV; see also 2 Thess 3:14). In all these cases Paul was forging community values using honor and shame to foster holiness.[93]

When asked what Bible passages helped them in times of conflict, interviewees responded with values and virtues the Bible espoused: "Blessed are the peacemakers" (Matt 5:9), "Do not let the sun go down on your anger" (Eph 4:26 ESV), and "Be merciful" (Luke 6:36). It is up to Christian leaders, pastors, disciplers, and parents to reinforce these values and challenge aspects of the culture that are contrary to Scripture. They must inculcate in believers the desire for honor arising from virtue. In Corinth, Paul called a man's sexual behavior shameful in a culture where this male privilege did not fall into the categories of honor and shame.[94] Similarly, values of humility, mutual

---

92. deSilva, *Honor, Patronage, Kinship*; *Despising Shame*.
93. Fernando, "Proclaiming the Gospel."
94. Witherington, *Conflict and Community*, 154.

submission, truth telling, and holiness must become part of the character, or as Wu puts it, "the DNA" of the church family.[95]

The researcher's interviews revealed that Sri Lankan men will probably find this harder to accept. In many walks of life honor is given to those whose character is not virtuous. There is a lack of good role models. The Sri Lankan church has a tendency to value titles and position, efficiency, and giftedness rather than a good character. In choosing leaders, it often seeks to elevate to leadership people with influence, entrepreneurial skills, and charisma rather than those with a proven track record of faithful discipleship and growing maturity.

Recommendations for Further Study

This study is a preliminary research into urban Sri Lankan church culture. It was limited in scope in that it only addressed one subculture within the nation. "Sri Lankan" culture is not monolithic. Further research could target various sub-groups such as Tamils affected by the war in the north, urban youth, or a village community. Differences could also emerge from gender-specific research. This study was also limited by the use of English language literature and participants whose first language is English. Further research could probe the differences between these findings and those from using resources in the vernacular.

Other fields of study that the researcher suggests would be:

- Research into the implications of a shame-oriented culture for national reconciliation. The process of national reconciliation has been fraught with failure, disappointment, and inconsistencies.[96] An analysis on the process from a shame-oriented culture lens could aid national reconciliation movements.
- The presentation of the gospel for a shame-oriented audience. Further biblical and theological study could present a more indigenous gospel presentation for a collectivistic shame-oriented culture.

---

95. Wu, "Biblical Theology," 25.

96. One notable example is the Lessons Learnt and Reconciliation Commission which was found to have intimidated witnesses and brought little closure to victims, unlike its South African counterpart.

- Teaching material for various levels of Christian education to propagate the recommendations of this study. Some attention is now being given to Sunday school curricula but on the whole the church does not have a systematic approach to Christian education for its members. Curricula for Bible study groups, youth groups, and adult Sunday schools would allow for the systematic education of the church in peace making.
- A culture-specific model for mediation could be studied. Case studies and interviews revealed that mediation paves the way for conflicting parties to move towards direct communication. Several models exist for mediation. Further study could propose a model that is effective in shame-oriented cultures.

Conclusion

This study began by considering the consequences to the church of broken relationships between its members. Perhaps we should not be surprised that the answer to the problem in the church lies with the church and primarily with its leaders and teachers. If we have confidence in the power of the gospel and the Holy Spirit to redeem cultures and to transform lives, then it is time for the leadership of the church to take the bold, and somewhat unpopular step, to address unresolved conflict in the church as an intolerable slur on the character of God.

The research has shown that shame-oriented cultures contain elements that impact conflict resolution. Believers need to be re-socialized to develop a biblical worldview that challenges cultural norms. Since conversion of the worldview occurs in the realm of cognitive, affective, and behavioral, change must be brought about in all these arenas. Material that helps believers understand their cultural tendencies and that offers help and hope should permeate the church's education system and pastoral care. The values of the church will then include reconciliation, and holiness, both of which bring honor to the church but also to God. Systems for discipling and for disciplining church members should be laid down with sensitivity and consistency. Honor should be attached to virtue and removed from mere status. Leaders in the church bear the biggest responsibility to teach and to lead by example.

APPENDIX A

Integrated Basic Values Model

Guilt Orientation	Shame Orientation
The person tries to be right, to be found innocent	The person seeks harmony, honor, prestige, glory/power, virtue/pride
Feels guilt after specific act of failure. "My act was bad"	Feels shame about self, after transgression is discovered. "I am bad"
Specific failure	Global failure
Peace is restored after fault is repaired through restitution	Peace is restored when harmony and honor are experienced by the group
Individualism/Individual identity	Collectivism/corporate identity
High level of independence, self-sufficiency, initiative	Interdependence, conformity, regard for the group
Identity is as self perceives it	Identity is as group perceives it
Security through feeling right in regard to rules and standards	Security through right relationships and acceptance
Personal achievement more importance than attention to community	Good human relations a priority, personal achievements sacrificed for group interaction
Direct communication	Indirect communication
Honesty, frankness, incorruptibility, steadfastness, perseverance (may be seen as rude by shamed)	Modesty, compliance, pliability, willingness to compromise (may be seen as dishonest)

Guilt Orientation	Shame Orientation
Competition and confrontation, self-critical in order to achieve greater heights	Cooperation, co-existence, will sacrifice to rise in the ranks
Time oriented	Event oriented
Concern for punctuality, deadlines, efficiency	Concern for event, laid back attitude to deadlines
Achievement focus	Status focus
Prestige is attained	Prestige is ascribed
Identity comes from personal achievements, knowledge, possessions	Identity is based on formal credentials like age, birth, rank, title
Respect depends on one's achievements as well as failures	Amount of respect is fixed; attention given to those of high status regardless of personal failings
The individual is extremely self-critical and will make sacrifices and changes to accomplish more	The individual is given a role to play and will sacrifice in order to gain status or higher rank
People associate with those of equal status	People associate with others of like status
Equal rights and opportunities for all (egalitarian)	One's rights and opportunities are based on one's status (hierarchical)
Analytical thinking (dichotomizing)	Synthetic thinking (holistic)
Judgments are black and white / right or wrong according to specific criteria	Judgments are open-ended. The whole person and all circumstances are considered
Either/or	And/and
Reductionist, fragmented knowledge: specific criteria are uniformly applied and specific aspects evaluated in others	Holistic, integral, totality knowledge: the whole person and all circumstances are taken into consideration
Willingness to lose face	Fear of losing face
Relative unconcern about mistakes and failure	Protection of image at all costs. Avoidance of error and failure

Guilt Orientation	Shame Orientation
Openness to alternative views and to criticism	Refusal to accept alternative views or criticism. Criticism is seen as personal attack
Openness about personal life	Vagueness about personal life
Willing to admit faults, weaknesses	Denial of culpability, hides weaknesses and shortcomings by withdrawing
Truthfulness is more important than harmony of relationships	Harmony in relationships is more important than truthfulness

Source: Lingenfelter and Mayers (*Ministering Cross-Culturally*, 156–177) and Wiher (*Shame and Guilt*, 428).

APPENDIX B

Interview Protocol

Questionnaire – Part 1

The anatomy of a conflict

What, in your experience, are the most frequent causes of conflict among believers?

What are key contributors to the *prolonging* of conflict among believers? (Style of communication? Motives? Fear of losing face?)

How does the offended party react? (words, actions, emotions, effect on those around, confidantes)

How does the offender react?

What discrepancy is there between what parties say they believe they should do and what they really do?

If someone is sorry for what they have done, how will they show it? (Will it be through some action or through words?) What will they expect of the person they have offended?

Are people typically ready to forgive? What is their understanding of forgiveness?

How does reconciliation come about? (How do people show they are repentant and seek reconciliation? Who takes the initiative? Is there a mediator?)

The contribution of the church

In what way does the church help people find their way from conflict to resolution? (How do they deal with offenders? Offended? Is there a process of church discipline? What biblical teaching do they offer?)

What Bible passages if any do you find most helpful in dealing with conflicting parties?

Case study

Can you share two case studies which illustrate what you have said in questions 1–8?

Specific cultural attributes that affect conflict

In the Sinhala /Tamil culture, what terms are used for "shame" and "honor"?

Describe what you understand by *ladja baya*

Give a secular example of this at play

APPENDIX C

Table of Characteristics

Questionnaire – Part 2

To what extent do you see these features at play in conflict situations? Using the guide below, insert a number in each column.

1: Not at all descriptive
2–3: Rare
4: Somewhat descriptive
5–6: Quite common
7: Very descriptive

Rating Grid

Cultural Attribute	Symptoms	Church	Secular
Indirect communication	Will not express feelings especially to someone of a different status. Tells others rather than going to people concerned		
Harmony in relationships is more important than truthfulness	Will say everything is okay when it is not. May lie to preserve harmony or honor		
Vagueness about personal life	Reserved about sharing feelings, motives		

Cultural Attribute	Symptoms	Church	Secular
Relative morality (Values)			
Group values are internalized. They are relational not intrinsic	An unbiblical response may be seen as right because significant others endorse it. (Internalization of biblical values that are at odds with family/society is difficult)		
Confession is seen as self-shaming	Does not like to admit to fault	·	
Limitation of good will to own circle	No necessity to treat those not from kin group with same integrity as kin group		
Modesty, compliance, pliability, willingness to compromise	Honesty, frankness may be laid aside for harmony's sake and may come across as dishonest		
Limited good. Honor is seen as limited and to be gained at another's expense	Envy, competitiveness, backstabbing		
Holistic, integral, totality knowledge: the whole person and all circumstances are taken into consideration[1]	Gives impression of lack of consistency in discipline		
Face saving techniques			
Protection of image at all costs. Avoidance of error and failure	Wanting to keep others from finding out, not wanting to ask for help		
Refusal to accept alternative views or criticism	Criticism is seen as personal attack		

---

1. Wiher, *Shame and Guilt*, 290, 430.

Table of Characteristics

Cultural Attribute	Symptoms	Church	Secular
Offer of repentance must be met by restoration of honor	Idea of offering restitution or being penalized (e.g. not allowed to be treasurer after incident of stealing) is construed as lack of forgiveness		
Denial of culpability, hide weaknesses/shortcomings by withdrawing	Denial, passive-aggressive behavior		
Motivation			
Desire for honor, power, harmony	Spirals of vengeance to regain lost honor or to shame adversary		
Identity formation			
Interdependence, conformity, regard for the group. Security through right relationships and acceptance	Raising issues of a potentially conflictual situation may be seen as disloyal. May choose to stay silent to keep the peace		
Identity is as group perceives it	May choose what is accepted over what is biblically prescribed		
Identity based on formal credentials like age, birth, rank, title. One's rights and opportunities are based on one's status (hierarchical)	Cannot question someone senior. May be ignored or silenced if attempt is made		
High power distance			
Amount of respect is fixed; attention given to those of high status regardless of personal failings	Cannot question someone senior in age, position		
Those from non-kin group are a threat	No necessity to show the same honor to outsiders or those of less status		

APPENDIX D

Case Summaries Compared

Comparison of Cases by Elements

CASES	**Amal and David**	**Youth Ministry**
Case Number	C1CODaAm	C2COYo
Parties involved	Two males	Two organizational "communities"
Relationship	Patron-client	Volunteers and leaders
Location	Christian organization	Christian Organization
Conflict cause	What was owed to a client by his patron. Identity affected	Change in organizational structure: Identity issues
Goal	Amal: substantive issues, restoration of honor, vengeance. David: substantive issues	Relational
Style of communication	Amal: Indirect David: direct	Indirect changes to direct.
Conflict Management style	Amal: Confront David: confront	collaborative

Gihan and Suraj	Ramona	Malini and Samanthi	Harin and Joseph
C3CHGiSu	C4ChRam	C5ChMaSa	C6ChHaJo
Two males	Female church member and church	Two females	Two male church leaders
equal status friends	Church member and leaders	Equal status friends	Unequal status leadership
Church	Church	Church	Church
Challenge to leadership Leadership undermined. Identity issues	Unfair dismissal.	Criticism of Samanthi's parenting skills. Identity as parent undermined	Criticism of leader's project. Challenge to leadership
Suraj: honor restored, acquisition of prestige Gihan: vindication, relationship	Ramona: substantial Church leaders: substantial	Samanthi: avoidance. Maintain status quo. Malini: unaware Third parties: reconciliation	Appearance of harmony
Indirect becomes direct after third-party intervention	Direct	Indirect	Indirect
Initially: avoidance until mediation	Confront	Avoidance	Avoidance

CASES	**Amal and David**	**Youth Ministry**
Third-party involvement	Taking sides. Fueling Amal's anger	Incites and undermines
Relative Morality	Deception Corruption Envy Pride. Slander	Ethnic tension, suspicion of other
Face saving techniques	Criticism of other; Refusal to acknowledge wrong	
Extreme reactions	Amal: Rage, vengeance: litigation	None
Status/power distance	High power distance	High power distance reduced by organizational ethos

Case Summaries Compared

Gihan and Suraj	**Ramona**	**Malini and Samanthi**	**Harin and Joseph**
Ignore, avoid, gossip, take sides	Yamuna attempts to mediate	Friends appealed for help from pastor	No intervention
Gossip, Deception Envy	Vilifying "opposition"	None	Pride
	Pastor sends message rather than speak directly to Ramona. One year later, leaders refuse to change their position		Refusal to acknowledge wrong
Suraj: Anger	None	None	None
Low power distance. Peers. Perceived difference due to official position in church	High power distance between Ramona and the church leaders	Low power distance	Low power distance

APPENDIX E

Case Studies

Grid for case studies:

1. Goal of Conflict Resolution
2. Identity of self and other
3. Style of communication
4. Conflict resolution style
5. Status orientation
6. Relativistic morality
7. Extreme reactions

Case Study 1: C1CODaAm

David met Amal while Amal was a seminary student. David was sympathetic to Amal who had gone through several stormy relationships with people and institutions and even his church. Over the years a relationship developed with David taking a keen interest in Amal's ministry, advising and financially supporting him. Although Amal had a history of poor working relationships with others, he worked well with David. Seeing his progress, David felt that people did not really understand Amal, and was sorry for him.

David was recruited to a leadership position in a Christian organization. His department was looking for some volunteer help and he suggested Amal as one of the candidates for this work. Amal received a monthly allowance for his work. Amal did not get on with others in the department. He was often belligerent, and wanted his own way. Occasionally when he was refused something by the staff, he would go over their heads to David. David, not knowing he had already been refused would give him permission. Amal took great delight in going back to the department and telling them how David had agreed with him.

The administrator of the department was leaving and David suggested that a young man who he had known for some time, apply for the post. This young man, Luke, had had his share of problems and was a rather diffident, quiet man, but he had been mentored by David and had shown potential. He was interviewed, and was given the post. About a year before this, the organization had decided that it could no longer pay its volunteers the monthly allowance and would only pay for work that was completed. David, knowing that Amal was in need of financial assistance, privately continued to support him financially. After some time, the department decided to ask all the volunteers to report on their progress. Luke, in his new capacity as administrator, sent out a letter to all the volunteers requesting this information, including asking for a list of any assets of the organization held by them. It was during these months that David was especially busy and was less available to Amal. He was also becoming stricter with Amal having noticed certain attitudes and traits he felt should change.

When Amal received the letter, he was very angry. He felt that Luke had no right to ask him for such information. David then heard from the governing board members that they had received letters and calls from Amal. David was shown the letter by one of the members of the Board.

In the letters, Amal criticized the way the department was being managed by David. He also challenged the recruitment procedure of the organization, the correctness of Luke writing to him and so on. He also complained that the position Luke held had not been advertised and that he, Amal, had not been informed when the Department Administrator had left. He also subsequently rang several of the senior staff and David's own supervisor to protest and make allegations against David. He also communicated with several of the other volunteers asking them to support him. If anyone seemed sympathetic or agreed with him on anything, Amal immediately quoted them to others. He also recorded their telephone calls.

When David realized the extent to which Amal had gone with his grievances, he called him to meet. He cautioned Amal about his behavior and reminded him of previous conflicts he had had with others. In response Amal criticized the organization and then began to launch personal insults against David. David was appalled and immediately told Amal that since he was behaving in this fashion towards the organization of which David was a leader, David could no longer support him in his private capacity as a friend. He told Amal that the financial support he had extended would be stopped with immediate effect. Amal left and as he was going, he saw Luke and a young lady from the same department laughing. Amal later told David that he knew they were laughing at him.

From the conversations Amal had with the people he called, it transpired that he felt he should have been told that the administrator had left. He felt that Luke had been appointed purely because of David's influence. He insisted that the job should have been advertised. He felt that Luke was unqualified for the post.

In his conversations, he also mentioned several internal matters that he could not have known about unless he had an insider passing on this information. It transpired that the administrator who had been asked to leave had been very friendly with Amal. In fact, he too was found to be spreading rumors about various members of the department, although he had always declared himself to be loyal to the organization and grateful for what he had received. He also had been in some trouble and the organization had offered him a job in spite of that.

Subsequently David called for a meeting where two of the management staff and Amal met along with David to ascertain what Amal's grievances were against the organization. In that meeting Amal made many allegations and demanded that the organization pay him monies that had already been paid. Amal continued to call people in the organization to voice his grievances. Many people who spoke to him were convinced by what he said and some approached David and tried to bring resolution to the problem. When the leadership of the organization did not take his side, Amal sought legal advice and sued the organization for nonpayment of services. The leaders including David were forced to attend various hearings at which it seemed obvious, some influence had been exerted by Amal on the officials. Although there was no basis for his law suit and the evidence he produced was either ambiguous or in one case a forgery, the officials accepted his case as valid and preliminary hearings went in his favor.

While this was going on, the organization made its own case for the returning of various assets held by Amal on behalf of the organization which he was then forced to hand over after much argument. Another charge was made against the organization for a minor infringement of the law of which they were not aware. The complaint was made anonymously and officials followed up only when the caller had made threats against the officials that they would be reported to their superiors if they did not follow up on the tip.

The court case drags on and Amal continues to make various attempts to contact David who has not taken his calls. David now feels that Amal was manipulative from the beginning of their relationship.

Analysis

Goal

In this case, Amal does not seek a relational rather than substantive goal. Although David starts off by attempting to maintain relationships, he too eventually opts for the substantive settlement over the relational. Amal wants to receive money in compensation for the loss of honor he feels at losing his connection with the organization. David wants to be vindicated by the legal processes.

Identity of self and other

Perhaps tied in with the previous observation, Amal does not seem to have the typical sensitivity to the needs and opinions of his closest "in-groups," his family, church or fellow workers. Why is this?

Amal has a history of falling out with those in authority, in church, school, government. The roots of this type of behavior probably lie with events in his past we do not know about. However, he found in David someone who was willing to give him the benefit of the doubt and give him a chance to start over. We see signs that Amal felt a measure of honor that was his because of his relationship with David. He delighted in showing the other staff members that he was close to David. David was his "patron." However, when that relationship broke down, Amal seems to have had nowhere else he "belonged." As research shows, sometimes we hate the one who has found us out. David has become part of the "out-group" to whom Amal no longer owes anything.

Throughout this episode, it did not seem that Amal had strong relationships with a church community, even though he held a leadership position in one. This appears to be a case in which Amal, although exhibiting shame culture characteristics, is also individualistic, acting against all the groups with which he is associated. This is unusual and could reflect the fact that the gospel brings a disjunction in the way people perceive their identity (God and I, rather than we). Instead of relying on what the group thinks, Amal acts against cultural norms of respect and honor for patrons (David) and leaders (the organization, his family). David acts with the backing of his organization and seems to be closely connected to the members of the board and leadership.

Mode of communication/conflict management style

In this study we see different styles of communication and conflict management within the same organization. Amal interprets David's actions as being a betrayal of the solidarity between patron and client.

Amal receives a letter that offends him. He does not go to David with it. It is quite possible that he attributes motives and actions to David and Luke that were imaginary, such as that David was losing interest in him, or that Luke was deliberately trying to demonstrate the new powers he had. So, Amal goes to members of the board, going over David's head. It is a way to flaunt his own power and show that he is capable of finding patrons from a higher status than David.

Luke does not get involved in the conflict, although it is his letter that has triggered the final severing of relationships between David and Amal. He shows the avoidance style of conflict management.

David on the other hand, is more direct. He uses the confrontational method of conflict management. Seeing that Amal is using tactics that he does not approve of, he sets out what is right and wrong in the situation as he sees it and stops the monetary aid to Amal.

Status orientation

Although the relationship between David and Amal has been close, there is a power distance between them. Amal in turn shows a desire for status. He achieves some of that through his relationship with David. Later, he is angered that someone of lesser status than he (only a driver), without his education has been given a permanent role in the organization when he has not.

The relationship between David and Amal is complex. They are not of equal status. David is Amal's patron, in which capacity, he is expected to provide resources, and support to Amal in his ministry. But when Amal becomes a volunteer for the organization, David also in a sense becomes a supervisor. Obviously, what Amal expected of the relationships is not the same as David's expectations. David and Amal are not equal in status but David is expected to see himself as being in an interdependent relationship with Amal. If Amal is expecting this from David, he is expecting to be treated as a member of a family, that David would treat him with special favor and not just the same as everyone else. He would expect David to protect his honor in a conflict with other employees.

Relative morality

In this episode, Amal frequently bent the truth to suit his case. He was willing to engage in behavior that he would have known was contrary to the teaching he had received at seminary. He was also a leader in a church and did not at any time feel that he had compromised his position as a pastoral worker. When he did not get the satisfaction he wanted from the courts, he took his revenge by attempting to get David into trouble with his employer and the law.

What are we to make of the fact that Amal, in spite of his theological training and leadership position in the church, resorts to lies and to taking revenge by attempting to sabotage David's position in the organization and the organization itself?

Hiebert explains conversion in terms of the transformation of the three dimensions of culture: cognitive (beliefs), affective (feelings) and evaluative (norms).[1] While in churches and seminaries we have traditionally laid most emphasis on beliefs, the transformation must be at the level of worldview, those hidden, unexamined, and unconditionally accepted assumptions that make sense of the world. In spite of the intentions of the church, seminary, and mentoring relationships, it appears that Amal's conversion has not extended to the evaluative aspect of culture.

Fear of losing face

In all the interactions in this case, Amal was trying to protect his image and interests. We do not see in Amal's case a desire to save face for others as is typical in collectivistic cultures. We see face saving techniques that serve Amal's

---

1. Hiebert, *Transforming Worldviews*, 312.

interests and keep him from taking responsibility for his actions, and showing repentance, such as transference of blame, envy, manipulation and rage.

Amal is more shamed by the fact that the person who has got the job he wanted is "lower" than him in status. His shame at being laughed at (so he thought) by others whom he considers lower than him in status, probably triggers the rage response.

Extreme reactions

In this case Amal shows an extreme shame-rage spiral. It causes him to act against cultural and church norms that operate in stable conditions. He takes the step of going to litigation, even using lies and bribes to pervert justice, or in his eyes, ensure justice.

We see the rage he felt at being laughed at, especially by someone he felt was less worthy of honor than he was. He was making sure he was protected if at any time his financial support stopped. Perhaps partly because of what had been done to him in the past but also because of his own mode of operation, he did not trust others.

New discoveries

At the foundation of the relationship there is low trust. Loyalty is expected but betrayal is common. We see two opposing conflict and communication styles, indirect (Amal) and direct (David).

Case Study 2: C2COYo

In a Christian youth ministry organization, a decision was made to change the structure of the organization from a language based to a regional based ministry. The committee that discussed the changes was composed of young members and senior ones, full time and volunteer. Every attempt was made to have a wide representation. Even so, when this was communicated to the organization, there was a lot of opposition. The communication from leaders to the others was not done well – cliques formed, there was anger. Because of the cultural differences between the language groups, each language ministry was different from the other. Each had a unique style and structure, which they felt suited them. Now for the first time, there would be a mix of languages in each regional ministry. Some people who had been used to having a lot of power in their own ministry structure would now have to adjust to a new system. There would be loss of power. The dissatisfaction was communicated to the leader. It was decided that the organization would hold a camp in which the plan would be presented.

At first there were teaching sessions on Acts 6 and 15 where the church discussed issues, made concessions and moved forward together, but it was sensed that this also was not enough. The leadership decided to allow everyone concerned to voice their opinion. People got into groups and discussed the issues. Deep-seated hurts and prejudices came out. Sinhala youth asked the question "Why do the Tamil youth support India when there is a cricket match between Sri Lanka and India?" Tamil youth were able to answer, and share their feeling of anger and pain that they were made to feel they did not belong in Sri Lanka. One youth shared with the others how badly he had been treated at the police check points, even being slapped when he had questioned the officers.

God came down on the gathered crowd in a powerful way. One young man spoke of how this was a special moment for the organization just as there had been moments like this in history and urged the others to make a commitment to move on from this point. The move of the Spirit was evident as people held hands, prayed and worshipped together.

This shows again the importance of talking and also listening. This was also shown by the fact that those who had not been part of this continuous dialogue were unable to come on board and were sometimes a negative influence.

The plan was launched after about a year of preparation. There were some who moved out but now after almost a year, the positive results are slowly emerging. The success of the project was based on volunteers being able to discuss and debate until they felt ownership of the changes and feel part of the decision-making process. Structural change is slow because people work by consensus. The lengthy process may have been seen as slow and bungling but the result was that most volunteers stayed.

We need to offer people generous justice. The Bible doesn't look at justice the Western way (blindfold and scales). The weak are always given concessions (e.g. give the poor their wages daily). When people leave us in anger, disciplined etc., we work on their behalf, look for jobs for them, and pay their salary until they find their feet. Not bending the rules but going beyond the rules. They are still family and must be treated as such. Sometimes, you may have to ask a person to leave their job because they have done something that makes it impossible to stay, but still look after them.

The bottom line is don't put people to shame. Treat the one offending you as vulnerable.

Question: Isn't grace offered at someone else' expense?

Answer: It cannot be offered so as to insult the victim. But the price can be paid by you.

Don't take seriously the ranting of angry people. Absorb it and minister to them.

Analysis
Goal

In this case, it appears that the conflict was the result of a change in the organizational structure. Lack of proper communication led to the forming of factions and the underlying feelings of anger, confusion, and hurt. There was also the threat of loss of power, the movement of people from their comfort zones into close relationships with those from whom they might have preferred to be distant. However, as time goes on, we see that the real cause of the conflict is deep-seated feelings, questions, and prejudices that have never been aired.

Identity of self and other

The issue of identity seems to loom large in this case, although here it is to do with ethnic identity rather than with status or power, though there is an element of that too. It reflects the larger problem in the country that a long running conflict has been running along ethnic lines. This issue is seldom brought up in the church, on the mistaken belief that Christians are somehow exempt from the effects of the conflict. Generally speaking, people associate in their ethnic groups to discuss the ethnic conflict deeply. They seldom share their own feelings and perspectives with members of the other ethnic group. When amongst people of a different ethnic group, one would stay silent because at the very least, the other person cannot understand what they are going through. The decision to change the structure of the organization along regional lines would break up the close community, within the language groups. Perhaps there has been some competitiveness between the groups, there is fear of losing one's identity in a mixed group.

Mode of communication

Unusually in this case, although there seems to have been a degree of unhappiness that was talked about within cliques, communication becomes direct, due to the sensitivity of the leadership. We see though, that it was the method of communication that initially caused the conflict. What was supposed to be a management decision on structure as far as the leadership was concerned was perceived by the organization as a family matter that should have been communicated more personally and with greater opportunity for input.

Conflict management style

Although there was a representative cross section at the meetings where changes were discussed it is possible that not everyone was able to speak what was on their mind. In cultures like Sri Lanka, people might fear to speak up because they might appear to be trouble makers, jeopardize their position by disagreeing with powerful leaders or make their leaders look small. We do not have sufficient evidence to state categorically that this happened, but it might have contributed to it. Although it is probable that many people who did not want the change spoke to other like-minded staff rather than the leaders, the general dissatisfaction was communicated to the leaders. The leaders did not take advantage of their positional authority to force the change on the people. This is the only case study in which a deliberate attempt was made to study Scripture together and pray together over the way forward.

The case shows that the causes of the conflict were a complex mixture of issues of identity, insecurity, and prejudice which had been buried until this disruption unearthed it.

Status focus/high power distance

The organization seems to have empowered the mostly young people in the organization to be able to speak openly about their feelings and even to disagree with decisions their leaders have made. As the interviewee said

> Although we are traditionally a hierarchical society, young people don't respond to that any more. For example in the Korean

church many young people are leaving in reaction to the rigid hierarchical structure (may be to do with globalization). But people, including pastors are looking for spiritual "fathers," for elders with the wisdom and care to help them move forward.

Relative morality

The interviewee stated that the organization places a high value of Christian virtues like truth telling; it also ensures its members are in close fellowship with small groups in which they are disciple. These values seem to have made an impact on the way the community reacted.

Extreme reactions

None.

New discoveries

This case study shows some differences from the others studied. It reflects an organizational culture that has a system of values that challenges the wider cultural norms. There is wide representation at the decision-making level. The goal is relational. Although the decision-making group has made its decision and does not reverse it, the decision is not implemented until it is explained, studied in the light of Scripture, and the body of believers moves together. Not everyone moves, but perhaps it is significant that those who were not part of the process and only heard of it from others often chose to leave. Since the level of consensus and commitment was high, those who attempted to make trouble did not succeed.

Case Study 3: C3ChGiSu

Gihan and Suraj have been friends since they were young men and are both respected leaders in their church. For some time, it had become apparent that Suraj was finding his many responsibilities stressful. He had become short tempered with various people in the church and there was more than one person who had been hurt by or was angry with the way they had been treated by Suraj. Many people knew about the various incidents but no one spoke to Suraj about it. Eventually, Gihan attempted to make Suraj aware that he was hurting his relationships in the church but Suraj would not listen. He was very committed to his ministry, was very protective of his own ministry team and took great care of them and was generally a very caring and diligent worker for the Lord. His family were also involved in his ministry and well known in the church.

Things came to a head when some of Suraj's team, in their dissatisfaction with the ministry's general direction, and feeling that Suraj had ignored their feelings in the past, asked the committee that headed the ministry, to make changes. Gihan who was in the leadership of that committee was the first to know about it. The team members asked him to meet with Suraj and the team and try to mediate. Suraj was hurt and very angry. He confronted the team members and accused them of betraying his friendship, and destroying his leadership. He called them up individually and said their behavior was un-christian. When the team asked Suraj to meet with them to respond to their concerns and voice his own, Suraj refused and resigned from the team.

Suraj also blamed Gihan for what had happened, believing that Gihan had known and approved of the team's decision to complain about the way the ministry was going. He did not tell Gihan that he was angry about his involvement in this incident or that he blamed him. However, his attitude to Gihan became hostile. Suraj and Gihan served on other committees together. An occasion arose when a committee in which they both served was divided on how to tackle a difficult situation in the church. Suraj sided with those who disagreed with Gihan. Thereafter, Suraj constantly challenged Gihan, questioned his loyalty to the committee, went against the committee's decisions, and generally made Gihan feel he was being constantly undermined. Every action was justified since it was being done for the good of the church. Eventually in a telephone call, Suraj let slip his grievance that Gihan had not supported him when he was being challenged by his team.

While this was going on, both families were also drawn into the conflict. Though spouses and children had been friends for years, now their relationship was strained. Friends had to choose sides. It became clear that some of Suraj's friends were now thinking negatively about the church. Suraj would often say things like "everyone is saying that . . ." and end up with a negative remark about the church. Eventually Gihan decided to ask a mutual friend to be a mediator. This friend, Yohan, undertook to initiate some meetings between Gihan and Suraj. Eventually, after prolonged conversation, Suraj revealed that he had believed Gihan to be instrumental in his initial problems with his team. Gihan was able to explain clearly that he was only responding to the team's request for help rather than being personally involved.

After this was openly discussed, the relationship between Gihan and Suraj has improved. However, Suraj still continues to criticize the team he left and although active in church leadership through various committees, attends church services more infrequently, and has begun to attend other churches. He maintains a relationship with the team he once led. He talks to them, is openly friendly, but has not forgiven them.

Analysis
Goal

In the first instance, when Suraj is obviously showing signs of stress and causing rifts in relationships, no one speaks to him about it. Many people know about it but though they speak to one another about it, the desire for the appearance of harmony, and the fact that Suraj is likely to refuse to listen and lose his temper, leaves people in the church talking behind Suraj's back, and using the avoidance style of conflict management. Everybody avoids the issue, and hopes that the various contentious issues and damaged relationships will heal themselves. If the step had been taken to get involved at this stage, perhaps the greater conflict could have been mitigated somewhat. The majority of the church seem to prefer a relational rather than substantive goal. However, the relationships remain at a surface level and it is the appearance of harmony and closeness that seems more important than depth and actual fellowship.

In this case, there is an unusual element in that although the relationship between Suraj and Gihan is a long standing one, Suraj in particular has shown no signs of wanting the relationship to be restored to the way it was. However, it is my belief that Suraj's norm or value is the relational goal. He assumes that whatever conflict arises, there will be protection for the honor of all. However, when he is shamed, his reaction is extreme. Suraj does expect the conflict process to be appropriate, to be satisfactory, not just the outcome. To him, the way the conflict has been handled is not appropriate. The actions of the team seem to him disloyal and done with evil intent. While he was prepared to support his team, his "in-group," and protect them against any attacks from outside the team, he expected a similar loyalty from them. Their behavior shames him as a leader and he will not accept that any blame is his. The effect of being shamed is described as "betrayal," "unworthy of Christians." He finds in Gihan a scapegoat. Gihan as Suraj's friend was supposed to support and defend him whatever the charges against him.

It raises the question of how loyalty is demonstrated in this culture. On the one hand, Suraj expects total loyalty from a friend, indicating high expectations of friendship. However, when he is betrayed, as he perceives it, he makes no effort to restore the friendship, to question his assumptions or take any blame.

Gihan and the team, both show a desire for the substantive elements of the conflict to be dealt with. Suraj expects the status of leader to protect him from the attacks that he perceives have come on him.

Identity of self and other

We saw that in collectivistic culture, the needs of the group and the honor of the group are of paramount importance in construction of the self. Here we see that the families of the conflicting parties are also drawn into taking sides, as are close friends. It seems clear that family and friends are one's closest kin-groups. There does not seem to be an overwhelming feeling that others in the church are also to be regarded as family.

It would seem that the cause of the conflict between Suraj and Gihan is brought to a head when Suraj is shamed by the actions of his group. The group's actions are unusual in that they have challenged the leadership of the team, rather than avoiding and complying with what has been asked of them. Suraj is not prepared to accept any criticism. Criticism of his actions is taken as a personal attack.

Mode of communication/conflict management style

In this case, we see indirect communication in the following

(i) The fact that Suraj is acting in a manner that is detrimental to his relationships for some time while no one in the church advices him, or offers pastoral support to discover if there are any ways in which his ministry burdens could be eased, for example.

(ii) The fact that Suraj does not openly tell Gihan that he believes Gihan has been the instigator of a move against him in his ministry and that he is angry or hurt by it. Instead, Suraj vents his anger by allowing it to surface in other areas where it seems reasonable, for example by disagreeing with whatever suggestions Gihan makes in other committees. We also see the familiar pattern of friends and family having to choose where their loyalties will lie.

Although people are aware that something is wrong, they do nothing, other than taking sides. Gihan has to ask for a mediator. However, the process of talking together does allow Suraj to admit what he has secretly believed, that Gihan betrayed his friendship.

Status focus/high power distance

One of the factors that has possibly kept people from approaching Suraj earlier on could be the fact that he is a leader in the church. Certainly, it seems that Suraj desires the status of leader and is shamed by the fact that his leadership in the ministry is challenged. It is perhaps unexpected. While in some churches and ministries in Sri Lanka there might be a high power distance between Suraj and his team, in this particular church, all the people involved seem to consider themselves peers.

Relative morality

There are aspects of behavior that are cultural rather than biblical that are not addressed. It is possible that an element of competitiveness, even envy, is driving a wedge between what was once a strong friendship. Suraj and Gihan are both leaders. Gihan is in effect agreeing with those who are challenging Suraj's leadership and questioning his actions. Anger, gossip, and scapegoating are all seen in this case.

Extreme reactions

In this case extreme shame reactions seem very clear. Suraj, when met with opposition, as he sees it, flares up and speaks critically of those he sees as the cause of his shame to his friends, though he refuses to meet with the team and hear their concerns. Since they have used a process that is unsuited to a shame-oriented personality, Suraj cannot accept their cause as valid.

New discoveries

The participants in this case tend to be unusual in their behavior from the typical model. The team members of the ministry who ask for change are unusual in bringing the matter out in a way that potentially causes a loss of face for Suraj. While this seems the way that an individualistic culture would advocate, being open and honest, the process has not protected Suraj's face. Suraj is the most shame-oriented personality in this case. It is the shame of being exposed as lacking in his leadership that provokes shame and rage, as well as passive-aggressive behavior, in undermining Gihan at every opportunity.

Cultural sins that need to be addressed by the church are gossip, lack of love (shown in watching relationships deteriorate and doing nothing), and the avoidance style which allowed leaders, including Gihan, to allow Suraj to continue in his destructive behavior. Virtues to be cultivated are humility in leadership, an attitude of stewardship in ministry that allows a person to separate their identity from their ministry, and speaking the truth in love, which seeks to uphold the honor of all. The necessity for a ministry of mediation is also demonstrated in this case. In addition to that, an awareness that those who are most closely involved in ministry are very likely to be in conflict with others, perhaps purely out of a passion for the furtherance of the kingdom, needs to be recognized. This recognition should lead to viewing conflict as a necessary and potentially healthy way of growing as a family, with Christian "rules of engagement" learned early in Christian discipleship. Just as providing counsel in times of trouble used to be part of the church's natural ministry of nurture, peacemaking should also be so. Unfortunately, both have become the province of "professionals."[2]

Case Study 4: C4ChRam

Ramona, who was very involved in the life of her church was given a job in the church office. It was later discovered that some money was missing and that Ramona was responsible for the loss. By this time, Ramona's behavior had already raised concerns, one being about an unsuitable relationship. The church did not consider any of these to be sufficiently serious to bring up with her. However, when the money was found to be missing, they took action. The leaders of the church met and discussed the issue and asked Ramona to leave. Another lady in the church, Yamuna, opposed this decision feeling that the case had been badly handled. For example, there were no written

---

2. While professional counsellors are needed for certain types of problems, many other difficulties in the Christian life ought to be part of the church's ongoing pastoral member care.

policies that could be applied in Ramona's case and her situation was open to interpretation.

Several people in the church disapproved of Yamuna's attitude, saying she was "soft on sin." Ramona tried to plead her case to the church leaders, but when they would not listen, she sought out others who had influence in the church. They listened to her, and agreed to represent her position to the leaders. They then went to speak to the leaders. They returned to Ramona and told her she was wrong and that after having heard the other side, they agreed with the leaders' decision. The pastor was told of what had happened and he sent word to Ramona that he supported the decision of the church leadership. Ramona decided, with Yamuna's support, that since her appeals had failed, she would go to court.

A concerned member of the congregation offered to mediate between Ramona and the leaders but the leaders refused the offer. Ramona prepared to go to court. Yamuna asked a lawyer to appear for her but the lawyer refused because of links he had to someone in the church. However, the prosecutor was a member of the church. Rumors spread in the church about what was happening. Those who had been part of the leadership team who made the decision to dismiss Ramona, together with a group who supported their decision started vilifying those who spoke against their decision or defended Ramona.

One year later, the leadership changed. One of those who was newly appointed appealed for reconciliation. Those who had been involved in the original decision refused to hear it. The new leaders were silent. Eventually, a financial payment was made to Ramona but there was no apology.

Analysis
Goal
It appears that in this case, Ramona and Yamuna both insists that the substantial issues of the case be central. So do the leaders of the church. There seems to be no attempt at restoration. It is hard to know what Ramona would have done if she was not supported by Yamuna.

Collectivism/corporate identity
Ramona, by her behavior, threatened the well-being of the group and thus is being treated as an outsider. Since she has done something that is recognizably against the norms of Christian community (stealing), people would feel

quite self-righteous about what was being done. Hence, Yamuna is accused of being soft on sin and those who are newly appointed and want to take a fresh look at the case are vilified. Quite likely leaders in the church would also be defensive if questioned by members of other churches.

Mode of communication/conflict management style

To begin with, there seem to have been areas in Ramona's life that needed to be dealt with, such as her relationships, but no one in the church has spoken to her to discuss them. It appears that as long as she did her job, she was accepted. This is in line with the typical shame-oriented reaction to a potential conflict. The issue was avoided. The missing money has triggered a mode of interaction which is not natural to the fellowship. It is unfortunate that it appears that material losses are what would prompt the church to address character issues in Ramona.

Yamuna is more guilt-oriented in her response. By encouraging Ramona to take the matter to court, she is standing for justice for the weaker party. This is commendable. However, since she is dealing with more traditional leaders in the community, this would have been seen both as disloyalty and an attempt to shame those who have status in the church.

Status focus/high power distance

In this case, the leadership of the church forms the high-status group who have the power to make decisions on the church's behalf. No one wants to be seen to be going against the leadership because that would be a challenge to their status. It would also suggest disloyalty to the in-group, which is the church. There is a power distance between Ramona and the leaders of the church. Their status and authority make their decision hard to question. The pastor of the church displays a certain weakness in allowing a distance between Ramona and himself. It allows him to avoid dealing with recriminations or pleas.

Relative morality

In this case there is a clear sense of right and wrong when it comes to the financial dealings of the office. Ramona is clearly in the wrong. Justice demands that she be let go. However, other sins such as pride, lack of love, and self-righteousness are not addressed.

Fear of losing face

The unwillingness of the newly appointed leaders to re-visit the situation a year later arises partly from a desire to protect the reputation of those who originally took the decision. To make a contrary decision would be to implicitly criticize them. The "in-group" in this case seems to be the leaders rather than the church as a whole.

Extreme reactions

Litigation.

New discoveries

At the point when Ramona is dismissed, the leaders take a decision that they feel entitled to take. However, they act in a way that is not supposed to be compatible with a shame-oriented culture. Rather than protecting a member of the "in-group," the church, they expel her. She is clearly not seen as part of a family. There seems to be no attempt to help her take responsibility, repent, and find restoration. There is no appearance of sorrow or pain at the fallenness of this sister. Although the church and its leaders are going by biblical principles of honesty in holding Ramona responsible for her theft, they show little grace, preferring to emphasize justice over mercy.

Case Study 5: C5ChMaSa

Two ladies, Malini and Samanthi, were friends. They both had young children. Malini had very clear views on child rearing. In her view, if parents adhered to certain principles, their children would be well behaved and develop satisfactorily. However, Samanthi was going through a rough patch with her children. One day in conversation, Malini put forward her opinion that Samanthi was not doing a good job of bringing up her children. Samanthi was very hurt by what her friend had said to her. She told another friend what had happened. She began to avoid activities that she had previously attended, if she knew that Malini was going to be there. Another friend of Samanthi's realized what was happening and told the pastor about the situation. However, she requested that the pastor not approach Malini about the situation.

The pastor was due to make a visit to a group which both Malini and Samanthi would normally attend. At this group, the pastor made a point of speaking about family life. He talked of how different people have different life experiences. He also shared incidents from his own family life to illustrate the struggles that he and his wife had gone through when their own children were younger. Both Malini and Samanthi were present and both gradually returned to their normal group activities. Neither of them mentioned the incident to each other. In fact, Malini never knew that what she had said had offended and hurt her friend. Malini and Samanthi continue to be friends but to others it seems that their relationship is no longer as strong as it was.

Analysis
Goal – relational versus substantive goal/seeks harmony, honor, prestige

In this situation, Malini is unaware that there is a rift in the relationship, or if she feels the relationship has altered, she does not know the reason. We do not know for how long Malini and Samanthi were friends but it appears that the relationship is not strong enough for Samanthi to express her feeling of hurt. It does not appear as if Samanthi wanted a resolution of the situation. She has attempted to avoid admitting that there is a problem. To those around them, there is the appearance of harmony but it is not real. We could say that the Samanthi's goal is harmony but this raises the question of the meaning of "harmony." It could be, though, that Samanthi's goal is for Malini to be taken to task, be made to retract what she has said, although she cannot admit that openly.

Conflict resolution style

Following on from the previous point, we can see that Samanthi's response to conflict is avoidance. Rather than tell Malini she is hurt, or refute Malini's assumptions about child rearing, she turns to another friend to express her feelings. Although we might say that, according to New Testament principles she ought to speak to Malini, her friend does not encourage her to do so.

Perception of self and other

The conflict here is between peers. Yet even in this situation, the person who perceives themselves as herself will not risk exposure. There could well be an element of anger or resentment or even envy on Samanthi's part, towards Malini whose children are apparently giving her no problems. There are quite likely feelings of guilt common to Christian parents when their family life is somehow below the standards expected from the church. All these emotions combined would add to her feeling of being unable to tell Malini directly how she feels. Samanthi has been shamed. Joseph George in his article on aspects of therapy speaks of "external shamers" who "infuse pathological shame," especially in the vulnerable.[3] Her identity as a parent is a major part of her overall identity. She is experiencing shame as a "violation" of her identity.[4] It is not just her parenting skills but herself as a person that has been undermined. Since shame has the effect of undermining self-esteem and affects one globally, in a sense, she is no longer Malini's equal. The criticism has affected her identity as mother.

Third-party help is well meaning and does help heal Samanthi's damaged self-esteem. However, it stops short of restoring the relationship because Malini is unaware of what she has done.

Indirect communication

The method of dealing with the conflict is diffuse. Samanthi tells her friend about the hurt she feels over Malini's statement. The friend tells the pastor. The pastor does not speak directly to either Malini or Samanthi. By avoiding this direct communication, he spares Samanthi the embarrassment of realizing that her family situation is now known about by others. Malini too is saved from having to face what she has done and the attendant reaction to being talked about by others. However, one has to wonder if Malini would have realized that her behavior must change. The problem with speaking to whole groups is that often the wrong people feel that the talk is aimed at them, while those who need to hear the message are quite oblivious to it.

The pastor, as spiritual leader plays an important role in teaching on the topic of parenthood. He is acting as mediator by indirectly explaining to Samanthi that she should not feel ashamed. He also helps to heal some of the hurt by explaining how he and his wife have faced similar challenges. Implicitly he is telling the group that it is not appropriate to judge another parent in the light of one's own experience because families are all different. People who may not listen to their peers will listen to the pastor. This means

---

3. George, "Shame, Guilt and the Rites," 76.
4. Albers, *Shame*, 22.

that the pastor's ability to help is related to his willingness to be open about his own struggles. This would not be easy for some pastors who might be tempted to elevate their own status by presenting themselves as perfect examples of parenthood.

Relativistic morality

There does not seem to be other moral issues involved here, although we might speculate that envy might be playing a part in either or both parties' behavior towards one another.

Face saving techniques

Criticism is seen as a personal attack. Samanthi saves Malini's face by not telling her what she feels.

Extreme reactions

None. Withdrawal.

New discoveries

The importance of being confident in one's identity is a recurring theme in these cases.

Case Study 6: C6ChHaJo

Harin is a church leader and has an idea for a new project for the church. When he made his proposal to the rest of the leadership team, one of them, Joseph, spoke up. In Joseph's opinion, there were flaws in the plan and he did not think it was a good option for the church. Harin heard him out. However, he made it clear that he thought Joseph was lacking in vision, was archaic in his thinking, and was leading the church astray by disagreeing with the proposed plan.

After the meeting Joseph realized that Harin took every opportunity to undermine him. Joseph was left out of various events and decisions and his influence in the church was undermined. Harin also made it clear that the plan would go ahead without Joseph's help. He went out of his way to show that Joseph was not important to the progress of this project. The project went ahead. Harin was very enthusiastic, put in extra hours, and even invested his own money to ensure its success. However, much negative feedback was received, from a wide spectrum of people. The project was then shelved. It appeared that Joseph was right to have reservations about starting on the project.

Harin never spoke to Joseph about the failure of his pet project, but he included Joseph in the discussions about future plans and matters progressed as usual. Joseph had been surprised and hurt by Harin's reaction to his opinion on the project, but never raised the issue with Harin. The two men continue to work with other. Other leaders did not seem to be aware of the tension between the two men and no one intervened at any time.

Analysis
Goal

Only Harin and Joseph seem to be aware that their relationships has been weakened by the meeting to discuss the project. Neither of them openly addresses the situation. They do maintain the working relationship in spite of their feelings and emotions. We do not know what motivates Joseph to continue the working relationship but a person in Christian ministry will often put up with issues feeling that they must be obedient to their calling and stay where they are. There appears to be a level of fear that if the issue is forced, only more disruption will ensue. The relationship is not strong enough to bear an open discussion. Apparent harmony exists, but not shalom.

Conflict resolution style

Although Joseph has been hurt by Harin's deliberate attempts to undermine his influence in the church, he has not spoken to Harin about it. This is even though, in Joseph's mind at least, what happened was unfair and Harin had behaved in a manner that was less than expected of a leader. One wonders why no one else foresaw the problems Joseph did and we could speculate that other leaders who might have had misgivings chose not to say anything because they foresaw Harin's reaction. In that case we see that the majority of leaders had an avoidance style. Joseph seems to have a collaborative style while Harin's style is competitive. When attacked, Joseph goes into avoidance mode.

Perception of self and other

Harin is offended that Joseph criticizes his ideas. Harin has perceived Joseph's objections to his plan as a personal attack on his ability as a leader and visionary. His identity is wrapped up in the success of the project. Joseph becomes a threat and an enemy and is labelled to prevent his influence in the church.

Face saving techniques

It would be reasonable to assume that Harin realizes that Joseph had a valid reason for objecting to the project. Therefore, he includes Joseph in future planning but he does not acknowledge that he has behaved badly towards him. Harin shows his regret, even repentance, by re-instating Joseph to his rightful place. Joseph understands that this is what has happened and slips back into his role although the experience will not easily be forgotten.

Power distance

We might assume that the lack of open discussion at the initial meeting was due to Harin's status in the church. We do not know what form the negative feedback took but possibly this came in an indirect fashion.

Indirect communication

We see that there was ostensibly an opportunity for direct communication in the meeting. However, the person who took advantage of that mode of communication was seen as a hindrance to the church's mission. Harin uses indirect communication to show his displeasure rather than talking through and arguing his case with Joseph.

Relativistic morality

Pride.

Extreme reactions

No extreme reactions. However, by side-lining Joseph, Harin gets his revenge.

New discoveries

Reinforces previous observations that relationships are not robust enough to bear facing weakness in self or the other. Harmony rather than shalom is maintained.

Bibliography

Aasgaard, Reidar. *"My Beloved Brothers and Sisters!": Christian Siblingship in Paul*. London: T&T Clark, 2004.

Abu-Lughod, Lila. "The Romance of Resistance: Tracing Transformations of Power through Bedouin Women." *American Ethnologist* 17, no. 1 (1990): 41–55.

Adams, Jay E. *Handbook of Church Discipline*. Grand Rapids, MI: Zondervan, 1986.

Adamson, James B. *The Epistle of James*. Grand Rapids, MI: Eerdmans, 1976.

Adeney, Bernard T. *Strange Virtues: Ethics in a Multicultural World*. Downers Grove, IL: InterVarsity Press, 1995.

Aden, Leroy, and David G. Benner. *Counselling and the Human Predicament: A Study of Sin, Guilt, and Forgiveness*. Grand Rapids, MI: Baker Books, 1989.

Albers, Robert H. *Shame: A Faith Perspective*. New York: Haworth Pastoral Press, 1995.

Albright, William Foxwell, and C. S. Mann. *Matthew*. New York: Doubleday, 1971.

Augsburger, David W. *Conflict Mediation across Cultures: Pathways and Patterns*. Louisville, KY: Westminster John Knox, 1992.

———. *Pastoral Counselling across Cultures*. Philadelphia: Westminster, 1986.

Auli, Vahakangas. "Shame, Guilt and Church Discipline." *Africa Theological Journal* 27, no. 2 (2004): 53–69.

Bailey, Kenneth. *Paul through Middle Eastern Eyes*. Downers Grove, IL: IVP Academic, 2011.

Baird, William. *The Corinthian Church: A Biblical Approach to Urban Culture*. New York: Abingdon, 1964.

Barclay, John M. G. "Paul, Philemon and the Dilemma of Christian Slave-Ownership." *New Testament Studies* 37, no. 2 (1991): 161–186.

Barclay, William. *The Gospel of Matthew*. Vol. 2. Edinburgh: Saint Andrew Press, 1975.

———. *The Letters to Timothy, Titus and Philemon*. Edinburgh: Saint Andrew Press, 1975.

———. *The Letters to the Philippians, Colossians, and Thessalonians.* Louisville, KY: Westminster John Knox, 2003.

Baroja, C. J. "Honour and Shame: A Historical Account of Several Conflicts." In *Honour and Shame: The Values of Mediterranean Society*, edited by Jean G. Peristiany, 79–137. Chicago, IL: Chicago University Press, 1966.

Bartchy, S. Scott. "Divine Power, Community Formation, and Leadership in the Acts of the Apostles." In *Community Formation in the Early Church and in the Church Today*, edited by Richard L. Longenecker, 89–104. Peabody, MA: Hendrickson, 2002.

———. "Undermining Ancient Patriarchy: The Apostle Paul's Vision of a Society of Siblings." *Biblical Theology Bulletin* 29, no. 2 (Summer 1999): 68–78.

Barth, Markus, and Helmut Blanke. *The Letter to Philemon: A New Translation with Notes and Commentary.* Grand Rapids, MI: Eerdmans, 2000.

Benedict, Ruth. *The Chrysanthemum and the Sword: Patterns of Japanese Culture.* Cambridge, MA: Riverside Press, 1946.

———. *Patterns of Culture.* New York: Houghton Mifflin, 1934.

Berger, Peter. "On the Obsolescence of the Concept of Honour." In *Revisions: Changing Perspectives in Moral Philosophy*, edited by Stanley Hauerwas and Alasdair Macintyre, 172–181. Notre Dame, IN: Notre Dame University Press, 1983.

Bieberstein, Sabine, and Brian McNeil. "Disrupting the Normal Reality of Slavery: A Feminist Reading of the Letter to Philemon." *Journal for the Study of the New Testament* 23, no. 79 (2001): 105–116.

Binau, Brad A. "Shame and the Human Predicament." In *Counselling and the Human Predicament: A Study of Sin, Guilt, and Forgiveness*, edited by Leroy Aden and David G. Benner, 127–143. Grand Rapids, MI: Baker Books, 1989.

Blomberg, Craig. *Matthew.* Nashville, TN: Broadman & Holman, 1992.

———. "On Building and Breaking Barriers: Forgiveness, Salvation and Christian Counselling with Special Reference to Matthew 18:15–35." *Journal of Psychology & Christianity* 25, no. 2 (2006): 137–154. Religion and Philosophy Collection, EBSCOhost (accessed 18 March, 2014).

Bonhoeffer, Dietrich. *The Cost of Discipleship.* London: SCM Press, 1959(57/63/95).

———. *Ethics.* New York: Macmillan, 1967.

———. *Life Together.* San Francisco, CA: Harper, 1954.

Bowman, James. "Decline of the Honor Culture." *Policy Review* 156 (2009): 27–39. Religion and Philosophy Collection, EBSCOhost (accessed 15 August, 2013).

Brew, Frances P., and David R. Cairns. "Styles of Managing Interpersonal Workplace Conflict in Relation to Status and Face Concern: A study with Anglos and Chinese." *International Journal of Conflict Management* 15, no. 1 (2004): 27–56.

Bruner, Frederick Dale. *The Church Book: Matthew 13–28*. Dallas, TX: Word Books, 1990.

———. *The Gospel of John: A Commentary*. Grand Rapids, MI: Eerdmans, 2012.

Burke, Trevor J. *Family Matters: A Socio-Historical Study of Kinship Metaphors in 1 Thessalonians*. London: T&T Clark, 2003.

Cairns, Douglas. "Honour and Shame: Modern Controversies and Ancient Values." *Critical Quarterly* 53, no. 1 (April 2011): 23–41. Religion and Philosophy Collection, EBSCOhost (accessed 16 July, 2013).

Capps, Donald. *The Depleted Self: Sin in a Narcissistic Age*. Minneapolis: Fortress, 1993.

Carson, D. A. *God with Us: Themes from Matthew*. Ventura, CA: Regal Books, 1985.

———. *The Gospel According to John*. Leicester: Apollos, 1991.

Carter, Warren. *Matthew and the Margins: A Socio-Political and Religious Reading*. JSNT Supplement 204. Sheffield, UK: Sheffield Academic Press, 2000.

Chan, Kwok Leung Darius K. S. "Conflict Management across Cultures." In *Social Psychology and Cultural Context*, edited by John Adamopoulos and Yoshihisa Kashima, 177–188. Thousand Oaks, CA: Sage, 1999.

Chiu, C. Y., S. C. Tsang, and C. F. Yang. "The Role of Face Situation and Attitudinal Antecedents in Chinese Consumer Complaint Behavior." *The Journal of Social Psychology* 128, no. 2 (1988): 173–180.

Chow, John K. *Patronage and Power: A Study of Social Networks in Corinth*. JSNT Supplement 75. Sheffield: Sheffield University Press, 1992.

Chance, John K. "The Anthropology of Honor and Shame: Culture, Values, and Practice." *Semeia* 68 (1994): 139–151.

Chua, Elizabeth, and William B. Gudykunst. "Conflict Resolution Styles in Low- and High-Context Cultures." *Communication Research Reports* 4, no. 1 (1987): 32–37.

Christensen, M., and Kristy M. Brumfield. "Phenomenological Designs: The Philosophy of Phenomenological Research." In *Counselling Research: Qualitative, Quantitative and Mixed Methods*, edited by Carl J. Sheparis, J. Scott Young, and M. Harry Daniels, 135–149. Upper Saddle River, NJ: Pearson Education, 2010.

Conzelmann, Hans. *1 Corinthians: A Commentary on the First Epistle to the Corinthians*. Philadelphia, PA: Fortress, 1975.

Coser, Lewis A. *Functions of Social Conflict*. New York: FreePress, 1956.

Creighton, Millie R. "Revisiting Shame and Guilt Cultures: A Forty Year Pilgrimage." *Ethos* 18, no. 3 (1990): 279–307.

Crook, Zeba. "Honour, Shame and Social Status Revisited." *Journal of Biblical Literature* 128, no. 3 (2009): 591–611.

Davies, W. D., and Dale C. Allison. *The Gospel According to St Matthew: A Critical and Exegetical Commentary*. Volume 2. Edinburgh: T&T Clark, 1991.

Dean, Aaron. "Clashing Cultural Views of Sin." *Evangelical Missions Quarterly* 38, no.1 (2002): 48–53.

deSilva, David A. "Despising Shame: A Cultural-Anthropological Investigation of the Epistle to the Hebrews." *Journal of Biblical Literature* 113, no. 3 (1994): 439–461. Academic Search Premier, EBSCOhost (accessed 13 May, 2014).

———. *Despising Shame: Honor Discourse and Community Maintenance in the Epistle to the Hebrews*. Atlanta: Society of Biblical Literature, 2008.

———. *Honor, Patronage, Kinship and Purity: Unlocking New Testament Culture*. Downers Grove, IL: InterVarsity Press, 2000.

———. *The Hope of Glory: Honour Discourse and New Testament Interpretation*. Collegeville, MN: Liturgical Press, 1999.

———. *An Introduction to the New Testament: Contexts, Methods and Ministry Formation*. Downers Grove, IL: InterVarsity Press, 2004.

———. "Patronage and Reciprocity: The Context of Grace in the New Testament." *Ashland Theological Journal* 31 (1999): 32–84.

———. *Perseverance in Gratitude: A Socio-Rhetorical Commentary on the Epistle "To the Hebrews."* Grand Rapids, MI: Eerdmans, 2000.

De Silva, Lynn A. *Buddhism: Beliefs and Practices in Sri Lanka*. Colombo: Wesleyan Press, 1974.

de Vos, Craig S. "Once a Slave, Always a Slave? Slavery, Manumission and Relational Patterns in Paul's letter to Philemon." *Journal for the Study of the New Testament* 23, no. 82 (2001): 89–105.

Dibelius, Martin, and Hans Conzelmann. *The Pastoral Epistles: A Commentary on the Pastoral Epistles*. Philadelphia: Fortress, 1972.

Domenici, Kathy, and Stephen W. Littlejohn. *Facework: Bridging Theory and Practice*. Thousand Oaks, CA: Sage, 2006.

Downing, F. Gerald. "'Honor' among Exegetes." *Catholic Biblical Quarterly* 61, no. 1 (1999): 53–73. ATLA Religion Database with ATLASerials, EBSCOhost (accessed 19 August, 2013).

Duling, Dennis C. "The Matthean Brotherhood and Marginal Scribal Leadership." In *Modelling Early Christianity*, edited by Philip Esler, 159–182. London: Routledge, 1995.

———. "Matthew 18:15–17: Conflict, Confrontation and Conflict Resolution in a 'Fictive kin Association.'" In his *A Marginal Scribe*, 212–244. Eugene, OR: Cascade, 2012.

Dye, T. Wayne. "Toward a Cross-Cultural Definition of Sin." *Missiology* 4, no. 1 (1976): 27–41. ATLA Religion Database with ATLASerials, EBSCOhost (accessed 14 May, 2014).

Edwards, Mark J. *Ancient Christian Commentary on Scripture*. Leicester: Inter-Varsity Press, 1999.

Elliott, John H. "Patronage and Clientele." In *The Social Sciences and New Testament Interpretation*, edited by Richard Rohrbaugh, 144–156. Peabody, MA: Hendrickson, 1996.

Elmer, Duane. *Cross Cultural Conflict: Building Relationships for Effective Ministry*. Downers Grove, IL: InterVarsity Press, 1993.

———. *Cross Cultural Connections*. Downers Grove, IL: InterVarsity Press, 2002.

Esler, Philip Francis. *The First Christians in their Social Worlds: Social-Scientific Approaches to New Testament Interpretation*. London: Routledge, 1994.

———. "Making and Breaking an Agreement Mediterranean Style: A New Reading of Galatians 2:1–14." *Biblical Interpretation* 3, no. 3 (1995): 285–314. ATLA Religion Database with ATLASerials, EBSCOhost (accessed 24 September, 2013).

———, ed. *Modelling Early Christianity*. New York: Routledge, 1995.

Evans, Craig. *Matthew*. New Cambridge Bible Commentary. Cambridge: Cambridge University Press, 2012.

Fee, Gordon D. *The First Epistle to the Corinthians*. Grand Rapids, MI: Eerdmans, 1987.

Fernando, Ajith. *Jesus Driven Ministry*. Wheaton, IL: Crossway, 2002.

———. *Leadership Lifestyle*. Wheaton, IL: Tyndale House, 1985.

———. "Proclaiming the Gospel in Sri Lanka: Some Lessons from the Methodist Heritage," paper presented at Methodist Church in Sri Lanka: Bicentenary Celebrations Theology Conference. Moratuwa, Sri Lanka. October 2013.

———. *Sharing the Truth in Love: How to Relate to People of Other Faiths*. Grand Rapids, MI: Discovery House, 2001.

———. "Wesley Groups and Holiness." In *World Mission in the Wesleyan Spirit*, edited by Darrell L. Whitman, 235–243. Franklin, TN: Providence House, 2009.

Fleckenstein, Cheryl M. "Congregation as Family? No, Know the Pitfalls." *Word & World* 33, no. 2 (2013): 189–191. ATLA Religion Database with ATLASerials, EBSCOhost (accessed 4 April, 2014).

Finney, Mark T. "Honor, Rhetoric and Factionalism in the Ancient World: 1 Corinthians 1–4 in Its Social Context." *Biblical Theology Bulletin* 40, no. 1 (2010): 27–36.

Fisher, Roger, and William Ury. *Getting to Yes: Negotiating Agreement Without Giving In*. New York: Penguin Books, 1991.

Flanders, Christopher L. *About Face: Rethinking Face for 21st Century Mission*. Eugene, OR: Pickwick, 2011.

———. "Shame." In *Global Dictionary of Theology*, edited by William A. Dyrness and Veli-Matti Karkkainen, 813–819. Downers Grove, IL: InterVarsity Press, 2008.

France, R. T. *The Gospel According to Matthew: An Introduction and Commentary*. Grand Rapids, MI: Eerdmans, 1985.

Friedmann, I. M. *Helping Resolve Conflict: True Experiences of a Christian Anthropologist*. Scottsdale: Herald Press, 1990.

Frilingos, Chris. "'For My Child, Onesimus': Paul and Domestic Power in Philemon." *Journal of Biblical Literature* 119, no. 1 (Spring 2000): 91–104.

Fung, Ronald Y. K. *The Epistle to the Galatians*. Grand Rapids, MI: Eerdmans, 1988.

Geertz, Clifford. "From the Native's Point of View: On the Nature of Anthropological Understanding." *Bulletin of the American Academy of Arts and Sciences* 28, no. 1 (1974): 26–45. Accessed online at http://hypergeertz.jku.at/GeertzTexts/Natives_Point.htm, 14 October 2013.

———. *The Interpretation of Cultures*. New York: Basic Books, 1973.

Genade, Aldred A. *Persuading the Cretans: A Text-Generated Persuasion Analysis of the Letter to Titus*. Eugene, OR: Wipf & Stock, 2011.

George, Joseph. "Shame, Guilt and the Rites of Reconciliation." *Bangalore Theological Forum* 35, no. 2 (2003): 60–82.

Gibbs, Jeffrey A., and Jeffrey Kloha. "'Following' Matthew 18: Interpreting Matthew 18:15–20 in Its Context." *Concordia Journal* 29, no. 1 (2003): 6–25. ATLA Religion Database with ATLASerials, EBSCOhost (accessed 4 April, 2014).

Gilmore, David D. *Honor and Shame and the Unity of the Mediterranean*. Washington, DC: American Anthropological Association, 1987.

Gooding, D. W. *True to the Faith: The Acts of the Apostles*. London: Hodder & Stoughton, 1990.

Gosnell, Peter W. "Honor and Shame Rhetoric as a Unifying Motif in Ephesians." *Bulletin for Biblical Research* 16, no. 1 (2006): 105–128. ATLA Religion Database with ATLASerials, EBSCOhost (accessed 24 September, 2013).

Govier, Trudy, and Wilhelm Verwoerd. "The Promise and Pitfalls of Apology." *Journal of Social Philosophy* 33, no. 1 (2002): 67–82.

Greenwood, Jean E. "Beyond Shame: Toward an Understanding of Church Conflict." *Clergy Journal* 81, no. 8 (2005): 3–5. Religion and Philosophy Collection, EBSCOhost (accessed 4 April, 2014).

Gudykunst, William B., Lea P. Stewart, and Stella Ting-Toomey, eds. *Communication, Culture and Organisational Processes*. Beverley Hills, CA: Sage, 1985.

Gudykunst, William B., Stella Ting-Toomey, and Elizabeth Chua. *Culture and Interpersonal Communication*. Newbury Park, CA: Sage, 1988.

Gunatilleke, Gehan. *Confronting the Complexities of Loss: Perspectives on Truth, Memory and Justice in Sri Lanka*. Colombo, Sri Lanka: Law and Society Trust, 2015.

Gundry, Robert H. *Matthew: A Commentary on his Handbook for a Mixed Church Under Persecution*. 2nd ed. Grand Rapids, MI: Eerdmans, 1994.

Hagner, Donald A. *Matthew 14–28*. Dallas, TX: Word Books, 1995.

Hanson, K. C. "How Honourable! How Shameful! A Cultural Analysis of Matthew's Makarisms and Reproaches." *Semia* 68 (1994): 81–112. http://www.kchanson.com/ARTICLES/mak.html, accessed 26 August 2013.

Harinck, Fieke, Saïd Shafa, Naomi Ellemers, and Bianca Beersma. "The Good News about Honor Culture: The Preference for Cooperative Conflict Management in the Absence of Insults." *Negotiation and Conflict Management Research* 6, no. 2 (2013): 67–78.

Harris, Gerald. "The Beginnings of Church Discipline." In *Understanding Paul's Ethics*, edited by Brian S. Rosner, 129–154. Grand Rapids, MI: Eerdmans, 1995.

Hauerwas, Stanley. *Matthew*. SCM Theological Commentary on the Bible. London: SCM, 2006.

Hays, Richard B. *First Corinthians*. Louisville, KY: Westminster John Knox Press, 1997.

Heine, Steven J. "Culture and Motivation: What Motivates People to Act in the Ways That They Do?" In *Handbook of Cultural Psychology*, edited by Shinobu Kitayama and Dov Cohen, 714–733. New York: Guilford Press, 2007.

Heller, Agnes. "Five Approaches to the Phenomenon of Shame." *Social Research* 70, no. 4 (2003): 1015–1030. EBSCOhost (accessed 22 April, 2014).

Herzfeld, Michael. "Honour and Shame: Some Problems in the Comparative Analysis of Moral Systems." *Man* 15 (1980): 339–351.

Hesselgrave, David J. "Missionary Elenctics and Guilt and Shame." *Missiology* 11, no. 4 (1983): 461–483. ATLA Religion Database with ATLASerials, EBSCOhost (accessed 19 August, 2013).

Hiebert, Paul G. *Anthropological Insights for Missionaries*. Grand Rapids, MI: Baker Academic, 1985.

———. *Cultural Anthropology*. Grand Rapids, MI: Baker Books, 1983.

———. *The Gospel in Human Contexts*. Grand Rapids, MI: Baker Academic, 2009.

———. *Transforming Worldviews*. Grand Rapids, MI: Baker Academic, 2008.

Hofstede, Geert. *Culture's Consequences*. Beverley Hills, CA: Sage, 1984.

Hollander, John. "Honor Dishonorable: Shameful Shame." *Social Research* 70, no. 4 (2003): 1061–1074. Academic Search Premier, EBSCOhost (accessed 22 April, 2014).

Holmberg, Bengt. *Paul and Power: The Structure of Authority in the Primitive Church as Reflected in the Pauline*. Eugene, OR: Wipf & Stock, 1978.

Horning, Estella B. "The Rule of Christ: An Exposition of Matthew 18:15–20." *Brethren Life and Thought* 38, no. 2 (1993): 69–78. ATLA Religion Database with ATLASerials, EBSCOhost (accessed 4 April, 2014).

Hsu, F. L. K. *Clan, Caste and Club*. Princeton, NJ: D. Van Nostrand, 1963.

Illian, Bridget. "Church Discipline and Forgiveness in Matthew 18:15–35." *Currents in Theology and Mission* 37, no. 6 (2010): 445–450.

Jandt, Fred E. *An Introduction to Intercultural Communication: Identities in a Global Community*. Thousand Oaks, CA: Sage, 2007.

Jewett, Robert. *Saint Paul at the Movies: The Apostle's Dialogue with American Culture*. Louisville, KY: Westminster John Knox, 1993

———. *Saint Paul Returns to the Movies: Triumph over Shame*. Grand Rapids, MI: Eerdmans, 1999.

———, ed. *The Shame Factor: How Shame Shapes Society*. Eugene, OR: Cascade, 2011.

Johnson, Lee A. "Satan Talk in Corinth: The Rhetoric of Conflict." *Biblical Theology Bulletin* 29, no. 4 (1999): 145–155.

Johnson, Luke Timothy. *The First and Second Letters to Timothy*. New York: Doubleday, 2001.

Kaufman, Gershen. *Shame: The Power of Caring*. Cambridge, MA: Schenkman, 1980.

Kaufman, Whitley. *Honor and Revenge: A Theory of Punishment*. New York: Springer, 2013.

———. "Understanding Honor: Beyond the Shame/Guilt Dichotomy." *Social Theory and Practice* 37, no. 4 (2011): 557–573. Academic Search Premier, EBSCOhost (accessed 27 May, 2013).

Kistemaker, Simon J. "Deliver This Man to Satan (1 Corinthians 5:5): A Case Study in Church Discipline." *Master's Seminary Journal* 3, no. 1 (1992): 33–46. ATLA Religion Database with ATLASerials, EBSCOhost (accessed 28 April, 2014).

Knight, Henry F. "From Shame to Responsibility and Christian Identity: The Dynamics of Shame and Confession Regarding the Shoah." *Journal of Ecumenical Studies* 35, no. 1 (1998): 41–62. ATLA Religion Database with ATLASerials, EBSCOhost (accessed 11 April, 2014).

Kraft, Charles H. *Anthropology for Christian Witness*. Maryknoll, NY: Orbis Books, 1996.

———. *Christianity in Culture: A Study in Dynamic Biblical Theologizing in Cross-Cultural Perspective*. Maryknoll, NY: Orbis Books, 1979.

Kraus, C. Norman. *Jesus Our Lord: Christology from a Disciple's Perspective*. Scottsdale, PA: Herald Press, 1990.

Kreider, Alan, Eleanor Kreider, and Paulus Widjaja. *A Culture of Peace: God's Vision for the Church*. Intercourse, PA: Good Books, 2005.

Laney, J. Carl. "The Biblical Practice of Church Discipline." *Bibliotheca Sacra* 143 (October 1986): 353–364.

———. *A Guide to Church Discipline*. Minneapolis, MN: Bethany House, 1985.

Lawrence, Louise Joy. *An Ethnography of the Gospel of Matthew*. Tubingen: Mohr Siebeck, 2003.

———. "'For Truly, I Tell You, They Have Received their Reward' (Matt 6:2): Investigating Honor Precedence and Honor Virtue." *Catholic Biblical Quarterly* 64, no. 4 (2002): 687–702. ATLA Religion Database with ATLASerials, EBSCOhost (accessed 15 August, 2013).

Lea, Thomas D., and Hayne P. Griffin, Jr. *1, 2 Timothy, Titus*. Nashville, TN: Broadman & Holman, 1992.

Lebra, Takie Sugiyama. "The Social Mechanism of Guilt and Shame: The Japanese Case." *Anthropological Quarterly* 44, no. 4 (1971): 241–255.

Lewis, G. Douglas. *Resolving Church Conflicts: A Case Study Approach for Local Congregations*. San Francisco: Harper and Row, 1981.

Lewis, Michael. *Shame: The Exposed Self*. New York: Free Press, 1992.

Lienhard, Ruth. *Restoring Relationships: Theological Reflections on Shame and Honour Among the Daba and Bana of Cameroon*. Yaounde, Cameroon: Bell & Howell Information and Learning Company, 2001.

Lingenfelter, Sherwood G., and Marvin K. Mayers. *Ministering Cross-Culturally: An Incarnational Model for Personal Relationships*. Grand Rapids, MI: Baker Books, 1986.

Little, D. "A Different Kind of Justice: Dealing with Human Rights Violations in Transitional Societies." *Ethics & International Affairs* 13 (1999): 65–80.

Loewen, Jacob A. *Culture and Human Values: Christian Intervention in Anthropological Perspective*. South Pasadena, CA: William Carey Library, 1975.

———. "Four Kinds of Forgiveness." *Practical Anthropology* 11, no. 4 (1970): 153–168.

———. "Self-Exposure: Bridge to Fellowship." *Practical Anthropology* 12, no. 2 (1965): 49–62.

———. "The Social Context of Guilt and Forgiveness." *Practical Anthropology* 17, no. 2 (Mar-April 1970): 80–96.

Lucas, R. C. *The Message of Colossians and Philemon*. Leicester: Inter-Varsity Press, 1980.

Luzbetak, Louis, J. *The Church and Cultures: New Perspectives in Missiological Anthropology*. New York: Orbis Books, 1988.

Luz, Ulrich. *Matthew 8–20*. Minneapolis: Fortress, 2001.

Lynd, Helen Merrell. *On Shame and the Search for Identity*. New York: Harcourt Brace, 1958.

Lyons, Kirk D., Sr. "Paul's Confrontation with Class: The Letter to Philemon as Counter-Hegemonic Discourse." *Cross Currents* 55, no. 3 (2005): 322–339.

Malina, Bruce. *The New Testament World: Insights from Cultural Anthropology*. Louisville, KY: Westminster John Knox Press, 2001.

———. "Understanding New Testament Persons." In *The Social Sciences and New Testament Interpretation*, edited by Richard R. Rohrbaugh. Peabody, MA: Hendrickson, 1996.

Malina, Bruce J., and Jerome H. Neyrey. "First Century Personality: Dyadic not Individualistic." In *The Social World of Luke-Acts: Models for Interpretation*, edited by Jerome H. Neyrey, 67–96. Peabody, MA: Hendrickson, 1991.

Malina, Bruce J., and Richard L. Rohrbaugh. *Social Science Commentary on the Gospel of John*. Minneapolis: Fortress, 1998.

Martyn, J. Louis. *Galatians: A New Translation with Introduction and Commentary*. New York: Doubleday, 1997.

Mason, Jennifer. *Qualitative Researching*. Thousand Oaks, CA: Sage, 2002.

Mayers, Marvin K. *Christianity Confronts Culture: A Strategy for Cross-cultural Evangelism*. Rev ed. Grand Rapids, MI: Zondervan, 1987.

———. *Christianity Confronts Culture: A Strategy for Cross-cultural Evangelism*. Grand Rapids, MI: Zondervan, 1974

McKnight, Scot. *The Letter of James*. Grand Rapids, MI: Eerdmans, 2011.

Mead, Margaret. *Cooperation and Competition among Primitive Peoples*. New York: McGraw Hill, 1937.

Meeks, Wayne. *The First Urban Christians*. New Haven, CT: Yale University Press, 1983.

———. *The Origins of Christian Morality*. New Haven, CT: Yale University Press, 1993.

Michaels, J. Ramsey. *John*. Peabody, MA: Hendrickson, 1989.

Miranda-Feliciano, Evelyn. *Filipino Values and Our Christian Faith*. Manila: OMF Literature, 1990.

Morris, Leon. *1 Corinthians*. Grand Rapids, MI: Eerdmans, 1987.

———. *The Gospel According to John*. Grand Rapids, MI: Eerdmans, 1995.

———. *The Gospel According to Matthew*. Grand Rapids, MI: Eerdmans, 1992.

Morris, Michael W., Kathrine Y. Williams, Kwok Leung, Richard Larrick, M. Teresa Mendoza, Deepti Bhatnagar, Jianfeng Li, Mari Kondo, Jin-Lian Luo, and Jun-Chen Hu. "Conflict Management Style: Accounting for Cross-National Differences." *Journal of International Business Studies* 29, no. 4 (1998): 729–747.

Mounce, William D. *Pastoral Epistles*. Word Biblical Commentary 46. Carlisle: Paternoster, 2000.

Moxnes, Halvor. "Honour and Shame." In *The Social Sciences and New Testament Interpretation*, edited by Richard L. Rohrbaugh, 19–40. Peabody, MA: Hendrickson, 1996.

———. "Patron-Client Relations and the New Community in Luke-Acts." In *The Social World of Luke-Acts: Models for Interpretation*, edited by Jerome H. Neyrey, 241–270. Peabody, MA: Hendrickson, 1991.

Munck, Johannes. *The Acts of the Apostles*. New York: Doubleday, 1967.

Muller, Roland. *Honor and Shame: Unlocking the Door*. Philadelphia, PA. Xlibris, 2000.

Nelson, Randy A. "Exegeting Forgiveness." *American Theological Inquiry* 5, no. 2 (July 2012): 33–58. ATLA Religion Database with ATLASerials, EBSCOhost (accessed 4 April, 2014).

Neyrey, Jerome H. *Honour and Shame in the Gospel of Matthew*. Louisville, KY: Westminster John Knox Press, 1998.

———, ed. *The Social World of Luke-Acts: Models for Interpretation*. Peabody, MA: Hendrickson, 1991.

Newbold, R. F. "Personality Structure and Response to Adversity in Early Christian Hagiography." *Numen* 31, no. 2 (1984): 199–215.

Nicholls, Bruce. "The Role of Shame and Guilt in Cross Cultural Mission." *Evangelical Review of Theology* 25, no. 3 (2001): 231–241.

Nicholls, Bruce, and Brian C. Wintle. *Colossians and Philemon*. Singapore: Asia Theological Association, 2005.

Nida, Eugene A. *Customs, Cultures and Christianity*. London: Tyndale Press, 1954.

Noble, Lowell L. *Naked and Not Ashamed: An Anthropological, Biblical and Psychological Study of Shame*. Jackson, MI: Jackson Printing, 1975.

Nordling, John G. "The Gospel in Philemon." *Concordia Theological Quarterly* 71, no. 1 (2007): 71–83.

Nolland, John. *The Gospel of Matthew: A Commentary on the Greek Text*. Grand Rapids, MI: Eerdmans; Bletchley: Paternoster, 2005.

Opler, Morris Edward. "Themes as Dynamic Forces in Culture." *American Journal of Sociology* 51, no. 3 (1945): 198–206.

Osborne, Grant E. *Matthew*. Grand Rapids, MI: Zondervan, 2010.

Overman, J. Andrew. *Church and Community in Crisis*. Valley Forge, PA: Trinity Press International, 1996.

Pattison, Stephen. *Shame: Theory, Therapy, Theology*. Cambridge: Cambridge University Press, 2000.

Peristiany, J. G. *Honour and Shame: The Values of Mediterranean Society*. Chicago: University of Chicago Press, 1966.

Petersen, Norman R. *Rediscovering Paul: Philemon and the Sociology of Paul's Narrative World*. Philadelphia: Fortress, 1985.

Peterson, David G. *The Acts of the Apostles*. Grand Rapids, MI: Eerdmans, 2009.

Panichas, George A. "The Absence of a Culture of Shame." *Modern Age* 45, no. 1 (2003): 3–6. Religion and Philosophy Collection, EBSCOhost (accessed 19 August, 2013).

Pfitzner, Victor C. "Purified Community – Purified Sinner: Expulsion from the Community According to Matt 18:15–18 and 1 Cor 5:1–5." *Australian Biblical Review* 30 (1982): 34–55. ATLA Religion Database with ATLASerials, EBSCOhost (accessed 25 April, 2014).

Piers, Gerhart, and Milton B. Singer. *Shame and Guilt: A Psychoanalytic and a Cultural Study*. New York: W. W. Norton, 1971.

Pitt-Rivers, Julian. "Honor and Social Status." In *Honour and Shame: The Values of Mediterranean Society*, edited by Jean G. Peristiany, 19–78. Chicago: Chicago University Press, 1966.

Pilch, John J., and Bruce Malina, eds. *Handbook of Biblical Social Values*. Peabody, MA: Hendrickson, 1998.

Priest, Robert J. "Missionary Elenctics: Conscience and Culture." *Missiology* 22, no. 3 (1994): 291–315. ATLA Religion Database with ATLASerials, EBSCOhost (accessed 20 May, 2014).

Ramshaw, Elaine J. "Power and Forgiveness in Matthew 18." *Word and World* 18, no. 4 (1998): 397–404.

Riezler, Kurt. "Comment on the Social Psychology of Shame." *The American Journal of Sociology* 48, no. 4 (1943): 457–465.

Roberts, Richard Owen. *Repentance: The First Word of the Gospel*. Wheaton, IL: Crossway, 2002.

Robertson, C. K. *Conflict in Corinth: Redefining the System*. New York: Lang, 2001.

———. "Courtroom Dramas: A Pauline Alternative for Conflict Management." *Anglican Theological Review* 89, no. 4 (2007): 589–610. Religion and Philosophy Collection, EBSCOhost (accessed 3 April, 2014).

Robson, Colin. *Real World Research*. Oxford: Blackwell, 1993.

Rodriguez Mosquera, Patricia M., Agneta H. Fischer, Antony S. R. Manstead, and Ruud Zaalberg. "Attack, Disapproval, or Withdrawal? The Role of Honor in Anger and Shame Responses to Being Insulted." *Cognition & Emotion* 22, no. 8 (2008): 1471–1498. Academic Search Premier, EBSCOhost (accessed 22 April, 2014).

Sande, Ken. *The Peacemaker: A Biblical Guide to Resolving Personal Conflict*. Grand Rapids, MI: Baker Books, 2004.

Santos, Narry F. *Turning Our Shame into Hope: Transformation of the Filipino HIYA in the Light of Mark's Gospel*. Lifechange, 2003.

Sapir, E. *Selected Writings in Language, Culture and Personality*. Berkley, CA: University of California Press, 1949.

Schirrmacher, Thomas. *Culture of Shame, Culture of Guilt*. Bonn: Berlag, 2013.

Schmidt, Thomas E. *Trying to be Good*. Grand Rapids, MI: Zondervan, 1990.

Schneider, Carl. *Shame, Exposure and Privacy*. Boston: Beacon Press, 1977.

Sheperis, Carl J., J. Scott Young, and M. Harry Daniels. *Counselling Research: Qualitative, Quantitative and Mixed Methods*. Upper Saddle River, NJ: Pearson Education, 2010.

Smedes, Lewis B. *Shame and Grace*. New York: Zondervan, 1993.

Smith, David Raymond. *"Hand this Man over to Satan": Curse, Exclusion and Salvation in 1 Corinthians 5*. London: T&T Clark, 2008.

Smith, Peter B., Shaun Dugan, Ark F. Peterson, Wok Leung. "Individualism, Collectivism and the Handling of Disagreements: A 23 Country Survey." *International Journal of Intercultural Relations* 22, no. 3 (1998): 351–367.

Stackhouse, Max L. "Social Ethics: Some Basic Elements East and West." In *A Vision for Man: Essays on Faith, Theology and Society*, edited by Samuel Amirtham and Joshua Russell Chandran, 326–338. Madras: Christian Literature Society, 1978.

Taylor, Nicholas H. "The Social Nature of Conversion in the Early Christian World." In *Modelling Early Christianity: Social-Scientific Studies of the New Testament in its Context*, edited by Philip F. Esler, 128–136. London: Routledge, 1995.

Tennent, Timothy C. *Theology in the Context of World Christianity*. Grand Rapids, MI: Zondervan, 2007.

Theissen, Gerd. *Social Reality and the Early Christians*. Minneapolis: Fortress, 1992.

Thompson, Marianne Meye. *Colossians and Philemon*. Grand Rapids, MI: Eerdmans, 2005.

Thompson, James W. *Moral Formation According to Paul: The Context and Coherence of Pauline Ethics*. Grand Rapids, MI: Baker Academic, 2011.

Thompson, William G. *Matthew's Advice to a Divided Community*. Rome: Biblical Institute Press, 1970.

Ting-Toomey, Stella. *Communicating across Cultures*. New York: Guilford Press, 1999.

———. "Towards a Theory of Conflict and Culture." In *Communication, Culture and Organisational Processes*, edited by William B. Gudykunst, Lea P. Stewart, and Stella Ting-Toomey, 71–86. Beverley Hills, CA: Sage, 1985.

Ting-Toomey, Stella, and John G. Oetzel. *Managing Intercultural Conflict Effectively*. Thousand Oaks, CA: Sage, 2001.

Toorman, Alex. "Selfless Love: The Missing Middle in Honor/Shame Cultures." *Evangelical Missions Quarterly* 47, no. 2 (2011): 160–167.

Towner, Philip H. *The Letters to Timothy and Titus*. Grand Rapids, MI: Eerdmans, 2006.

Turner, David L. *Matthew*. Grand Rapids, MI: Baker Academic, 2008.

Turner, Max. "Human Reconciliation in the New Testament with Special Reference to Philemon, Colossians and Ephesians." *European Journal of Theology* 16, no. 1 (2007): 37–47.

Vahakangas, Auli. "Shame, Guilt and Church Discipline." *Africa Theological Journal* 27, no. 2 (2004): 53–69.

Verhezen, Peter. "Respect, Integrity and Trust: A Cross Cultural Interpretation of 'Corruption' beyond the (Conflictual) Shame and Guilt Concepts." Working paper. Accessed 21 January 2014. https://www.verhezen.net/index.php/en/insights.

Ury, William, and Roger Fisher. *Getting to Yes: Negotiating Agreement Without Giving in*. London: Random House, 1991.

Weerasingha, Tissa. *The Cross and the Bo-Tree: Communicating the Gospel to Buddhists*. Taiwan: Asia Theological Association, 1989.

Wiher, Hannes. *Shame and Guilt: A Key to Cross-Cultural Ministry*. Bonn, Germany: Verlag, 2003.

Witherington, Ben, III. *The Acts of the Apostles: A Socio-Rhetorical Commentary*. Grand Rapids, MI: Eerdmans, 1998.

———. *Conflict and Community in Corinth*. Grand Rapids, MI: Eerdmans, 1995.

Wright, N. T. *Colossians and Philemon*. Grand Rapids, MI: InterVarsity Press, 1986.

Wu, Jackson. "Biblical Theology from a Chinese Perspective: Interpreting Scripture through the Lens of Honor and Shame." *GlobalMissiology*, 2011. Accessed 27 March, 2014. http://ojs.globalmissiology.org/index.php/english/article/viewFile/1217/2821.

———. *Saving God's Face: A Chinese Contextualization of Salvation through Honour and Shame*. Pasadena, CA: William Carey, 2012.

Yang, Wong Fong. *Discipline or Shame?: The Dynamics of Shame in Church Discipline*. Malaysia: Kairos Research Centre, 1998.

Yin, Robert K. *Case Study Research: Design and Methods*. Thousand Oaks, CA: Sage, 2009.

You, Young Gweon. "Shame and Guilt Mechanisms in East Asian Culture." *Journal of Pastoral Care* 51, no. 1 (1997): 57–64. ATLA Religion Database with ATLASerials, EBSCOhost (accessed 19 August, 2013).

Zavalloni, Marisa. "Values." In *Handbook of Cross-Cultural Psychology*, vol. 5, edited by Harry C. Triandis and Richard W. Brislin, 73–120. Boston: Allyn and Bacon, 1979.

Langham Literature, with its publishing work, is a ministry of Langham Partnership.

Langham Partnership is a global fellowship working in pursuit of the vision God entrusted to its founder John Stott –

> *to facilitate the growth of the church in maturity and Christ-likeness through raising the standards of biblical preaching and teaching.*

Our vision is to see churches in the Majority World equipped for mission and growing to maturity in Christ through the ministry of pastors and leaders who believe, teach and live by the word of God.

Our mission is to strengthen the ministry of the word of God through:
- nurturing national movements for biblical preaching
- fostering the creation and distribution of evangelical literature
- enhancing evangelical theological education

especially in countries where churches are under-resourced.

Our ministry

Langham Preaching partners with national leaders to nurture indigenous biblical preaching movements for pastors and lay preachers all around the world. With the support of a team of trainers from many countries, a multi-level programme of seminars provides practical training, and is followed by a programme for training local facilitators. Local preachers' groups and national and regional networks ensure continuity and ongoing development, seeking to build vigorous movements committed to Bible exposition.

Langham Literature provides Majority World preachers, scholars and seminary libraries with evangelical books and electronic resources through publishing and distribution, grants and discounts. The programme also fosters the creation of indigenous evangelical books in many languages, through writer's grants, strengthening local evangelical publishing houses, and investment in major regional literature projects, such as one volume Bible commentaries like the *Africa Bible Commentary* and the *South Asia Bible Commentary*.

Langham Scholars provides financial support for evangelical doctoral students from the Majority World so that, when they return home, they may train pastors and other Christian leaders with sound, biblical and theological teaching. This programme equips those who equip others. Langham Scholars also works in partnership with Majority World seminaries in strengthening evangelical theological education. A growing number of Langham Scholars study in high quality doctoral programmes in the Majority World itself. As well as teaching the next generation of pastors, graduated Langham Scholars exercise significant influence through their writing and leadership.

To learn more about Langham Partnership and the work we do visit **langham.org**

www.ingramcontent.com/pod-product-compliance
Lightning Source LLC
Chambersburg PA
CBHW070234240426
43673CB00044B/1785